Reconstructing Prehistory

Reconstructing Prehistory

Scientific Method in Archaeology

James A. Bell

Temple University Press

Philadelphia

Temple University Press, Philadelphia 19122

Copyright © 1994 by Temple University. All rights reserved
Published 1994
Printed in the United States of America

⊗ The paper used in this publication meets the minimum
requirements of American National Standard for Information
Sciences—Permanence of Paper for Printed Library Materials,
ANSI Z39.48-1984

Library of Congress Cataloging-in-Publication Data
Bell, J. A. (James A.)
    Reconstructing prehistory: scientific method in archaeology
/ James A. Bell
        p.   cm.
    Includes bibliographical references and index.
    ISBN 1-56639-159-8 (cl : alk. paper). — ISBN 1-56639-160-1
(pb : alk. paper)
        1. Archaeology—Methodology.   I. Title.
    CC75.B38   1994
    930.1'01—dc20   93-25727

Contents

Preface

In the public imagination fieldwork is often synonymous with archaeological work. Fieldwork does absorb much of the time and energy of archaeologists, and, arguably, it should. Planning and organizing a dig, careful excavation, and painstaking preservation, recordation, and publication of the results are all demanding tasks. They are what yield the artifactual record, however, and that record provides the most important ingredient for archaeological theory.

Recent decades have seen an expanding interest in archaeological theory. When building theories, certain issues cannot be avoided. How should theories about the unwritten past be formulated, for example, and how should they be assessed against the artifactual data? These and related methodological issues have come to the forefront of the theoretical revolution in archaeology. Indeed they should. At stake are confidence in explanations in archaeology and the hope that these explanations can be improved.

The search for method reveals different and incompatible views. There are no less than four in the philosophy of science, and each is at odds with its competitors. In the confusion some archaeologists and philosophers insist upon just one view, while others conclude that rational use of method must be a hoax. Neither response is desirable. Turning method into a dogma chokes the advance of knowledge, but discarding method leads to indiscriminate theorizing. Fortunately, scientism (the former) and relativism (the latter) are not the only alternatives.

Because the goal of archaeological theory is to improve our knowledge of the unwritten past, it is crucial that archaeologists attempt to formulate theories that are refutable, or testable; that is, vulnerable to error. In this book methodological guidelines are developed to help increase testability. Although the guidelines are forged primarily from the refutationist view of science, effective use is enhanced by the contributions of the inductive, paradigmatic, and anarchic views as well. That is why all four views figure prominently here.

The philosophy of archaeology is not an entirely new field, so it would be helpful to state what is different about the approach in this book. The reader will find a refutationist flavor in these pages, whereas much of the literature in the philosophy of archaeology has an inductive thrust. The refutationist view is certainly not adequate in itself, but I hope to show that it is the most fruitful philosophical framework for the development of archaeological theory. Another difference may be even more crucial. Much of the systematic literature in the philosophy of archaeology tends to project philosophical issues onto archaeology. Although some of those issues are relevant and helpful to archaeologists, others are less so. That mixture can be confusing and we philosophers are not always aware of it. Furthermore, some issues relevant to archaeologists are conceptualized so differently by philosophers that practicing archaeologists can be thrown for a complete loss. This last point requires further comment.

Archaeologists must confront a host of methodological and philosophical issues when building theories about the past. That is no surprise, but I have learned that issues are unearthed by practicing archaeologists in a context quite different from the way they are normally formulated and understood by philosophers. The lesson became obvious as I proceeded to coax the issues out of an archaeological context. My philosophical colleagues may find some of the differences surprising, and I hope intriguing as well. One cannot help but suspect that such differences would be revealed whenever philosophers do applied work tied closely to the issues actually faced by those in an applied field.

In short, I intend this book to provide a philosophical framework and specific methodological recommendations useful to archaeologists in their theoretic deliberations. I also hope it will be interesting to philosophers, especially as an illustration of the ingredients necessary to make applied philosophy easily accessible and useful to those in another field. Lists of suggested readings at the end of each chapter include references to supplement the discussion for archaeologists and philosophers.

In 1984 I found myself at a professional crossroads. My research had hit a cul-de-sac, and a change was in order. Where should my energies be directed in the future? Happily, the answer came quickly. I most wanted to write a full-length study on method in archaeological theory. I outlined a proposal and sent it to Colin Renfrew in Cambridge, England. You can imagine my disbelief when I received a letter from him a few days later, asking that I consider undertaking just such a project. We had not been in touch for quite some time, but our letters must have crossed over the Atlantic. My interest in the project was heightened further by this startling coincidence.

Let me retreat further into the past. In 1978 I met Colin Renfrew and Jeremy Sabloff. I had been invited to participate in a conference in Santa Fe on simulation modeling in archaeology (see Sabloff 1981). That started a love affair with archaeology that eventually blossomed far beyond my rather technical methodological contribution to that conference (see Bell 1981).

I have had the opportunity to deliver numerous papers at archaeological conferences, especially over the past seven years. Nearly every major idea in this book was initially conceived in those papers, and the feedback on them has been crucial in its development. In 1987 the University of South Florida granted a sabbatical so that I could pursue the work on this book full-time. My wife Catherine and our younger daughter Cristin moved to Cambridge, England, where I was able to concentrate on the development of the manuscript as a Visiting Scholar at Wolfson College. Yet another love affair broke out, this one with Cambridge and the university. All three of us were smitten. The time in Cambridge was quite productive despite the romance, or perhaps because of it. Particularly helpful was my seminar on scientific method in archaeological theory for students and staff, and my daily association with the "computer-room crowd" in the Archaeology Department on Downing Street. Early drafts of each chapter in this book received cogent and lively analysis both at the seminar and in the computer room.

The encouragement and editorial comments of Colin Renfrew, Jeremy Sabloff, and Christopher Peebles have been crucial from the inception of this book. In the later stages Christopher Peebles played a particularly important role. His rather remarkable command of the philosophical, anthropological, and archaeological literature was invaluable, as was his critical acumen. That is not all. I would work into the morning hours at his dining room table in Bloomington. This infringed on his own sleep, but he would awaken with the enthusiasm—and coffee—to keep me going. I can never be thankful enough.

Many other archaeologists and anthropologists have also contributed their suggestions and moral support. They include Ian Hodder, Steven Mithen, Valerie Pinsky, Olivier Montmillon, E. M. Melas, Nigel Holman, Matthew Johnson, James McGlade, Sander van der Leeuwe, Kenneth Dark, Tom Patterson, Robert Preucel, Tim Earle, Ezra Zubrow, Joel Gunn, Jim Strange, and Ailon Shiloh. Philosophers who have done the same include Kristin Shrader-Frechette, Stephen Turner, Ellen Klein, Joseph Agassi, Lester Embree, and Alison Wylie.

Ms. Jane Cullen at the Temple University Press guided the manuscript over the many hurdles to publication. Her substantial enthusiasm has certainly been gratifying to me, and helped make revision work a source of pleasure rather than drudgery. I can only hope it has also made her many onerous editorial tasks more bearable. Ms. Linda Gregonis' work as copy editor put the manuscript in better form than I could have imagined possible. Even declined recommendations were invariably appropriate. For example, the word "prehistory" is too narrow, at least in its literal sense. The methodological proposals in the book are designed for all explanations of the unwritten past, regardless of whether an explanation is set in a prehistoric, protohistoric, or historic context. I nevertheless decided to leave "Prehistory" in the title, simply because alternative words and phrases seemed either awkward or too lengthy.

Many who helped with this book have been specifically mentioned above, but the number of people to whom I am indebted seems limitless. Two anonymous archaeologists who reviewed the manuscript for the Temple University Press were also philosophically sophisticated. Each provided many helpful comments throughout the manuscript. The comments of an anonymous philosopher who reviewed the manuscript also led to noticeable improvements. I can remember the faces if not all the names of those who offered comment on my papers at archaeological conferences in Southampton, Cardiff, Glasgow, Cambridge, London, and Newcastle, not to mention Atlanta, Bloomington, Carbondale, Santa Fe, and Tampa on the western side of the Atlantic. Improvements in the manuscript are largely the result of suggestions by the reviewers, the people at these conferences and the others mentioned previously. Its remaining faults are entirely my own responsibility.

A few ideas and themes in this book appear in some of my other publications. Even though those ideas have been developed and elaborated further in this book, I would like to acknowledge the other sources. Chapter 3 incorporates an elaboration of some parts of "Universalization in Archaeological Explanation," which appeared in *Metaarchaeology: Reflections by Archaeologists and Philosophers* (Embree 1992: 143–63). Chapter 7 is an amplification of "Anarchy and Archaeology," in *Processual and Postprocessual Archaeologies* (Preucel 1991: 71–80). Chapter 8 is a further development of "On Capturing Agency in Theories about Prehistory," which appeared in *Representations in Archaeology* (Gardin and Peebles 1992: 30–55). Chapter 9 is an elaboration of some parts of "Interpretation and Testability in Theories about Prehistoric Thinking," in *The Ancient Mind: Elements of Cognitive Archaeology* (Renfrew and Zubrow 1993).

Finally, this book is dedicated to research and graduate students in archaeology. Those at Cambridge University are typical. They were principal players at my seminar and in the computer room. Their keen interest in matters methodological was unwavering. I have encountered that interest in all students of archaeology, no matter where they might be. It was and continues to be a deep source of inspiration to me.

Dade City, Florida
29 October 1993

Reconstructing Prehistory

Introduction

Methods of science can be productive for theory-building in any field. In this book they are forged into tools helpful to archaeologists. The methodological tools will be particularly useful when making decisions about theories, by enabling those decisions to reflect answers to questions such as the following:

- How can theories be formulated so that they increase understanding and insight?
- How can theories function usefully even when they do not further understanding or provide insight?
- How can theories be structured so that they can be improved?
- How can theories be adjusted when anomalies are revealed?
- How can theories be tested against the artifactual record and assessed against competing theories?
- When should theories be abandoned, and when pursued further?

Methods of science provide no definitive answers to these or related questions. They are not and never will be a substitute for the creativity, intuition, and even luck that is integral to theory development. What they *can* do is provide a fruitful framework within which to explore answers to such questions, and to trace the potential consequences of each answer. More informed and judicious decisions about theories are the payoff.

The goal of this book is none other than that of the New Archaeology: to improve theory development through better use of method. In this book, however, the route toward that goal differs from others already taken. A few comments on the New Archaeology will serve to explain the differences.

The New Archaeology burst upon the scene in the late 1960s. It quickly turned a river of methodological controversy into the contentious torrent that has characterized methodological discussion ever since. Despite disagreement over the benefits of alternative approaches to the New Archaeology, attention to method has led to more effective assessment of theories. It is also reflected in theoretical publications, where an archaeologist can no longer assume or assert an explanation without offering a critical discussion of the reasons in its favor. The upshot has been an increase in the breadth and pace of theoretical development.

Accompanying the New Archaeology has been an expanding body of literature devoted exclusively to method. The arguments for and against specific methodological approaches have piqued the interest of archaeologists, contributing at least indirectly to methodological sophistication. Unfortunately, significant portions of the methodological literature do not provide many insights directly useful for making productive decisions about theories. The underlying reasons are explored here.

Numerous proposals for method in archaeology have either been modeled after an exclusive conception of scientific method, or have been formulated to avoid scientific method altogether. These alternatives provide the extremes of a continuum, to be sure, but much of the discussion is carried out at or near the extremes rather than on the possibilities that lie between (a theme running throughout Trigger 1989b).

Proposals to use one conception of science and its method easily slip into *scientism*: the belief that there is one and only one method of science, and that science is identified with that method. A corollary of scientism is that method, correctly applied, is the best guarantor of worthwhile ("scientific") theory. Scientism is seldom endorsed explicitly, but it does cast a shadow over such well-known works as *Archaeological Explanation: The Scientific Method in Archaeology* (Watson et al. 1984) and *Philosophy and Archaeology* (Salmon 1982). By proposing a formal model of science and recommending that archaeological theory meet its standards, both books offer hope that archaeological theory will be more productive, and more credible. Watson, LeBlanc, and Redman "reiterate our belief that the generalized CL [covering-law] model is important because it illustrates crucial aspects of archaeological method" (Watson et al. 1984: 41). Salmon, who proposes statistical-relevance models of science in place of covering-law models, intends "to seek in works of philosophy of science, fairly specific guidelines for ways to make their discipline [archaeology] more scientific, that is, to ensure that archaeological claims embody knowledge rather than guesswork" (Salmon 1982:2; for a review see Bell 1984).

Scientism follows from the assumption that there is a unique conception of science, and that it alone confers legitimacy. That is why it tends to encourage the "law and order" approach to method, that is, the rather rigid application of one set of methodological rules. The scientistic tendencies in the two books discussed are compounded by the fact that each incorporates a variation of inductive method. Inductive method is an approach to establishing the truth, or probable truth, by attempting to determine how well data verifies theory. The covering-law model is not itself inductive, but it often is associated with inductive method. The statistical-relevance model is explicitly inductive. In Chapter 3 it will be argued that inductive method is not very fruitful for theory development even though it is embraced in a variety of forms by numerous philosophers of science.

An inductive approach to archaeological theory is also advocated by Jane Kelley and Marsha Hanen, authors of a 1988 book called *Archaeology and the Methodology of Science.* Fortunately they do take pains to avoid scientism. They also augment their inductive approach with other methodological suggestions that render it more workable.

Although scientistic approaches assume a monolithic conception of science, there are actually numerous views of science. Four will be reviewed in this book. Each view yields starkly contrasting standards for science and disparate guidelines for building theory. Depending upon the context, a particular set of methodological rules can be helpful, irrelevant, or harmful. They can be helpful when specific guidelines are carefully used to make a decision about an explanation in a particular theoretical context. Alternative guidelines can be useful when a theoretical context changes.

Another reason some methodological recommendations are not entirely useful is found in the attempts to separate archaeology from science (see Cole 1980; Sabloff 1982, ed. 1982; and Trigger 1989b and 1989c). Because its hallmark is the rejection of scientific method, I call such approaches *anti-scientific*. Noting that a field such as archaeology is not a physical science, and perhaps not even a biological or social science, proponents of anti-scientific approaches conclude that the methods of science are inappropriate or even deleterious. Ian Hodder's *Reading the Past: Current Approaches to Interpretation in Archaeology* provides a salient example of an extreme anti-scientific approach. In his view, human agency demands rejection of scientific models of explanation: "It will be necessary, then, in the quest for an adequate archaeology of mind, to ditch decisively the natural science, covering law approach" (Hodder 1991:32).

The following is a typical sketch of how anti-scientific approaches can emerge in a field like archaeology. The goals of archaeological theory are not always the same as those of scientific theory. For example, the search for universal laws should be a goal in the sciences. It should also be a goal in archaeology (Bell 1992b). There is, however, more to it than that. In a historical discipline such as archaeology, explaining the uniqueness of occurrences—not just the universality of phenomena ("covering-laws")—can also be a goal. Many accounts of history (and prehistory) are narratives, and narrative history explains unique events (Goode 1977). Indeed, the uniqueness of events and cultures is inseparable from the "historical particularist" assumptions favored by such influential thinkers as Franz Boas (Trigger 1989b:190). Certainly there is no reason to limit archaeological explanation to narrative explanation, but neither is there good reason to categorically exclude narrative accounts from archaeology.

Furthermore, the constituents of archaeological explanations are sometimes different from those in physical and biological explanations. For example, at least some theories in archaeology can incorporate distinctly human elements, such as cognition and decision making. It is assumed—although incorrectly this time—that theories in the sciences must be reducible to deterministic elements and hence exclude such human variables.

If archaeological theory can sometimes explain uniqueness, and if human agency can sometimes be a constituent of archaeological theory, it is not surprising that scientific models for archaeological explanation have come into question. To these concerns add the scientistic overtone in widely known methodological literature. No wonder that some question the effectiveness of the methods of science for theory development in archaeology.

Despite questions about attempts to build archaeological explanations with the methods of science, the anti-scientific attacks are misguided. Explaining uniqueness, hence using narrative reconstruction, is sometimes an appropriate goal in archaeology, but it is not the only goal. Human agency can be included in some archaeological explanations by using fruitful methods of science. Most important, anti-scientific approaches attack the rigid standards and guidelines of scientism and hardly touch the fruitful methods of science. Scientism should be dismissed in archaeology or any other field. The mistake is to dismiss methods of science along with it.

Scientism and anti-scientific approaches are opposites. The first merges archaeology with a (mistaken) perspective on science, the second separates archaeology entirely from science. Nevertheless, scientism and anti-scientific approaches are intimately related. The inevitable failure of scientism leads to skepticism about science and its methods. That encourages a boomerang to anti-scientific approaches. The reasoning captured in the earlier quotation from Ian Hodder (1991) is an example. In *Reading the Past*, Hodder's endorsement of a quasi-irrational approach to theory building is spurred on by his rejection of scientistic approaches (for detailed criticism see Bell 1987a).

The arguments in this book are as critical of scientism as those of any anti-scientific approach, but the approach in this book is far from anti-scientific. In this book methodological guidelines of science are recast for building and assessing theories in archaeology.

The goal is to provide archaeologists with tools that will help them make productive decisions about their theories.

Despite shortcomings, the thirst for methodological insight continues unabated. Watson, LeBlanc, and Redman's *Archaeological Explanation*, published in 1984, is a revision of *Explanation in Archaeology: An Explicitly Scientific Approach* (Watson et al. 1971). Hodder's *Reading the Past* sold off the shelves almost as soon as it could be stocked. At Cambridge University, interest in method enhanced the attendance at a 1987 series of seminars based on an early draft of this book. In short, archaeologists sense that method does matter, and clearly it should. At stake are confidence in theories about the past, and optimism that they can be improved.

This book draws upon numerous intellectual resources. Methodological fruit has been picked from each of four views of science. The refutationist view has made the largest contribution. It was systematized by Karl Popper and elaborated upon by him and others. The refutationist view provides many insights into the advance of science and knowledge, including the notions of testability and theory adjustment that maintains testability (Popper 1957, 1959, 1962, 1983).

Contributions to the refutationist view by Imre Lakatos and Joseph Agassi are particularly significant. My notions of increased understanding and new insight are taken from Lakatos' concepts of theoretical progress and empirical progress, respectively (Lakatos 1970). Joseph Agassi's many ideas on scientific method and historiography have been as pivotal as his insights into institutionalized academia (Agassi 1963, 1964, 1975, 1977). He also insisted that his graduate students develop the intellectual courage to pursue their own interests rather than follow the fashions in the philosophical profession. Erazim Kohak is another courageous professor whose many interests and independent thinking were an inspiration during my graduate studies. A book like this might not have been undertaken without the good fortune of having worked under these men twenty-five years ago.

Important ideas have been adopted in this book from the paradigmatic view of Thomas Kuhn (1962) and the anarchic view formulated and argued so forcefully by Paul Feyerabend (1978). Although inductive approaches are heavily criticized in this book, the number of inductive theorists to which this book is indebted are too many to list. Prominent among them is Carl Hempel (1952, 1965, and 1966). Furthermore, major works advocating induction in archaeology include the clearest expositions and defenses of inductive themes that I have ever encountered in the philosophical literature. For that I am particularly grateful to Merrilee Salmon (1982) and Jane Kelley and Marsha Hanen (1988).

There are also notable differences between the goal and approach of this book and the intellectual traditions in which it is rooted. Three stand out.

First, this book is intended to be more like a manual than a discourse on views of science. The goal is to provide methodological tools for theoretical work in archaeology. Each view is assessed critically in light of what it can or cannot provide archaeologists. Each view provides at least some valuable methodological insights for archaeologists, and none are without serious drawbacks as well.

That this book draws upon various and inconsistent views of science and method does not mean that each view has made comparable contributions to its arguments. The refutationist view is by far the most important, especially because of its conception of the goal of science—to make progress—and its central tool for moving toward that goal—testability. On the other hand, it is not the purpose of this book to provide a general defense of, or attack on, any given view of science and method. Nevertheless, the flow of argument in the book clearly does reflect many themes in the refutationist camp and does criticize numerous ideas from other camps. In this indirect and modified way the book can be considered supportive of the refutationist view of science.

Although the book incorporates many refutationist ideas, it is very important to note that the methodological battlefield is not the traditional one. Philosophers in particular are used to arguing about abstract concepts and logical problems in views of science and method, normally with little or no interest or regard for application in a practicing field. Many philosophers will be confused because their usual focal point is different from the one proposed in this book, where application is the central purpose. The battlefield should be quite recognizable to archaeologists even if they disagree on minor or even major points.

Second, different battlefields do necessitate different tactics. Some features of views of science and method will be important to archaeologists but will seem trivial to many philosophers. Other points of interest to philosophers will be bypassed when they are unimportant to archaeologists. In general, methodological controversies will be avoided where they have little or no bearing on application.

The third difference is related to the other two. Because methodological approaches will be reconstructed for application in theoretical archaeology, some methodological elements are included with each view that would not normally be addressed in a purist exposition. Excluded are other elements that purist manuscripts would include. For further reference, the list of suggested readings at the end of each chapter will be helpful.

In short, this is a book in applied philosophy, in this case the philosophy of science. I will be satisfied if archaeologists find the ideas helpful. I hope it may lead some to consider changing the way they theorize. I hope it will *not* change the way others theorize, but that it will help the latter gain a clearer understanding of the reasons underlying their approach. That should at least enable them to do their theorizing more systematically and confidently. It should also provide them with more tools to battle their methodological critics.

Part I, The Context and the Issues, provides the background and outlines the methodological issues faced by archaeologists. The central idea—testability—is discussed and applied in archaeological contexts. Part II, The Philosophical and Methodological Roots, has a chapter on each of the four views of science: the inductive view (Chapter 4), the paradigmatic view (Chapter 5), the refutationist view (Chapter 6), and the anarchic view (Chapter 7). The goal is to identify in each view those elements particularly helpful for theorizing in archaeology. Part III, Individualism and Cognitive Archaeology, is focused on individualistic method, method that assumes that indeterminant elements such as thinking and acting are crucial in the structure and change of social organization. The goal is to show how individualistic elements can be incorporated into archaeological theory without sacrificing methodological rigor.

The reader should exit this book with more resources for making productive decisions about theories. Replete with its share of ironies and anecdotes, the fascinating story behind scientific method might also prove to be absorbing. In the eyes of the author, however, that story will be hollow if the ideas are not also useful in the reader's theoretical deliberations.

Part I The Context and the Issues

Chapter 1   Controversy Over Method in Theoretical Archaeology

"The Loss of Innocence" by the late David Clarke was a landmark paper in the New Archaeology. Clarke stressed the need to investigate theoretical assumptions and procedures of inference in archaeology, a field in which both had often been presumed without sufficient critical reflection (Clarke 1973). Clarke's concern about theory analysis arose from a transformation in archaeology. An era in which fieldwork was the only significant focus had come to an end. Although fieldwork has continued and arguably should continue to be the centerpiece of archaeological endeavor, explaining what is revealed in the "dirt" has also taken a place at or near the center stage of archaeology.

Almost any history of archaeology will reveal that explaining the past has been part of archaeology since its inception (for example, see Sabloff and Willey 1980; Trigger 1989b). Furthermore, some contend that problems in proposed explanations and conflicts among competing explanations have provided and always do provide the impetus for intellectual work. This view of the interests of researchers and the motivation for their work has been argued for the sciences (Agassi 1964) as well as for social sciences such as anthropology (Jarvie 1964). Nevertheless, a more explicit awareness of theoretical assumptions and more conscious analysis of the methodological underpinnings of theory did sweep into archaeology. The movement began in the late 1960s and has been vigorous ever since.

Along with the rising interest in archaeological theory has come awareness that theory building and assessment should not be left to chance. It was realized that there are benefits to understanding method, and applying it more systematically. That is why *views of knowledge*, or *epistemological theories*, have also become a focus of attention. Such views or theories include methodological guidelines for formulating and evaluating explanations. The New Archaeology has become a generic label for attempts to improve archaeological explanation by focusing explicitly on methods of generating and testing theories.

Optimism has been another important characteristic of the New Archaeology. Not surprisingly, the emergence of interest in method was associated with a rise in optimism that the prehistoric past could be understood. Archaeologists began to hope and even believe that reasonably accurate interpretations of the past could be found. That is why the belief that reliable knowledge of the past could be culled from the artifactual record also came to be identified with the New Archaeology.

Optimism is absolutely crucial to attempts to improve theory. Without it there would be no motive to make the effort. The situation is similar to that during the modern revolution in science, which occurred in the seventeenth century. Attention to method along with the vociferous, exciting debates over method during that period would have been inconceivable without the Enlightenment. The core of an enlightened outlook, during the seventeenth century or any other time for that matter, is the view that there is truth and that truth can be discovered.

Although this book is focused on method, then, it should not be forgotten that use of method only makes sense for one who is optimistic that diligent and systematic attention to method can lead to a comprehension of the archaeological past, or at least better theories about it. This seems rather obvious, but the consequences are quite significant for archaeologists who do not share the optimism. A well-known early skeptic was M. A. Smith (1955). Paul Courbin's (1988) more recent skeptical musings have also become widely known.

Method and Theory

Method, methodology, and middle-range theory

At this point it would be helpful to comment on use of the terms "method" and "methodology." The goal is not to provide an exhaustive list of the meanings, a task that may very well be impossible, nor to straighten out the myriad confusions that arise when the meanings are crossed. My goal is considerably more modest: to clarify how the terms are used in this book. The usage is not dissimilar to that of many philosophers, and is consistent with usage in some of the significant archaeological literature.

Methodology sometimes refers to the study of method, but is normally a word that is synonymous with *method*. In this book the two words and the locutions of each are used interchangeably.

In the broadest sense, method consists of the guidelines used to structure and assess theories. In terms familiar to archaeologists, method consists of the tools used to formulate and evaluate "middle-range theory." A very brief presentation of middle-range theory is in order.

The concept of research or theory at the "middle-range" was introduced into the archaeological literature in the early to middle 1970s by Lewis Binford. It had become clear to Binford that the strategies needed to generate and test archaeological theory were not the same as those used to assess general theory. To avoid confusion, Binford began using the labels "middle-range theory" or "middle-range research" to designate theoretic work in which empirical methodological strategies can and should be used. (Binford 1983b:18fn5). At about the same time the concept was also introduced, independently, into archaeological circles by Mark Raab and Al Goodyear (see Goodyear et al. 1978). Raab and Goodyear suggested that archaeologists adopt Robert Merton's recommendation for sociology (Merton 1968). Merton argued that high-level theory is quite abstract and not amenable to empirical assessment, so that theories with empirical content—theories at the middle-level—should be the focus of theoretic activity (Binford 1983b:18–19fn5). The concepts of theory at the middle-ground developed by Binford and by Merton are similar enough that distinctions would be, for the purposes of this book, distinctions without a difference.

Middle-range theory is made up of the ideas, models, and other interpretative assumptions necessary to structure a link ("middle-range") between the low-level artifactual observations on the one hand and the high-level general theories on the other (Trigger 1989b). Low-level theories are the observations that emerge from fieldwork. Even though they are themselves interpretations—that is the reason for expressions like "observational theory," or "low-level theory"—they are normally considered the "data" or the "facts" to which explanations should be accountable. High-level theories are very general. That is why they are more an overarching framework that informs explanatory structure in the middle range rather than being part of that structure. High-level theories have been called "research strategies" by Marvin Harris and "controlling models" by David Clarke (Trigger 1989b:22). Examples include broad frameworks such as historical materialism, ecological determinism, and social individualism. The middle-level theories are or at least should be consistent with the high-level general theories, and they should explain at least some of the low-level artifactual observations.

Middle-range theory is quite different from either low- or high-level theory. Two differences are particularly noteworthy.

First, middle-range theories are explanations that are actively formulated and assessed. Unlike the low-level artifactual observations, they are not a given for generating and evaluating theory. Nor are they assumptions, as are the high-level research strategies or controlling models that inform the theory building in the middle range. In brief, both the low-level artifactual data and the high-level research strategies serve as rather inert inputs when the theoretic action is underway in the middle range.

To deflect possible misunderstanding, artifactual data and research strategies certainly do not always remain passive aspects of theory building and assessment. There are instances in which theoretic activity leads to data being challenged. As a result, data are sometimes reformulated, changed significantly, or even thrown out completely. Research strategies themselves also can and do undergo challenge. When the explanations that flow from research strategies do not provide adequate solutions to research problems, provide less adequate solutions than those from other strategies, or fail tests against the artifactual data, then those research strategies are typically brought into question. At times they are reformulated, and some may even abandon them in favor of other strategies.

Second, guidelines are needed to structure and evaluate the explanations that constitute middle-range theory. Such guidelines are always used in the middle range, regardless of whether the guidelines are explicit or not and regardless of whether those employing them are aware of them or not. Those guidelines are *method* or *methodology*. They are the focus of this book.

Conceiving of method as guidelines for formulating and assessing middle-range theory is quite insightful. It forces one to appreciate that there is indeed a gulf between artifact and general theory. It also forces archaeologists to explore and understand what fills or should fill that gulf. In addition, it forces archaeologists to explore the methodological guidelines that can or should be used for that purpose. A serious investigation of method is essential if archaeologists are to be confident that their theories do explain the artifactual record in a productive way.

The meaning of method outlined here is quite broad. The difficulty is not that the meaning is too inclusive, however, but that it can be confused with other meanings of method.

Four meanings of method can be identified: (1) method as techniques for recovering or establishing data, such as pollen analysis and radiocarbon dating; (2) method as approaches to finding and organizing field data, such as using statistical means for predicting site location and making an analytic survey of a site; (3) method as ways to interpret data, such as use of diffusionist models, processual models, and Marxist interpretations; and (4) method as tools for formulating and assessing theories, such as inductive method and refutationist method. This fourth meaning of method is normally called "scientific method." Nevertheless, discussion of the scientific method cannot avoid rather substantial reference to method as ways to interpret data (the third category). The intellectual and attitudinal framework within which the artifactual record is conceived has a major bearing on whether scientific method can be fruitfully utilized, much less used at all.

The first and second meanings of method fall more clearly onto the empirical rather than the theoretical side of archaeology. Empirical matters have an important bearing on archaeological theory. A number of arguments and examples in this book drive that point home; however, the empirical side of archaeology is largely beyond the scope of this book and hence is discussed only tangentially.

Theory

The word "theory" can be used in numerous ways. Misunderstanding can come about because of different meanings, and because writers switch between meanings.

Broadly speaking, in this book theory is interchangeable with explanation. The reason is that a theory is simply an attempt to explain. Such usage is quite common and is not in itself prone to misunderstanding. Confusion can arise, however, for other reasons, such as the different levels of theorizing or the number and variety of components that constitute an explanation.

The division of theories into three levels has already proven helpful. Recall that method is an active tool in the middle range, and the explanations with which an archaeologist is normally involved are in that range. In theoretic practice the low and high levels do function quite differently than the middle level: Low-level or observational theories are normally a given and high-level or controlling theories are usually assumed. Labeling the ideas at all three levels as "theories," however, can camouflage these rather substantial differences. For the sake of clarity, then, the word "theory" in this book will simply mean an explanation at the middle range. An explicit verbal flag will be waved whenever the discussion turns to low-level or high-level theories.

Incidentally, another convention is to distinguish between expressions such as "hypothesis," "theory," and "law." From this conventional perspective "hypotheses" are quite speculative and tentative, normally suggested before substantial research is undertaken to assess them. "Theories," on the other hand, are hypotheses that have been confirmed to the point where they can be held with reasonable confidence. "Laws" are theories that are so highly confirmed that they can be held without further question. These distinctions will not be used in this book for two reasons. First and foremost, all explanations are conjectural. Even though some may be more highly corroborated (by passing tests) than others, they are all prone to error. There are no "laws," then, and making a distinction between "hypothesis" and "theory" can mask a more important shared characteristic: vulnerability to error. Explanations had better be vulnerable, by the way, if they are to provide a route to further theory development. Second, the distinctions between "hypothesis," "theory," and "law" seem to reflect a subjective degree of confidence rather than an objective measure of corroboration. There is no workable measure of objective corroboration, to be sure, but making a subjective judgment of confidence is even more tenuous. The history of science is strewn with explanations that were held with great confidence but were overthrown, and explanations that inspired little confidence but eventually flourished.

The number and variety of components in an explanation can also lead to confusion in the use of the word "theory." Even in uncomplicated form, a theory is a conjunction of statements rather than just one statement. Consider the following example: Agricultural workers were redeployed to produce religious icons because of the declining prestige of priests, causing a further decrease in agricultural production. This explanation can be analyzed into three component statements: (1) Agricultural workers were redeployed to produce religious icons; (2) the prestige of priests was on the decline; and (3) whenever agricultural workers are redeployed to alternative types of production, all other factors remaining unchanged, there will be a decrease in agricultural production. Not only are there three statements, but there are different types of statements. Statements (1) and (2) are low-level assertions that summarize "facts," whereas (3) is a middle-level statement that is universalized. The word "theory" could apply to the original explanation, which contains all three statements, or it could refer to (1) or (2) or both (1) and (2), or it could refer to (3). Matters can become considerably more complicated than outlined here because the original explanation would typically be associated with numerous other explanatory statements. That would definitely be the case when a theory is only one part of a systemic explanation, for example. Is there a way around such potential problems of reference when using the word "theory?" I believe so, and it is not complicated.

Normally, there is no need to be overly specific about the precise referent of the word "theory." The context most often is clear enough that a general reference is sufficient. For example, in many contexts one can simply and appropriately refer to "the theory of relativity," or the "hydraulic theory of the origin of state structure." Each of those theories, needless to say, is made up of a web of different statements at different levels. Unless the context requires further specificity, however, there normally will be no confusion, and hence no need to be more precise. When more precision is required, then it can be provided. For example, when testing an explanation it is usually crucial to designate its theoretic components so that test(s) can be directed at the appropriate part(s) of a theory. In that way one can have a better chance of discovering which components are sound and which are questionable. But it is not necessary to go into such detail if ones task at the moment does not require it.

Foci of the controversy over method

The turn toward more intensive and critical discussion of theory formation and assessment, along with use of method for that purpose, constitutes a major revolution in archaeology. Like all revolutions, it has created storms of controversy. The controversy swirls around three foci.

First, there are numerous ways of attempting to improve archaeological theory. It is helpful to distinguish *internal* types of analysis—those that focus on the methodological approaches actually employed in archaeological theory building and testing—from *external* types of analysis—those that attempt to import methodology from other disciplines such as the physical sciences, biological sciences, social sciences, and the philosophy of science.

Those who put their faith in the internal approaches understandably tend to view archaeology as a unique discipline and have confidence that methodological insight lies within its resources. Those who search for external criteria tend, just as understandably, to conceive of archaeology as a subdiscipline of other fields—such as the physical, biological, or social sciences—and assume that wisdom on matters of method can best be obtained from those fields.

Second, it has been recognized that there are numerous views about how to build and test explanations. Faced with different and contradictory methodological positions, it is difficult to know which are preferable and why, much less how to apply method judiciously.

The controversies over internal and external approaches, and over the multiplicity of methods, are further complicated by a third type of disagreement: disagreement over the purposes of archaeological work. Theory building and assessment are endorsed by many. Yet there is also a backlash against theoretical concerns and a call to return to fieldwork (Smith 1955; Courbin 1988). Controversies over theory are a wasteful distraction to those less than enamored with the rising star of theoretical archaeology. To them, lack of consensus on theory and method only confirms the futility of theoretical speculation. They would prefer that time and energy expended on theoretical and methodological debate be spent in the field (for a humorous parable, see Flannery 1982).

The contentions concerning theory building and assessment in archaeology are somewhat caricatured here. They will, nevertheless, be recognized by nearly any contemporary archaeologist. In order to clarify and discuss the multiple issues underlying these contentions, in the following sections I review the rise of theoretical archaeology and its relationship to science, and outline the connection between theoretical archaeology and the New Archaeology.

Views of Science and the Revolution in Theoretical Archaeology

The revolution in theoretical archaeology is rooted in rejecting the tendency to write prehistory as a myth, or fairy tale, or some other type of fiction. It has not been denied, however, that there may be some truth in early accounts of prehistory. Recall, for example, how stories of Troy and the Trojan War were considered by many to be purely myth. Nevertheless, the supposedly mythical tales of Homer led to a spectacular discovery: Bronze-Age Hisarlik. Heinrich Schliemann's work in the summer of 1868 was pivotal. His faith that Homer's geographical commentary was accurate enabled him to find where Troy had stood. Another example occurred in 1880 when A. H. Sayce boldly postulated that there had existed in Anatolia an important but undiscovered empire, that of the Hittites. Few took Sayce's view seriously until excavations in the 1890s by Flinders Petrie in Egypt revealed clay tablets that proved Sayce correct (Renfrew 1989a:47–50).

To be more precise, then, the thrust of the revolution is not and should not be to reject uncritical accounts of ancient events out of hand. It is, instead, to make the procedures of theory building explicit, to improve upon them, and to use them repeatedly. The goal is to produce theories that can be criticized and evaluated, and hence modified or even replaced by other theories. Even if none among a set of competing theories seem satisfactory, at least the stage is open for consideration of alternative explanations rather than being closed to all but entrenched theories.

The revolution in archaeology introduced methods of science into theoretical discussion. The reason is plausible: Methods of science are designed to produce theories that can be criticized and evaluated, and thus modified or replaced. Fruitful use of scientific method also necessitates avoiding abusive use.

Many abuses follow from the attempt to use definitions of scientific rather than to deal with methods that help theory building and assessment. One difficulty is that labeling a theory "scientific" because it follows some definition does not in itself render the theory any more deserving of confidence. A related difficulty is that the term "scientific" has many meanings, none of which are likely to be entirely satisfactory from all perspectives. For these reasons it is helpful to think of scientific as simply meaning "arrived at by means of scientific method." Attention can then turn to different methodological proposals, and the advantages as well as disadvantages of using them in the formulation and assessment of theories. Whether or not the label "scientific" is also used would then be quite immaterial. Perhaps it would be less confusing if it were abandoned.

Another source of abuse is the ring of authority and respect conveyed by the word "scientific." Labeling a theory as "scientific" can give a stamp of legitimacy without aiding theory development, the consequences of which can actually be harmful. Unwarranted authenticity can discourage criticism. It can also encourage dogmatism on the part of those who claim scientific status for their theories.

Yet another abuse derives from the ill-guided attempts to establish whether theories meet some precast meaning of scientific. These attempts can easily lead to interminable and barren disputes. The disillusionment that follows can fuel the relativistic (but unwarranted) conclusion that there are no reliable guidelines for improving theories, nor criteria for judging some preferable to others. It is only a small step to the view that nonintellectual factors such as power or propaganda are the key to establishing theories, especially in archaeology and other disciplines with potential social and political consequences.

The New Archaeology: First and Second Meanings

There may be no label more confusing in the lexicon of archaeologists than that of the New Archaeology. It is assumed to have clear reference when it actually has multiple and incompatible meanings. It was pointed out earlier in this chapter that the New Archaeology is a generic label for explicit use of method to improve archaeological explanation, and for the associated optimism that reliable knowledge of the unwritten past can be culled from the artifactual record. In addition to these general references, four quite particular meanings of the New Archaeology can be distinguished. Each is related explicitly or implicitly to science or views of science. The first and second meanings are discussed here, and the third and fourth meanings are addressed later in the chapter.

The first meaning of the New Archaeology arose shortly after the advent of radiocarbon dating the early 1950s. It became established when radiocarbon dating was improved with calibrated dates from tree-ring analysis of the bristlecone pine. It is an old story now, but recall that the radiocarbon dating of many significant artifacts throughout Europe and the Mediterranean basin eventually overturned the accepted explanation of cultural development in those regions. The received view was that cultural progress had advanced in Mesopotamia and Egypt at an early date, diffusing from those regions into Europe. Radiocarbon dating showed that such could not have been the case: Many artifacts in Europe predated those from which they supposedly diffused. A prime example of *diffusionist theory* became highly suspect. Diffusionist theory is the view that culture spreads from more "advanced" centers to more "primitive" ones via contact among peoples.

The tidal wave from the downfall of the diffusionist explanation of the origins of European culture went much deeper than the reordering of the chronological record. Diffusionist theories in general came under siege, and diffusionist theories had dominated explanations of cultural development. It was recognized that cultural influences certainly do, at times, spread by diffusion. No longer, however, could it be uncritically assumed that diffusion was the explanation. Thenceforth it had to be argued, both empirically and in competition with other explanations (Renfrew 1973a). Of particular importance here is that the New Archaeology became a label for the emerging nondiffusionist perspectives.

The first meaning of the New Archaeology, then, designates any nondiffusionist theory. *Processual* explanations, which assume that social and cultural change are primarily a function of internal dynamics ("processes"), became the predominate nondiffusionist theories. That is why the New Archaeology is frequently used as a stand-in for processual archaeology. It is a more restricted version of the first meaning.

A second meaning of the New Archaeology also stems from the early 1950s. There were major shock waves in archaeological theory due to the advent of radiocarbon dating, but many other types of scientific techniques were also being developed for generating and analyzing field data. Examples are pollen analysis, archaeomagnetic dating, and osteoarchaeology. Such techniques are also called "scientific methods," although the meaning is clearly different from meaning of that expression in this book. In any case, these and other scientific techniques, including radiocarbon dating, are sometimes referred to as the New Archaeology. Most of the techniques became widely adopted and have remained relatively noncontroversial instruments for archaeological fieldwork. Use of the New Archaeology to refer to scientific techniques of data collection and analysis was made more popular when David Wilson's book on scientific techniques of data collection and analysis, *Atoms of Time Past* (Wilson 1975a) was published in an American edition under the title *The New Archaeology* (Wilson 1975b).

Notice that the second meaning of the New Archaeology is quite distinct from the first. The first refers to a change in archaeological explanation, whereas the latter refers to scientific techniques used to generate data and analyze data. They can easily be confused, however, because the downfall of uncritical diffusionist theory (associated with the first meaning) was closely associated with radiocarbon dating (an example of the second meaning).

Views of Science, Views of Knowledge, and Method

The third and fourth meanings of the New Archaeology emerge from approaches to structuring and evaluating theories. In short, they both have emerged from concerns over method.

Method—the guidelines for building and assessing theories—is implied by any view of science. It is often called scientific method for that reason. Not surprisingly, effective use of a method requires a solid understanding of the view of science with which it is associated. But there are different views of science.

It is best not to think of science as a monolithic entity, but as an enterprise composed of numerous and different goals and tasks. That is why the expression "scientific enterprise," rather than just "science," is often employed in this book. Alternative tools are often needed for the contrasting goals and tasks, however, and that is why there are different methods.

When it is realized that the scientific enterprise is comprised of a variety of goals and tasks, it comes as no surprise that there are multiple views of science and hence different formulas for generating knowledge and incompatible criteria for judging knowledge "scientific." Far from being a disadvantage, understanding contrasting views of science and method is absolutely crucial for effective use of methodological tools. The reason is not mysterious: Views of science, and the method implied by them, are addressed to different facets of science. Archaeologists are themselves faced by numerous and contrasting tasks when developing theory. When searching for method appropriate for a particular theoretical task, then, familiarity with different views of science enables the selection to be more judicious.

Four Views of Science and Method

The four views of science are the inductive, paradigmatic, refutationist, and anarchic.

According to the classical *inductive view*, knowledge grows by gathering facts and then generalizing—inducing—explanations from them. Knowledge is legitimate if it is reducible to the facts. The goal of method is to establish the truth of theories. Variations on induction have dominated the English-speaking world ever since the idea was formulated by Francis Bacon in the seventeenth century.

Contemporary versions of the inductive view relegate the generation of theories to the background, focusing on the legitimation of theories relative to available data. Contemporary induction is probabilistic, with a modified goal of establishing the probable truth of theories. Many are also *positivistic*; that is, they are hostile to speculation about causes, minds, and other entities underlying data. Positivists have even developed terminology that implies there are no assumptions about what underlies data; for example, they prefer the expression "correlation of data" to "induction from facts."

The most salient contribution of induction is its emphasis on the empirical side of theory. That is why induction is superior to the more subjective method of the Aristotelian view it replaced. The principal weakness is its goal of establishing truth, or probable truth. The goal cannot be realized, and attempts to reach it yield inadequate and even unworkable guidelines for making decisions about theories.

The inductive view of knowledge still dominates the English-speaking world. Very entrenched, inductive method tends to become ritualistic. That is why it is often imposed ideologically. Furthermore, its influence has been so pervasive that two other views—the paradigmatic and refutationist views—have emerged from criticism of the inductive view.

According to the *paradigmatic view*, science develops from a set of assumptions called a "paradigm." Tracing the implications of a paradigm by research is called "normal science." Although criticism of a paradigm is discouraged, normal science does uncover anomalies. Overlooked or downplayed during the course of normal science, anomalies eventually provide the impetus to launch "revolutionary science:" the questioning of an established paradigm along with an earnest search for a new paradigm. Revolutionary science ends with acceptance of a new paradigm. The establishment of a new paradigm ushers in another period of normal science and hence the beginning of another paradigmatic cycle.

The paradigmatic view, systematized in its contemporary form by Thomas Kuhn in the early 1960s, incorporates sociological forces and dogmatic elements into its account of the scientific enterprise. The principal weakness is that it underestimates the role of rational procedures in scientific change, providing only a rudimentary account of how reason can function in theory assessment and selection.

According to the *refutationist* view, science consists of theories about the empirical world. The goal of science is to develop better theories. Progress is made by finding mistakes in received theories and overcoming mistakes by proposing alternative theories. Theories are best regarded as stepping-stones toward better theories, and so it is crucial that theories be *refutable*, or vulnerable to error. If theories are refutable, they are vulnerable to empirical demonstration of error. The refutationist view was developed in the early 1930s by Karl Popper.

The principal strengths of the refutationist view are its goal—to make progress—and its workable means of moving toward the goal—finding and overcoming error in theories. Its major lacunae are an inadequate account of sociological and other less than rational factors operating in the scientific enterprise, and an insufficient account of the role of competing theories.

As discussed in greater detail in the final part of this book, theories can be developed that include distinctly individualistic elements such as cognition and decision making. In these theories individuals are interpreted as active agents, not passive automatons. Because active agents can change ideas and decisions, some transformations in human institutions are unpredictable. It is argued that the best approach to developing such theories is with *methodological individualism*. Methodological individualism can be understood from a variety of perspectives, but its methodological core is closely associated with refutationist method. A background in refutationist method is important for understanding methodological individualism thoroughly, and using it effectively.

According to the fourth view of science, the *anarchic* view, the goal of science is to increase understanding through theoretical development. That goal is similar to the goal in the refutationist view. Unlike in the refutationist view, however, the most efficient route is theoretical anarchy: proposing theories of any type, which necessitates there be *no* methodological constraints. Theories should be supported by any means possible, including deliberately propagandistic argumentation and accentuation of difficulties in competing theories.

Developed by Paul Feyerabend in the 1970s, the anarchic view provides excellent medicine for scientism and other ideological uses of method. The anarchic view also highlights the importance of creativity, argumentative skill, and sheer luck, factors that can never be captured by appeal to scientific method. Finally, it gives a detailed account of the role of multiple, competing explanations in theory development. Like the paradigmatic view, a serious weakness is its disregard for the role of rational criteria in making decisions about theories.

A Multiple Approach to Method

The variety of theoretical tasks in a field such as archaeology are best approached with numerous methodological tools. When searching for theory, for example, exploring correlative relations among data will sometimes suggest an explanation. Careful attention to correlative relations among data is a mandate of inductive method. When testing an explanation, however, focusing on points vulnerable to error is normally most fruitful. That focus is a mandate of refutationist method. Inductive testing is aimed at establishing the truth or probable truth of the explanation. It will later be argued that attempting to establish truth or probable truth is fruitless except in trivial cases, and that it is often detrimental as well. Generalizing from the examples already given, the method implied by one view of science can be fruitful for some theoretical tasks, but not for others. That is why it is argued that archaeologists should use a *multiple* approach to method; that is, archaeologists should pick and choose method that is appropriate for a specific theoretical task.

As pointed out in the Introduction, a common tendency in the methodological literature has been to adopt a monolithic view of science. Not only does that approach encourage scientism and its unfortunate consequences, but the use of one and only one methodological framework is simply not workable. It is one reason that methodological literature is not always very helpful. In contrast, use of the multiple approach to scientific method allows creation of tools more useful to archaeologists for making decisions about theories.

Incidentally, it is common for methodological purists to feel that "pollution" from other methods would open the door to relativism. Purists fear that methodological pollution would leave no reliable standards by which to criticize theories, much less to choose rationally among them or make productive decisions about them. The upshot would be a muddle that permits nearly any theory to gain scientific status. It comes as no surprise, then, that methodological purists are attracted to scientism. Unswerving application of the (supposedly) one and only one method—read "pure method"—is thought to be a defense against relativism.

The multiple approach does draw upon different sets of methodological tools rather than just one set. That step need not, however, put one on a slippery slope to relativism. For one thing, the choice of method is far from arbitrary. Building theory is like building a house: Different tasks require different tools, but one *must* pick an appropriate tool for a given task. Familiarity with an array of methodological tools along with the advantages and disadvantages of each enhances rather than decreases the ability to choose an appropriate tool. For relativists the choice of method is not intellectually judicious but arbitrary, usually functioning to reinforce ones own favored theories at the expense of others.

Second, despite the benefits of familiarity with numerous views of science and method, the contributions of each to theory development are not all equal. For example, testability is absolutely crucial for effective theory development, a point that will be argued and illustrated extensively. Testability is the heart and soul of the refutationist view of science. Testability is also fatal to relativism; it provides a rational way of discovering where theories are mistaken and an effective route to improving theories and developing new ones. Induction, on the other hand, is not so significant. I argue that much theory development could proceed without major inductive influences.

Although induction does not provide the central methodological framework for archaeology, it is still crucial to theory development for a number of reasons. One reason is its emphasis on the importance of a sound empirical basis for theorizing. A related reason is its encouragement of judicious fieldwork to yield an accurate artifactual record. Induction also provides useful guidelines for generating theories about prehistoric thinking when such theories cannot confidently be generalized beyond the data base from which they arise. Familiarity with induction is important for another reason as well. Disappointment with inductive approaches to theory building have amplified the relativistic tendencies among some archaeologists (see Bell 1987a). Separating the strengths of induction from its drawbacks can help one exploit the former while dampening the relativistic reaction to the latter. In short, then, the multiple approach provides weapons against relativism rather than leading to it.

The New Archaeology: Internal and External Meanings

The groundwork has now been laid to discuss the third and fourth meanings of the New Archaeology: the internal and the external. Although different, these two meanings are often confused. For that reason, and the fact that those embracing either meaning are trying to use method to improve theory, it will be important to offer a thorough discussion of each.

The *internal* meaning of the New Archaeology is aimed at improving theory by explicitly analyzing and improving methods already implicit in theoretical archaeology. It assumes that there has been productive theoretical work in archaeology, and that the method implicit ("internal") in that work has contributed to its success.

In philosophical circles, the search for and evaluation of method as actually employed are tasks within *naturalized* epistemology. A naturalized approach to the philosophy of science, for example, includes a study of what actually transpires in the scientific enterprise and among scientists rather than focusing exclusively on the formal properties of rational procedures (for example, see Giere 1988 and Hull 1988). The paradigmatic view of science is the product of a naturalized approach. It incorporates sociological forces and psychological factors. Furthermore, the intellectual procedures identified in the paradigmatic view emerge from attempted descriptions of scientific practice rather than prescriptions for it.

Naturalized approaches do not dominate professional philosophy even though they are being given more consideration. The trend toward naturalized approaches is an especially healthy one, in my view, especially when used in conjunction with prescriptive work. Naturalized approaches to understanding method can enhance the effectiveness of methodological recommendations. A naturalized study can reveal the context in which methodological decisions are actually faced by practitioners, and can expose recommendations that are irrelevant, or at least inapplicable.

In my view, most of the valuable methodological insights generated in the New Archaeology derive from the internal approach. Generating "scientific" theories is not a goal of the internal approach. Whether archaeological explanations can be labeled "scientific" or not, or should be labeled "scientific" or not, is not considered crucial. Salient examples of desirable methodology might be labeled "scientific" in a derivative sense, but the use of that label would add nothing to the rationale for a particular method. Also noticeable is the *lack* of highly generalized and formal guidelines. Methodological suggestions, as outgrowths of theoretical work in archaeology, tend to be embraced cautiously rather than universalized compulsively.

In addition, method has historically developed in the context of use. Progress was made in the physical sciences, for example, long before any of the contemporary methodological views were systematized. Furthermore, methodological suggestions and contributions by practicing scientists have been significant. For example, Isaac Newton was concerned with what would now be called methodological issues. Most notable was his concern about the empirical status of his gravitational theory, which seemed suspiciously akin to the astrological "emanations" he so deplored. Yet another reason is that methodological suggestions that emerge from actual theoretical work can be more readily grasped by those who would employ them. For all of these reasons methodological insights from the internal approach have the best chance of being relevant and effective in theoretical archaeology.

A noteworthy example of the internal approach to the New Archaeology is Jean-Claude Gardin's *Archaeological Constructs: An As-*

pect of Theoretical Archaeology, published in 1980. Gardin's lengthy but lucid analysis of the structure of archaeological reasoning includes many evaluative comments on method. His reflective prescriptions are elicited from archaeological "constructions," to use his expression. Although the constructions are hypothetical idealizations, they are constituted so that the methodological suggestions that emerge are applicable to archaeological theorizing.

Another fruitful example of the internal approach to the New Archaeology is David Clarke's recommendations for theory building in *Analytical Archaeology,* published in 1968. Clarke's methodological proposals arise from archaeological theory itself, and he avoids hypostatizing them into artificial generalities. Clarke did find some promise in methodological insights from the natural sciences but recommended only cautious use in archaeology. He did not blindly impose scientific method, and warned explicitly against doing so.

The *external* approach to the New Archaeology is the attempt to improve explanation by adopting a precast version of method for archaeology. Most often the method has been culled from fields outside ("external to") archaeology. In practice, however, the external approach has amounted to imposition of a methodological view on explanations in archaeology, more often than not for the purpose of legitimating certain explanations as "scientific."

The emphasis on a precast and inflexible standard to legitimate explanations as "scientific" is the reason why the external approach is sometimes called the "law and order" approach. Because satisfying methodological standards can demand more attention than assessing the content of theories, the external approach amounts to the "tyranny of methodology," to use yet another colorful expression. Whenever there exists an uncritical drive to be "scientific" one is almost sure to find an external approach, either endorsed explicitly or lurking in the background.

The external approach to the New Archaeology made its appearance in the 1960s, at about the same time as the internal approach. That the models of science were taken largely from the philosophy of science is not surprising. Philosophers of science devote much time and energy to explicating views of science and scientific method. The external approach was also encouraged by the philosophers themselves. It took root at a time when more philosophers were showing an interest in making their ideas relevant to other fields. The commendable trend toward applied philosophy was on the upswing and has fortunately remained so ever since.

If the external approach had been directed toward judicious use of method in an internal context, the external approach might have been more fruitful. By adopting the purist tendencies already rampant in the philosophy of science, however, the external approach tended toward the "law and order" imposition of method that has become its unfortunate hallmark.

A well-known example of the external approach from the philosophical profession can be found in Merrilee Salmon's *Philosophy and Archaeology*, which was published in 1982. The "law and order" flavor of the early chapters in Salmon's book is rooted in an inductive model of science. It is not surprising that those chapters are of little value to archaeologists (Bell 1984). Salmon does offer a number of insights and helpful suggestions, however, specially in the later chapters. Those suggestions, interestingly enough, arise from analysis of archaeological literature; they should be labeled internal rather than external.

Another example of the external approach to the New Archaeology is Watson's, LeBlanc's, and Redman's *Explanation in Archaeology: The Scientific Method in Archaeology*, a 1984 revision of *Explanation in Archaeology: An Explicitly Scientific Approach*, which was published in 1971. The title of the 1971 edition suggests its external orientation. The legitimation models in these books are also inductive, although they are covering-law models rather than the statistical-relevance models used by Salmon.

It should be noted that the external approach has yielded some benefits. The goal of improving theoretical work, shared in both the external and internal approaches, is commendable even if the external route has not been the most productive. Furthermore, difficulties encountered in the external approach have accentuated what science is *not*. Knowing what science is not helps ward off misuse of method. Finally, the external approach has also shaded into the internal approach, rendering methodological recommendations that can be helpful even when shrouded with an external mantle. Such is especially the case with methodological suggestions in Salmon's later chapters, where she does begin to explore the actual use of method in archaeological theory (Bell 1984).

North American and British Approaches to the New Archaeology

Partitions are also drawn between practitioners of New Archaeology in North America and advocates of New Archaeology in Great Britain. The North American New Archaeology is identified with Lewis Binford and those associated with his methodological ideas. The methodological position in the North American New Archaeology is largely positivistic. The insistence upon positivism does give the North American approach a scientistic flavor, and it also explains why the North American methodological orientation does not allow for cultural-historical or narrative models, both of which are considered unsuitable for generating scientific explanations. Instead, the high-level models assumed by this group are deterministic, typically ecologically and technologically deterministic for social organization and biologically deterministic at the level of the person. These high-level models are ideal for informing systemic explanations: A "system" can combine interactions between the social and the personal levels, and all in a deterministic way. Furthermore, a system can be iterated over time, making it possible to explain processes. Finally, such systemic explanations of processes can be highly testable, and hence improvable (Bell 1981).

A major drawback of deterministic high-level models is that humans are interpreted as being robotic. For example, humans are assumed to be products of ecological and technological constraints as well as biological necessity. They may indeed make decisions, but the decisions are predictable, much like those of conditioned animals. That is why archaeologists associated with the North American approach have been criticized for neglecting the role of human agency (for example, Hodder 1991) and have been accused of behaviorism (Peebles 1992).

The British New Archaeology is usually identified with Colin Renfrew and David Clarke and those associated with their approach. Like Binford and his followers they believe it important to develop theories that are testable against the artifactual record. They have also been enthusiastic users of the same deterministic research strategies as the North American school to inform the development of explanations in archaeology. Like the North American New Archaeologists, then, they have frequently generated systemic explanations of processes. Despite these important similarities, however, there are also significant differences.

Those following the British approach to the New Archaeology are not convinced that any precast view of science, such as positivism, should be used to exclude alternative types of explanations. Unlike those following the North American approach, then, they do give cultural-historical and narrative explanations further consideration. Rather than discard them as unscientific, they typically attempt to reformulate such explanations so that they are testable. If the explanations cannot be made testable, they are at least willing to consider them as interpretations that might offer some understanding.

Those following the British approach are also not committed exclusively to deterministic high-level models. Social individualism is now sometimes used as a high-level model in the British approach. From an individualistic perspective, social structure and its change are interpreted as the products of the thoughts, decisions, and actions of individuals. Because the thoughts, decisions, and actions of individuals are not always predictable, use of social individualism is an invitation to wild speculation from the North American perspective.

Incidentally, use of social individualism to inform theory development has given rise to a relatively new field: *cognitive archaeology*, or *archaeology of the mind*. The hallmark of this new field is the study of the ideas and decisions that may have guided human action in the past. True to their tradition in the New Archaeology, however, those following the British approach insist that theories in cognitive archaeology should be testable against the artifactual record; they should not just be interpretations (Renfrew 1982, 1987, personal communication 1987; Bell 1992a, 1993).

Although the North American approach has its historical roots in North America and the British approach in Britain, each has become defined by concepts rather than geography. That is why, for example, some North American archaeologists (such as Ezra Zubrow and Christopher Peebles) and some French archaeologists (such as Jean-Claude Gardin and Henri-Paul Francfort) are associated with the British approach.

Despite the differences, both the North American and British approaches to the New Archaeology have a common goal for method: to improve archaeological explanation. Furthermore, in practice both share the same methodological route to that goal: to make archaeological explanations testable. For these reasons the distinction between the North American and British approaches is not significant for the development of testability.

The Multiple Approach and the New Archaeology

The improvement of theory formulation and evaluation is the goal of any book on methodology. The methodological tools developed here come from views of the physical sciences, as seen by a philosopher of science. For those reasons, the multiple approach seems to be an example of the external approach, rather than an amplification of the internal approach that has proven so valuable to the New Archaeology. There are, however, other reasons that push this discussion closer to the internal camp.

First, the methodological tools are directed toward internal use. They must be clearly applicable to theoretical decisions in archaeology.

Second, that the tools originate in views of the physical sciences does not justify them. Even though the tools were developed through reflection upon method in the physical sciences, the entire justification for them in this book lies in the potential they hold to help archaeologists with theoretical work.

Third, the goal in this book is not to be scientific, which often characterizes the external approach. The goal is to enhance theory generation and assessment. Use of the methodological tools in this book will gain nothing by being labeled "scientific."

Fourth, the guidelines are multiple, whereas use of a single method is characteristic of the external approach. Recommendation of alternative methodological tools for different tasks makes it difficult to impose the "law and order" flavor that is frequently found in external approaches.

Fifth and finally, effective use of the tools recommended in this book is largely dependent upon the ingenuity of the people internal to the field, that is, to the archaeologists employing them. Having an adequate set of tools and a basic knowledge of how to use them can certainly help one become a competent carpenter. Becoming a competent carpenter requires more than that, however; it requires cleverness in actual work, and adaptability to new challenges. To become a master carpenter requires even more. A book like this can provide archaeologists with methodological tools, and a fundamental knowledge of how to use them, but the rest is up to the archaeologists who actually use the tools.

By the way, it would likely make little or no difference which area of science were used to develop methodological tools. For example, the methodological tools could have been developed by reflection upon the biological sciences. The reason is that methodological tools helpful for theory development in the biological sciences have been substantially the same as those in the physical sciences. I have chosen the physical sciences simply because the physical sciences have provided the usual turf for discussion of scientific method and because I am more familiar with them.

Views of Science Reified into Views of Knowledge

The external approach is so implausible that one must ask why it has ever been proposed much less seriously discussed. The reasons are rooted in the tendency to regard scientific knowledge as the model for other types of knowledge. That tendency can certainly be fruitful, as I hope this book will demonstrate. The trouble is that misconceptions about science, especially when encouraged by political forces and professional fashions, can and do become the "model" of science.

Views of science are reified for knowledge in general, even for areas far removed from what is generally considered science. A view of science extrapolated to include extra-scientific areas is often called a *view of knowledge*. Also, a theory of scientific method generalized for use beyond the confines of science is often called a *theory of rationality*.

There is little doubt that the reification of scientific views into views of knowledge and scientific method into theories of rationality are major reasons that science influences our lives far beyond its own domain (Snow 1959; Popper 1962; Bell and Bell 1980). The technological products associated with science have tended to buttress the influence of scientific views even more (Ellul 1964).

It is clear, then, that views of science and scientific method are reified, and that reification extends the influence of science far beyond its own realm. How and why reification takes place, however, is a complicated matter that is not completely understood. Both intellectual and sociological factors are certainly involved.

Even though the meaning of science has undergone numerous transformations throughout history, science has frequently served as a model for other intellectual endeavors. The eminent position of scientific knowledge was evident in Classical Greece, for example. In the fifth century B.C. geometrical mathematics became the model of knowledge (Popper 1962). Presentations of ideas as distant from science as ethics and politics were thought best explored using a geometrical model. During the high reign of theology in the Middle Ages, the Aristotelian view of knowledge underlying theological discourse was Aristotle's view of science (Bell and Bell 1980).

Extension of scientific views is also driven by additional factors: historical, cultural, and other elements. Sociological factors vary so widely it would be fruitless to summarize them here; particular sociological forces are addressed later in the discussions of each of the four views of science. What can be said here is that the effects of sociological forces are largely negative. They at least partly explain why a particular view of science becomes so dominant in a given intellectual era and largely explain why ideological overtones so frequently surround views of science and scientific method (Bell and Bell 1980). An ingrained view of science that is held ideologically leads without fail to scientism. Scientism, remember, is the (mistaken) belief that there is one and only one method of science and that science is identified with that method.

A number of reasons for the rise of scientism have already been suggested: the fear that multiple views of method will lead to relativism, the fact that one view of science tends to dominate most intellectual epochs, and the propensity for one view to be reified and institutionalized—read ossified—in institutions throughout a society. Additional reasons are explored here.

Scientism is partially the product of linguistic convention. The word "science" can be thought to have one referent, giving the impression that science is monolithic. It is only a short step to the belief that science has some timeless, unchanging "essence" that is the key to its success (Popper 1962). According to the essentialist view science should have but one set of methodological rules.

Scientism in its contemporary form is also a product of the structure of academia. It is widely recognized that research programs gain status if they are regarded as "scientific." This is especially the case in the social sciences, the academic area in which archaeology is often placed. Furthermore, many philosophers of science expend their energy defending one scientific view and attacking competing views. In other words, it is acceptable for an academic philosopher to be a methodological "purist," a euphemism for being a methodological ideologue (Feyerabend 1978, 1982). More than just acceptable, some schools and journals in the philosophy of science are organized along methodological divisions to the point where making a career can be difficult unless one is a purist of some sort.

Debates across sharply divided methodological positions can be productive by eliciting strengths and weaknesses of different views. The drawback is that intellectual commitment to a view of science often degenerates into the ideological conviction that there is only one worthy view of science. The barrenness of ideologically held views becomes particularly evident when philosophers of science attempt to "apply" method by projecting a purist view onto a field like archaeology (Salmon 1982; Bell 1984). The same misfortune can beset archaeologists who advocate one view (compare, for example, Watson et al. 1971 and 1984).

In brief, there is an array of rather powerful intellectual reasons and sociological forces that explain the rise and persistence of scientism. It is hardly surprising, then, that external approaches to theory building have been attempted in archaeology, and that they would continue to be discussed despite shortcomings.

In any case, familiarity with scientism along with its supporting intellectual and social currents is one effective defense against abusive use of method. Abuse is even better avoided by understanding how method *can* function usefully in building and assessing theories. Three important functions of method are outlined in the next section.

Functions of Method

Method helps one make decisions about theories in many ways. Broadly speaking there are three categories under which those ways can be grouped and understood: Method serves to clarify goals, method facilitates reaching goals, and method suggests characteristics of theories and theorizing. A brief discussion of each will show how methodological awareness can aid decision making about theories.

This section is strictly introductory; its main purpose is to convey a sense of how helpful—and basically simple—the application of method can be. Needless to say, using method to make decisions becomes considerably more complicated than portrayed here. Nevertheless, the reasoning at any stage of decision making should be as clear and seemingly obvious as outlined here.

It seems trivial to emphasize that methodological tools are forged for certain theoretical goals. For example, inductivist guidelines are formulated for the goal of establishing theories. On the other hand, refutationist guidelines are formulated not to *establish* theories, but to develop theories that are improvements on received ones.

When making a decision concerning theory, the guidelines one chooses should reflect goals. Ask questions such as "do I want to establish this theory, or do I want to use it to find even better theories, or do I want to win others over to a theory, or some combination of the above?" The answer(s) will help clarify one's goals. The method one then chooses can then help further clarify one's goals. Knowledge of methodological approaches enables one to know what can be reasonably accomplished with them, and what cannot. Goals may be modified or changed accordingly.

Clarifying goals can also suggest alternative goals. For example, suppose that the goal of testing a theory is to demonstrate its plausibility. Upon testing, however, anomalous data are encountered to the point where one should consider changing goals. Instead of further attempts to corroborate the theory, one might aim at discovering which element(s) of the theory are weak.

Method can also facilitate reaching goals. For example, suppose the accepted route to ones processual goals is via theories that do not incorporate decision making by humans. After research it is realized that an important change in social organization seems to suggest the influence of cognitive elements. The processual goal of explaining the change might be maintained in that case, but theories that incorporate decision making by humans could be explored.

Method also suggests characteristics of theories and theorizing. For example, suppose one wants to explore the strengths and weaknesses of a theory that relates irrigation and social organization. To find strengths and weaknesses, it would be important that the theory be testable. Furthermore, the testing should be done in different types of cultures. Testing the theory against data from different cultures would increase the likelihood of exposing other explanatory variables, variables that might be masked when testing against data from cultures that are similar.

The ways method aids the making of theoretical decisions can overlap and even become conflated. For example, clarifying goals can increase the number of possible goals as well as suggest alternative routes of reaching goals. As another example, the difficulties in testing one type of theory might provide the impetus to consider different types of theories, which in turn might reveal goals not originally apparent.

One need not always be aware of the ways methodological tools aid theory development, but when difficulty arises, separating the different functions of method can suggest a way out of an impasse. The next chapter is more specific. It outlines six specific issues important for building and assessing theories in archaeology, and explains in considerably more detail how method can help one grapple with those issues.

Suggested Readings

For additional information on an entry please refer to the bibliography at the end of the book.

1. David L. Clarke, 1968, *Analytical Archaeology*.
Pertinent to discussions on method and on the New Archaeology.
This book not only employs but discusses and defends an "internal" approach to method. Clarke culls methodological insight from archaeological work rather than importing it from external sources. Clarke also warns against reifying rules of method into artificial generalities. Although Clarke does find some promise in methodological insights from the natural sciences, he warns against blind imposition of preconceived notions of scientific method.

2. Paul Courbin, 1988, *What is Archaeology? An Essay on the Nature of Archaeological Research*, Paul Bahn, trans.
Pertinent to introductory comments, discussion of method and theory, and discussion of the New Archaeology.
Courbin criticizes theory building in archaeology and, in his view, the methodological puffery that gives it legitimacy. His prescription for the theoretical disease is a return to the empirical side of archaeology. Archaeologists should be absorbed in fieldwork. Courbin's views are typical of the

resistance movement; that is, the resistance to the theoretical side of archaeological investigation and the methodological concerns that accompany it.

3. Kent V. Flannery, 1973, "Archaeology with a Capital 'S.' "
Pertinent to discussions on method, the New Archaeology, and views of science.
This well-known article provides a clear, direct, and sometimes humorous criticism of scientistic imposition of method onto archaeological theory. The analysis is all the more credible because Kent Flannery is a highly regarded processual archaeologist whose theorizing incorporates elements of scientific method.

4. Jean-Claude Gardin, 1980, *Archaeological Constructs: An Aspect of Theoretical Archaeology.*
Pertinent to discussions on method and on the New Archaeology.
Gardin analyzes the structure of archaeological reasoning systematically and thoroughly, from data recognition through theory building. Gardin makes explicit the intricate patterns or "constructions" of archaeological thought, the goal of which is to evaluate the method that guides the pattern formation. Although the constructions are hypothetical idealizations, Gardin's approach is internal. The constructions emerge from reflection upon theoretical reasoning in archaeology.

5. James A. Moore and Arthur S. Keene, eds., 1983, *Archaeological Hammers and Theories.*
Pertinent to introductory comments, discussion on the New Archaeology, and discussion of science and method.
This is a book of essays addressing a variety of methodological issues in archaeology. The meaning of method is quite broad. In many essays the focus is on method in empirical research (fieldwork), and hence lies beyond the scope of this book. Nevertheless, the approach to method shares a significant characteristic with the approach recommended here. Method is viewed as a tool rather than a dogma, requiring careful thought for every application. That view is absolutely crucial, whether used on the theoretical or empirical side of archaeology.

6. Merrilee H. Salmon, 1982, *Philosophy and Archaeology.*
Pertinent to discussions on method, the New Archaeology, and views of science.
Salmon recommends a "statistical-relevance" model of scientific explana-

tion for archaeology. This contemporary inductive model is imported from the philosophy of science. The book provides an example of how far astray an "external" approach can wander. The later chapters do take an "internal" bent, however, in the discussion of the method actually employed in Lewis Binford's work.

7. Bruce G. Trigger, 1989, *A History of Archaeological Thought*.
Pertinent to discussions of method and theory, theoretical archaeology, and the New Archaeology.

This book is a history of the traditions in theorizing about the unwritten past. The author also offers many evaluative comments on those traditions, comments that can be very helpful to a practicing archaeologist. The book does not focus on method per se, but the author does suggest an eclectic approach to theorizing that is similar in spirit to the multiple approach to method recommended in this book. *A History of Archaeological Thought* is an excellent companion to this book.

8. Patty Jo Watson, Steven A. LeBlanc, and Charles L. Redman, 1984, *Archaeological Explanation: The Scientific Method in Archaeology*. Revised version of the 1971 book *Explanation in Archaeology: An Explicitly Scientific Approach*.
Pertinent to discussions of method and the New Archaeology.

Watson, LeBlanc, and Redman recommend "covering-law" models of scientific explanation for archaeology. Covering-law models are another contemporary idea imported from the philosophy of science. The search for universals and deduction to trace the consequences of theory are two fruitful elements of covering-law approaches. Other elements of covering-law models are less productive, notably, the inductive compulsion to establish theories and the scientistic rigidity of such models. As in Salmon's book, helpful methodological insights do emerge despite the inductive framework. Innumerable references to philosophical literature sometimes hinder the methodological discussion.

Chapter 2 Issues in Theory Building and Assessment

Methodological tools should be forged so that they can help archaeologists in their theoretical deliberations, but for what tasks should the tools provide help? Six can be identified: (1) searching for theories that increase understanding and yield new insight, (2) formulating testable theories, (3) using empirical tests and consistency tests, (4) avoiding ad hoc adjustments, (5) encouraging competing theories, and (6) making decisions about theories.

It will quickly be realized that these six tasks are interrelated. Gaining new insight, for example, requires testable theories. When deliberating on theory, however, it is often helpful to distinguish between the tasks. That is particularly the case when faced with a theoretical cul-de-sac, the resolution of which often requires astute and detailed analysis of a theoretical context. In this chapter the six issues are outlined, discussed, and illustrated with examples.

Searching for Theories

Theories can solve practical problems even when antiquated theoretically. For example, Newtonian physics gave way to Einsteinian physics early in the twentieth century, but Newtonian explanations are still perfectly adequate for many applications in engineering and for objects moving slowly relative to the speed of light.

In contrast to explanations with practical applications, the goal of archaeological explanation is almost exclusively theoretical: to increase understanding and gain new insight.

Increasing understanding

To increase understanding is to explain more, although that can be done in multiple ways. Among the most important are the following: A theory might be generalized to explain more phenomena, it might provide a more detailed and precise explanation, or it might provide further argument for other explanations.

Here is an example. Karl Wittfogel postulated that the need to manage water—sometimes for flood control, usually for irrigation—led to the development of state structure. This hydraulic theory increased understanding of the origins of complex societies. It was originally developed to explain the development of hierarchical social organization in arid regions of the Far East. The theory was not limited to explaining the origin of complex societies just in the Far East, however, or just in arid regions. It was generalized by Wittfogel to explain the origin of complex societies everywhere, including non-arid areas such as Hawaii (Wittfogel 1957).

Generalizing Wittfogel's theory was a bold move. It increased understanding by broadening its explanatory claims. Its broadened explanatory territory also rendered the theory more testable: There were more points at to which the theory could be put to a test. Increased testability also increased the potential for new insight.

Gaining new insight

Theories that increase understanding become more valuable when testing and other types of assessment reveal strengths or weaknesses. When a theory is found correct at a point of testing, new insight is gained. In other words, "new insight" is the product of testing a theory at some point and finding it correct at that point. The original Wittfogelian theory was tested in a number of arid contexts, and passed tests in those settings (Wittfogel 1957). Not only was understanding increased, then, but new insight was gained.

That gaining new insight is valuable for theoretical development seems so obvious that it hardly need be argued. What is counterintuitive, however, is that finding a theory mistaken or even question-able at a test point can also be invaluable. More mileage can be gained from the Wittfogel example. When testing in other contexts suggested that Wittfogel's theory was suspect, a new fact was dis-covered: Irrigation development need not always lead to the estab-lishment of hierarchical social organization. A new and unforeseen explanation also emerged: Irrigation could be used to buttress al-ready existing hierarchical structure, and could even be deliberately exploited for that purpose (Earle 1973, 1977, 1978). The original Witt-fogelian thesis became suspect, but unanticipated new understand-ing about hierarchical social structure was gained.

The development of Wittfogelian theory thus illustrates a crucial but often unappreciated facet of theoretical development. When the-ories are bold enough, they can make a contribution even when in-terpreted as mistaken. That is why theories that increase under-standing are valuable even if they do not yield new insight at every point.

Unanticipated understanding and insight

Increased understanding and new insight should, as far as possible, be unforeseen. That is, new understanding and insight should po-tentially be *unanticipated* by a theory under consideration. The origi-nal Wittfogelian thesis, which stipulated that irrigation need was a necessary condition for the formation of state society, led to a differ-ent theory—that building and control of irrigation works were ex-ploited in an already existent hierarchical structure, even though ir-rigation was not a necessary condition for the formation of the hierarchical structure.

Even more radical unforeseen theoretical development occurred in another example: the overthrow of the classical diffusionist theory. Ac-cording to this theory, European culture had its roots in the Classical World, having spread by cultural contact (diffusion) into Europe.

The classical diffusionist theory implies that the dates of the Euro-pean monuments should be later than those in the Classical World. When radiocarbon dating techniques were refined in the 1950s, it was found that many of the European monuments *predated* those of the Classical World. That shock left the door open for interpreting European culture as the product of endogenous development rather than exogenous input. Endogenous development is a process, and systems models are particularly helpful for linking together the numerous causal elements that constitute an endogenous process (Bell 1981). The upshot is that systemic models became the new high-level theories used to generate explanations of the origin of European culture.

The point here is that nothing in the classical diffusionist theory anticipated systemic explanations, much less any other type of processual explanation. The latter are informed by entirely different assumptions than the classical diffusionist theory.

The importance of generating unanticipated understanding and insight will now be illustrated via a counterexample. Marxist approaches and the critical theory often associated with them provide the basis for the counterexample.

Marxist approaches place ideational elements in dialectical relation with material factors. Marxist approaches also assume that the broad categories of interpretation—the material and ideational factors along with the dialectic between them—are always valid. Also, Marxist approaches often (but not always) have a political dimension with two notable themes. First, privileged or entrenched classes are always in exploitative position over disadvantaged or marginalized classes. Second, exploitation of the disadvantaged classes by the privileged classes is a central factor in all human institutions, including intellectual fields (such as science, philosophy, political theory, anthropology, and archaeology). Analyzing human institutions from the Marxist perspective with its associated political dimension is called *critical theory*. Because critical theory is an historic as well as thematic outgrowth of Marxist analysis, the terms are sometimes used interchangeably. That will be done here.

An acknowledgment of the contributions of Marxist approaches is appropriate before focusing on the methodological weaknesses. That an archaeologist's present material conditions (his or her "class") can influence an interpretation of the past is a critical perspective that has shed light on the fact that archaeological theories can be exploited for political purposes (Shanks and Tilley 1987b). The now discredited lost-race explanation for the Moundbuilders of the Hopewell culture provides an example from America. The view that the Hopewell culture of the Ohio region was the product of a sophisticated lost race served to deny, at least according to some, that native Americans of that region had a significant cultural heritage. It also served the desire to create the myth of a heroic past for the Americas (Silverberg 1968; Sabloff 1982). Furthermore, there have been noticeable refinements within the Marxist interpretative categories, and such refinements will likely continue to be made (Hodder 1991; Leone 1982a, 1982b; Shanks and Tilley 1987a). Hodder's contextual approach to theory building, for example, is partly the product of his criticism of cruder Marxist approaches (Hodder 1991). Crumley and Marquardt's approach is in the Marxist tradition, but is so different that it is called dialectical (Crumley and Marquardt 1987).

A major problem with Marxist approaches is that the broad categories of Marxist interpretation are not allowed to be rejected. That, along with the associated belief that alternative categories are not considered legitimate, leads to the conviction that only Marxist categories are valid. What this means is that the material and ideational factors, along with the dialectic between them, are the only high-level models that can validly inform theory. In critical theory it also means that the exploitative tendencies of the privileged classes will always be the controlling model for explaining social institutions. That is why some archaeologists insist that an archaeologist's present material conditions are *always* the source of his or her interpretations of the past, and that reconstructions of the "real" past are thus impossible (Shanks and Tilley 1987b). It is also why critical theorists can be so convinced their explanations are always correct. It is not surprising, then, that Marxist approaches can take on a dogmatic overtone. When they do, no anomalous data is interpreted as counterevidence. Also, attempts to offer explanations informed by alternative high-level models are interpreted as further examples of exploitation by the privileged.

The source of the difficulties outlined is that the broad interpretative categories that inform Marxist approaches and critical theory are not allowed to change. Since they are not allowed to change, only refinements are possible. As stepping-stones in a research program that can yield unanticipated understanding and new insight, then, Marxist interpretations falter. Significant unforeseen or unanticipated theoretical development cannot be realized when interpretative categories are not allowed to change (Bell 1987a).

Although a distinction has been made between theories that lead to unanticipated developments and theories that only allow refinements, in practice no hard line can be drawn between the two categories. When applying method, it is best to think of abstract distinctions as representing extremes of a continuum. In this case, the example of the overthrow of the classical diffusionist theory and its replacement by processual theories is near one end of a continuum, and Marxist approaches fall near the other. Theoretical development in the Wittfogelian program lies between the two, although it is closer to the diffusionist example. Earle's new theory for the formation of complex societies in damper climates did not necessitate that there be control of water. That is quite different from the original Wittfogelian theory, in which the need to control water was the central theme.

On the other hand, recognizing there is a continuum does *not* imply that it makes little difference where on the continuum a theory lies. All theories contribute less as they exhaust their potential for understanding and insight, but those that only allow refinements foreclose on major unanticipated theoretical developments. That is why theories that disallow unforeseen change also become so predictably repetitive, eventually sparking little interest except among those with a special stake in them.

The potential of theories to yield unanticipated understanding and insight is closely related to the testability of theories. It also depends on exploiting tests fruitfully, including avoidance of ad hoc adjustments in the face of anomalous data.

Formulation of Testable Theories

In order to yield new insight theories must pass tests. In order to serve as stepping-stones to unforeseen understanding and insight, they must also be capable of failing other tests. For these reasons theories must be *testable,* that is, they must imply at least some empirical consequences that, when tested, can be used to interpret the theories as right or wrong. Examples of testable and nontestable theories are given here.

Testable and nontestable theories

Classical diffusionist theory implied that cultural artifacts in Europe should postdate similar ones in the Classical World. In other words, the classical diffusionist theory was testable. As explained earlier, it failed the test when radiocarbon dating techniques were refined. Processual approaches to theory development replaced classical diffusionist theory when the latter was refuted. Note that processual approaches might not have gained an adequate foothold if the classical diffusionist theory had not been refuted, and the latter would not have been refuted if it had not been testable. A hypothetical counterexample will illustrate this point.

Imagine that the dominant explanation was that European culture was a gift from the Greek gods to the Barbarians. Furthermore, assume that the gift-of-the-Greek-gods theory is plausible, or at least that elements of it might be correct. The trouble is that there exists no reliable way to assess the theory as right or wrong because there are no empirical points at which the theory could potentially fail. The unanticipated understanding and insight that followed after the empirical failure of the classical diffusionist theory might not have been possible if this gift-of-the-Greek-gods theory had been the dominant view instead of the classical diffusionist theory.

The example given is hypothetical, generated to illustrate the importance of testability. Unfortunately, lack of testability has characterized many influential theories in the annals of archaeology. In addition to the lost-race explanation of the Hopewell culture, others include the wildly speculative theories about the builders of Stonehenge, the extraterrestrial explanations for the markings in the Peruvian Desert, and the multitude of fantastic explanations of the origins of the pyramids in both the Nile Valley and Central America. All of these have been discredited among professional archaeologists, largely because other theories have gained credibility, and a major reason other theories have gained credibility is *that they have been testable*. Theories that could not be assessed against the ever-increasing store of archaeological data have fallen by the wayside, and those theories that could be assessed against the data have gained the attention of archaeologists (Sabloff 1982).

It must be clearly understood that nontestable theories can be valuable. The understanding they offer can be interesting in itself. In addition, nontestable theories may contain elements of truth even if those elements cannot be sorted out confidently. Furthermore, nontestable theories sometimes evolve into testable theories. Recall from Chapter 1 the examples of possible myth leading to the discovery of Bronze-Age Hisarlik, and untested conjecture being confirmed with the discovery of the Hittite kingdom. Typically nontestable theories become testable decades or even centuries after being proposed, and sometimes in different and unforeseen problem-situations. Nevertheless, they do become credible when and if they become testable and pass some tests. Finally, nontestable theories can provide a perspective from which to discover weaknesses in competing theories, a point to be discussed later in this chapter. For all of the reasons listed, one should not dismiss a theory out of hand simply because it is not testable.

On the other hand, nontestable theories have serious drawbacks. Because they are not testable, they are not capable of providing new insight (when tested and found correct) or unforeseen increased understanding and potential insight (when tested and found incorrect). Unfortunately, these shortcomings are very severe. Nontestable theories are like finished paintings with little or no improvement possible. They are not daring sketches with clues for new development.

Implicative reasoning

A testable theory is, more precisely, a theory with testable implications. For that reason it is important to discuss *implicative reasoning*— tracing the implications of a theory. Stated in alternative idiom, to trace the implications of a theory is to deduce its consequences. It goes without saying that the most significant implications are those that can be tested. Often the implications of a theory can be deduced without an undue amount of reflection. Classical diffusionist theory, for example, implied that cultural artifacts in the Classical World should predate similar ones in Europe. More complicated implicative reasoning is used in the following example. Revelation of synthesized bricks at a site implies that kilns must have been used. The implication is complicated by the fact that correct characterization of the bricks (as synthetic) would have to be assumed, and what would qualify as evidence of a kiln might not be obvious.

Mathematics and formal techniques

For two reasons, mathematics and other formal techniques of deduction can be helpful when drawing implications. First, the implications of a theory can be drawn more clearly. Formal deduction makes use of highly specified rules. Formally deduced implications can thus be more reliable than intuitively deduced implications, especially when the intuitive distance between a theory and its implications becomes greater and greater. Second, formally deduced implications become more precise when quantitative parameters, usually numbers, are carried through the deduction to the implication. A numerical or quantified implication is more precise because it specifies more exactly what follows from a theory.

For both reasons, tests of formalized theories can be more severe: the more clear and the more precise the implications of a theory, the more vulnerable the theory to demonstration of error. The more vulnerable to error, the greater the opportunity to discover weaknesses in theories. When weaknesses are discovered there is more motivation to search for modified or new theories. If theories pass more severe tests, on the other hand, there is firmer ground for confidence in them. It is no wonder that formalized theories are so prized.

The introduction of mathematical and formal techniques into science was and still is a great aid in its advance. Yet one must be on guard against abuses as well. Two of the most obvious faux pas are discussed next. The first mistakenly renders tests more severe than warranted, and the second mistakenly yields tests that are less severe than they appear.

The first abuse is to quantify explanatory elements not amenable to quantification. The quantitative implications will be falsely precise and hence the tests will seem more severe than warranted. Two outcomes, both undesirable, can be the result. The theory might be mistakenly interpreted as suspect by not passing a misconceived quantitative test. Alternatively, one might be tempted to "smooth out" the quantitative test results, thus making it appear as if the theory has passed a more severe test than it actually has.

Archaeology is not a field particularly prone to the first type of abuse, perhaps because archaeologists do not automatically revere quantified theories. In fields such as sociology, however, quantification and formal techniques are such an integral part of acceptable method that placing numbers indiscriminately on parameters is much more tempting.

The second abuse is more subtle and counterintuitive. Certain quantifications can actually make testing less severe, and hence discourage the revelation of anomaly. By far the most common misuse is to use probabilistic conventions to establish confidence in a theory. This misuse arises from attempts to answer a question that is impossible to answer. Examples are "what is the probability that the classical diffusionist theory is true," or "what is the probability that Wittfogel's original theory is true?"

The reason it is impossible to calculate the probability of theories is that the *prior probabilities*—probabilities of the constituent events comprising an outcome—cannot be established. For example, one cannot establish the prior probability of Wittfogel's theory passing a particular test. Hence one could not calculate the probability of Wittfogel's theory, either, which would require establishing such prior probabilities. Even if probabilistic calculations could be made for theories, a probabilistic measure of a theory would be unfortunate for another reason: It could tempt one to accept improbable, but possible, anomalies rather than interpreting anomalies as errors to be exploited for further theoretical development. That is why interpreting an anomaly as acceptable within a stipulated range of probability can weaken the testing of a theory (Bell 1986). Incidentally, an insightful article by Martin Wobst on the use of statistical techniques in site location also includes comments on indiscriminate use of probabilistic measures (Wobst 1983). His analysis identifies confusions about the different functions of probability.

Attempts to use probabilistic measures to establish confidence in theories is not desirable, but such attempts must not be confused with exploiting stochastic regularities, that is, with using statistical patterns found in the real world. For example, finding a certain vase in the burial sites of the vast majority of women but only a few of the men is a regularity compiled from empirical evidence. It is the type of statistical evidence that indicates that such vases are likely to have had significance, evidence that can provide the impetus to search for an explanation or be used to evaluate explanations. Not surprisingly Wobst, in his exposition of beneficial statistical analyses in site location, and Stephen Shennan, in his recommendations for applying statistical techniques in archaeology, deal only with stochastic regularities and not with probabilistic measures of theories (Wobst 1983; Shennan 1988).

The difference between attempting to measure epistemological probabilities and exploiting statistical regularities found in the real world seems so obvious that it hardly need be mentioned. Yet the two are often conflated, and the resultant confusion is a major reason for the abuse of probability. In my view the responsibility for conflating the two lies squarely on the inductive tradition that still dominates the English-speaking world. Archaeologists have by no means escaped exposure to this confusion that lies at the heart of inductive theory. It runs throughout much of Merrilee Salmon's well-known book *Philosophy and Archaeology* (Salmon 1982; see also Bell 1984). Chapter 4 offers a more detailed discussion of the abuses of probability and why they can mesmerize us so easily.

Testable and weakly testable theories

It will come as no surprise that the distinction between testable and nontestable theories is bridged by a continuum. Theories range from highly testable to nontestable, with most situated somewhere between those extremes. Because the potential for a theory to yield new insight is directly related to its testability, the closer to the testable end of the continuum the greater the potential for new insight. Furthermore, the continuum between testable and nontestable theories generates the continuum discussed in the last section between theories that can lead to unanticipated understandings and theories that only allow refinements. The more testable a theory, the more potential it will lead to unanticipated developments and the less testable a theory the more likely it will only permit refinements. For these reasons the position of a given theory on the continuum between testable and nontestable theories is absolutely crucial. From a methodological perspective, *the degree to which a theory is testable is the most important single indicator of its potential to contribute to the advance of archaeological theory.*

If so much depends upon testability, is there some way of knowing where on the continuum a given theory lies? Clearly there is no definitive yardstick, much less quantifiable measure. Fortunately, such a measure is not crucial. What is crucial is that a theory can be analyzed to reveal characteristics that augment or constrain its testability. Diffusion theory and processual theory present an interesting contrast.

Diffusion theory is testable, as we have seen. Diffusion implies that diffused artifacts will post-date the sources from which they stem. A chronology, provided it is sufficiently accurate, can thus be used to refute a diffusion explanation. Furthermore, diffusion can be established if there is sufficient positive evidence. For example, the discovery of a ceremonial axehead made of lapis lazuli at Troy confirmed that there must have been at least some cultural contact between Bactria (modern Afghanistan) and Troy. Why? There were numerous sources of copper around the Eastern Mediterranean that were known during the Bronze Age, but no sources of tin. Lapis lazuli is normally associated with Afghan tin sources. Therefore the tin likely came from Afghanistan to Troy on its way to the Aegean.

A reasonably accurate chronology could refute a diffusion explanation, then, and strong positive evidence could establish a diffusion explanation. Other than that, however, diffusion theories are not subject to testing. The reasons are outlined here.

First, although chronologies can be used to refute a diffusion theory, chronologies are not sufficient to establish a diffusion theory. If the supposedly diffused artifacts postdate the sources, which they should, it only suggests that diffusion is possible. The reason is that the allegedly diffused artifacts could have been produced endogenously but simply at a later date than the supposed sources.

Second, and most important, the very structure of diffusion explanations curtails testability. The reason is that nothing, except for chronology, can provide definitive evidence *against* a diffusion explanation. If positive evidence of diffusion is not available, one can simply assume that the evidence for diffusion has yet to be found. If it is never found, one can still assume that diffusion took place but that the evidence has been lost.

Diffusion explanations can sometimes be refuted in more indirect ways. If artifacts supposedly diffused can be plausibly explained as the product of endogenous development, then there is reason to regard a diffusion explanation as refuted. For example, sourcing analysis could establish that the material sources of artifacts are local rather than external. The disadvantage is that such refutations can be more dependent upon an interpretive decision than direct refutation by chronology. To exploit the example further: Ideas important for generating certain artifacts might have arrived via diffusion even if the material sources for building the artifacts were local. Despite such interpretive problems, regarding a diffusion theory as refuted could still enhance theory development by providing the impetus to search out and consider seriously other types of explanation.

The relative lack of testability in diffusion theory explains why its contribution to the advancement of archaeological knowledge has been curtailed. Certainly diffusion did occur in the past. The trouble is that diffusion theories are not highly testable. Chronologies can sometimes directly refute a particular diffusion theory, and alternative explanations can sometimes indirectly refute a particular diffusion theory. At times, positive evidence can establish diffusion in a particular context. Otherwise, however, a diffusion explanation can be as empirically frustrating as a gift-of-the-Greek-gods explanation: It can neither be refuted nor established by the artifactual record. The upshot is that someone who wishes to believe in diffusion can do so irrespective of the evidence. Maintaining such beliefs is not consistent with the development of new understanding and insight. Thus, although diffusion theory is testable, it is only weakly testable. On the continuum it is more characteristic of the nontestable pole than the testable pole. Furthermore, attempts to adjust diffusion theory tend to render it completely nontestable. This issue is discussed later, in the section on ad hoc adjustments to theories.

Processual theories make explicit the network of causal links that explain a "process;" that is, how a given state of affairs is transformed into another. A key assumption in processual approaches is that the causal links are endogenous, rather than exogenous, unless there is clear evidence to the contrary. This assumption is critical for the testability of processual approaches.

When an explanation consists of a network of endogenous casual links—in other words, when an explanation is systemic—it yields an array of implications. Furthermore, because the causal links are internal to the system under study, the implications are also internal. Finally, processual explanations are often dynamic: They explain change over time. Dynamic explanations normally yield different implications when iterated over time. Each of these characteristics of processual explanations can increase testability.

A network of causal links tends to yield a large number of implications. All things being equal, the greater the number of implications, the greater the number of testable implications. Furthermore, internal or endogenous implications tend to be more testable than external or exogenous factors. One reason is that internal factors are generally more accessible than external ones. Another reason is that exogenous factors tend to be weakly testable if testable at all. Like a deus ex machina, an exogenous factor may not be refutable itself, and may also not be positively established. That is why exogenous factors can be methodologically suspect. Finally, the number of implications is multiplied if a processual explanation can be iterated over time. At one point in time a processual explanation may imply a certain artifactual array, and at another time it may imply a different artifactual array. If the artifactual evidence is sufficiently rich, then, a processual explanation may be testable at two or more different dating windows.

For an example that illustrates the testable qualities of processual explanations, I recommend "Simulation Model Development: A Case Study of the Classic Maya Collapse" (Hosler et al. 1977). The authors offer many causal links in the explanation of the rather rapid changes in the Maya world usually (but not always) referred to as a collapse. These many causal links do yield a plethora of implications, among them a sizable number of testable implications. Furthermore, the systemic explanation put forward in the study does not rely on exogenous factors such as invasion or economic competition to explain the collapse. The collapse is instead explained as the product of internal dynamics, particularly of the relationship between the priests and the commoners. The implications of internal dynamics are normally more accessible to testing than exogenous factors and do not have the exogenous tendency to be ad hoc. Finally, the model was dynamic and was iterated over time, yielding an array of different testable implications at different time windows. A static model would not have provided such an array. (For another simulation study of the Maya collapse, see John W. G. Lowe's 1985 book, *The Dynamics of Apocalypse*.)

Incidentally, processual archaeology is often called "scientific." If a hallmark of science is the testability of its theories, then the label is quite fitting. It should be added that the replacement of diffusion theory by processual theory is usually interpreted as more than just the overthrow of one type of theory by another. It is also viewed as a methodological revolution in which a less than scientific approach is replaced by a scientific approach. This view is appropriate. Diffusion explanations are weakly testable at best whereas processual explanations can be highly testable.

Exploiting Empirical and Consistency Tests

That data must be used in assessing theories is a healthy methodological rule, of course. The question is not whether to use data, but how to use it for testing.

Theories can be tested in two broad ways: by empirical tests—

evaluation directly against data—and by consistency tests—assessment of the compatibility of theoretical statements. Each type of test is discussed in this section.

Empirical testing

Whether under controlled conditions in a laboratory or under passive conditions in the field, empirical tests are crucial for evaluating theories. Empirical tests can help show where theories are correct and where they are mistaken. To be more specific, if a theory implies X and X is a testable point, then after testing one can interpret the theory as correct or mistaken at that point. Each possibility is discussed and illustrated in turn.

If X is discovered, the theory can be interpreted as correct at that point. To gain mileage from a prior example, A. H. Sayce's research led him to theorize that there had existed a significant but undiscovered empire in Anatolia. Flinders Petrie's analysis of clay tablets in Egypt proved Sayce's theory correct.

If data contrary to X are discovered—anomalous data—then the theory can be interpreted as mistaken at that point. Using another prior example, the classical diffusionist theory predicted that the monuments in Central and Northern Europe should have been built at a later date than those of the Eastern Mediterranean. With the establishment of reliable radiocarbon dating techniques it was discovered that many of the European monuments predated those of the Mediterranean. The classical version of diffusionist theory was proven incorrect.

It is important to remember that assessing explanations in the light of empirical data is more dependent upon interpretative decision than is normally assumed. Those of us nurtured on the inductive tradition tend to assume *res ipsa loquitur*—the facts speak for themselves. But data do not speak for themselves, nor do they even come close to it. How data are used to assess a theory is vitally dependent upon how one chooses to *interpret* the data with respect to the theory.

Interpretation of data becomes particularly important when it seems to conflict with a theory. If contrary data is interpreted as acceptable within some probabilistic range, or explained away as unimportant, or simply ignored, the impetus for further theoretical development is likely to be lost, or at least delayed. If such unfortunate decisions are made, remember that the culprit is not the data, but methodological decisions made in light of the data. Changing data is dishonest, of course. On the other hand, decisions about data certainly can and should be changed if there is methodological reason to do so. An illustration of the pivotal role of a decision about data is found in the research program that grew from Wittfogel's work.

Recall from the beginning of this chapter that Wittfogel generalized his theory that state society formed because of need to develop and manage water resources to explain the formation of *all* state societies in any climatic conditions. Earle concluded from his own research in Hawaii that Wittfogel's theory had been refuted, and then postulated his own theory—that irrigation development and management is not a necessary condition for the formation of complex societies, but can function to solidify state structures already extant. The first crucial methodological decision in this story was Wittfogel's willingness to generalize from his research in the arid regions of the Orient to the formation of state society in all contexts, including damp regions such as Hawaii (Wittfogel 1957). The importance of that bold move by Wittfogel was discussed earlier in this chapter. Another crucial methodological decision was Earle's conclusion that his Hawaiian data refuted Wittfogel's theory (Earle 1973, 1977, and 1978). The data did not simply "refute" Wittfogel's theory by itself. Rather, Earle *decided* that his data refuted Wittfogel's theory. That is why it not surprising that questions have been raised about whether the data from Hawaii does indeed refute Wittfogel's theory (Gandara 1981).

Two points merit highlighting here. First, Earle had to decide that his data were sufficient to refute Wittfogel's theory even though there are questions about whether they did. Second, Earle's decision was crucial in the development of his new, unanticipated theory. In short, without the bold decision that Wittfogel was refuted, a new unanticipated theory might not have been generated.

The importance of Earle's decision—that his data refuted Wittfogel's theory—becomes clearer if one hypothesizes what might have happened had Earle decided *not* to regard Wittfogel's theory as refuted. What might have happened if Earle had decided, for example, that Wittfogel's theory was plausible in the majority of contexts even though Earle had discovered an exception in Hawaii? Earle might have concluded that despite the exception, Wittfogel's theory is probable enough to merit confidence. Alternatively, Earle might have decided that Wittfogel's theory applies in arid regions but that it is not relevant in damp regions. Although Wittfogel had generalized his own theory to apply in all contexts, including Hawaii, Earle could have set a boundary on the theory by limiting its range to arid contexts. In either case—treating Hawaii as an improbable but possible exception, or declaring Hawaii beyond the boundaries of Wittfogel's theory—there would have been little or no incentive to search for an alternative explanation of the relationship between the formation of state society and irrigation development. Theory development would have been retarded rather than augmented. The culprit would not have been Earle's data, but the methodological decisions made from the data.

Incidentally, the two methodological strategies hypothesized earlier—explaining away anomalous data as a possible but improbable exception and excluding anomalous data by setting up boundary conditions—are methodological tools forged from the inductive view of science. They are explored further in Chapter 4.

This is a convenient point to say more about relativism, specifically, about data and relativism. Confidence in data normally provides a bulwark against relativism. The reason is that testing theories against data presupposes that there is an objective criterion for assessing theories. Surprisingly, however, misplaced confidence in data—unwarranted faith that data speak for themselves—unintentionally starts one down a slippery slope to relativism. Here is a sketch of how that can happen.

A critic of science can trot out typical truisms such as "facts and theories are not clearly separable" and "facts can never really confirm or refute a theory." These and related claims do have a modicum of truth: "Facts" only become relevant in a theoretical context, for example, facts are themselves interpretations of phenomena, and interpreting a theory as confirmed or refuted requires a methodological decision (as illustrated earlier).

A critic is unlikely to be satisfied with the modicum of truth in such claims. Instead, he or she can use truisms like those already mentioned as premises from which to draw conclusions that purportedly undermine science. A typical chain of such "reasoning" is the following: Because facts can never definitively confirm or refute a theory, empirical data cannot be crucial for making decisions about theories. Thus empirical data are not important for science. Science, in other words, is just another subjective product of our interpretative faculties. It should be regarded much like poetry, music, literary criticism, and other creative enterprises. Lest one think that this vision of science is so ridiculous it hardly need be addressed, a recent, widely read book espouses just such a view (Harding 1986; for a critical review see Shrader-Frechette 1988).

The chain of reasoning exemplified here is typical of how uncritical faith in facts can boomerang to relativism (Popper 1962). A similar chain of reasoning for relativism results from conflating empirical tests with consistency tests. I will return to that point after discussing consistency testing.

Consistency Testing

A consistent theory is one that harbors no contradictions. In practice, testing for consistency amounts to searching for an inconsistency—a contradiction—among the statements and assumptions that constitute a theory. An inconsistency can be productive if exploited. The reason is that an *inconsistent* theory—one with assumptions or statements that cannot all be true—is either empirically mistaken or contains interpretative mistake(s). That is why it is important to analyze explanations to ferret out inconsistency.

If inconsistency is found, search for factual error or interpretative mistake(s) should be undertaken. If an inconsistency is found within a theory, one can attempt to find an empirical error. One would separate the assumptions in the theory that might be erroneous and devise ways of testing them. Then one would proceed as with empirical testing.

If empirical error is not the source of the inconsistency, then there must be an interpretative mistake. In other words, the inconsistency can be treated as a *paradox*—an inconsistency due to misinterpretation. Treating an inconsistency as a paradox provides the impetus to rethink an entire problem, along with the theories and assumptions that surround it.

It is difficult if not impossible to foresee how a paradox will be resolved. Paradoxes are usually rectified in an unforeseen way, often in the context of startling and sometimes revolutionary changes in explanations. Even unresolved, however, paradoxes are valuable. They indicate something is wrong in a theory or the broad conceptual structure within which it is placed. That can provide the motive to search for a resolution, or at least prepare one to recognize and consider a resolution proposed by someone else.

Here is an hypothetical example of consistency testing. An archaeologist formulates an explanation for the social behavior of a prehistoric group. Their behavior as reconstructed from the artifactual record is characterized by benevolent relations, both within and without the group. Yet there is reason to believe that neighboring groups at the same time were not benevolent toward each other, implying there would have been conflict with the target group as well. In short, there is an inconsistency.

In face of the inconsistency, an archaeologist would, it is hoped, attempt to devise ways of isolating assumptions or claims within the postulated social behavior of the group, and then test them for error. For example, evidence of destruction may be found in the material record, but it might not be due to strife. A check on seismic activity might reveal the explanation of the destruction. If nothing of significance is found, the inconsistency could be interpreted as a paradox, and an entire rethinking of the social behavior of this group might bear fruit.

As with empirical testing, it is clear that the potential for greater understanding and new insight provided by consistency testing is very much dependent upon methodological decisions. One could simply ignore an inconsistency, or explain it away. If interpreted as a paradox, it might be regarded as superficial rather than indicative of need for rethinking. Such abuses of inconsistency can retard theoretical development.

Testing for inconsistency is pivotal in another example—Patty Jo Watson's and Mary C. Kennedy's analyses of theories about the development of horticulture in the eastern woodlands of North America (Watson and Kennedy 1991). This example is particularly interesting for another reason as well: It reveals how gender bias can interfere with theory development. The latter purpose of the example will be discussed after the former.

Watson and Kennedy note that anthropologists and archaeologists have typically let their theories about social organization in hunter-gatherer and foraging societies be informed by traditional (high-level) models. Such models include the following characteristics: (1) subsistence activities are divided according to age and sex, (2) for biological reasons adult women are primarily responsible for nourishing and socializing infants and small children, (3) for biological reasons adult men are primarily responsible for safeguarding the social unit and with tasks that require bursts of energy, such as running down game, and (4) therefore labor is divided such that women are responsible for passive activities that do not interfere with child care, such as the collecting of stationary resources such as plants and firewood, while men are responsible for exploiting mobile resources, such as the hunting of game (Watson and Kennedy 1991: 259). The upshot is that "Men are strong, dominant protectors who hunt animals; women are weaker, passive, hampered by their reproductive responsibilities, and hence, consigned to plant gathering" (Watson and Kennedy 1991:256).

It is interesting to note that biological reasons are cited as the ultimate basis for traditional conceptions of social organization in hunter-gatherer and foraging societies. "Biological" in this context does literally mean that the social organization has a biological basis. "Biological" in this context has an implied meaning as well, however: that the traditional models of social organization are necessary because their biological basis make them inevitable.

Fortunately, however, Watson and Kennedy are not prepared to foreclose on other models of social organization. The reason is that they find inconsistencies among the theories that are (supposedly) informed by the traditional models. Bruce Smith's (1987) reconstruction of the domestication of seed-bearing plants in eastern North America, for example, implies that women were active in processing, storage, fertilization, and consumption patterns. Yet, Smith's explicit reconstruction "downplays stress, drive, intention, or innovation of any sort on the part of the people involved, in this case the women" (Watson and Kennedy 1991:262). Another example of inconsistency is found in Guy Prentice's (1986) account of the origins of plant domestication in the eastern United States. Prentice's reconstruction incorporates innovation. Because innovation is not a product of deterministic forces, Prentice does not assume a strict biological model of explanation. Nevertheless, he postulates that the innovation would have to be "introduced by an individual of high status, a specialist, and ambitious person who is in contact with outsiders and who is oriented toward commerce rather than subsistence" (Watson and Kennedy 1991:263). In short, the individual would have to be a man. Watson and Kennedy object to that assumption, and rightly so. There is an inconsistency: Women are traditionally accorded the dominant role in plant domestication, but then are removed from that dominant position when innovation or invention is postulated as a precursor to a revolutionary event (Watson and Kennedy 1991:264).

Watson and Kennedy show further methodological acumen by arguing that the inconsistencies suggest the need for further empirical testing. They point out that the data are not conclusive as to whether men or women were involved in plant domestication, and in what ways. Moreover, further testing might yield answers, or partial answers. If so, there would be increased insight. Notice also that Watson and Kennedy did *not* simply jump to the conclusion that women must have been the sole agents of plant domestication, or that women must have been innovators. They correctly recognize that such conclusions would be no more empirically justified than that men played such roles. I might add that such conclusions would also blunt the impetus to do further empirical testing. The lesson? It is equally important that inconsistencies be recognized and that they be exploited for further empirical testing whenever possible.

Incidentally, in their article Watson and Kennedy do provide evidence that women were agents in plant domestication in the eastern woodlands of North America. Their chain of reasoning about the introduction of Northern Flint (or Eastern) eight-row maize is somewhat complicated, but their discussion does provide evidence that the acceptance and cultivation of eight-row maize was purposeful and deliberate, and that women were likely the ones who did it (Watson and Kennedy 1991:266). In short, Watson and Kennedy themselves provide some of the empirical argument that contributes to resolving the inconsistencies.

The gender bias in explanations of plant domestication seems so obvious that it hardly need be discussed further, but additional comment is warranted. First, Watson and Kennedy's article is so clearly argued that the gender bias seems self-evident. In my view it is the penetrating analysis of Watson and Kennedy that makes it seem so obvious. Second, if the gender bias is so obvious, why was it not revealed earlier? The answer is, I believe, the one suggested by the authors: the women's movement and the recognition that women can work outside the domestic sphere (Watson and Kennedy 1991: 256). Earlier there seemed to be little impetus to challenge the traditional conception of the division of labor among the sexes implied by the biological models. Third and finally, Watson and Kennedy avoid the temptation to create a reverse gender bias against men. There may be various reasons why they avoided this, but among the reasons must certainly be their loyalty to empirical standards and desire to exploit the inconsistencies for further theory development. In short, they have used sound method and much the same can be said of many other studies included in the same book (Gero and Conkey 1991). By way of contrast, sound method does not characterize the interpretative speculation recommended by some in the post-processual camp whose theorizing is associated with the women's movement (see Bell 1987a and Chapter 7 of this book).

By the way, there is a logical similarity between empirical tests and consistency tests. A "fact" is actually a *factual statement*: a statement about empirical data. For that reason empirical tests can be interpreted as consistency tests within a set of statement(s) that include theoretical statements and factual statements. Likewise, a fact that contradicts a theory can be understood to be a factual statement that is inconsistent with the statements constituting a theory. To a practicing archaeologist these points of logic might seem like philosophical quibbling, but there is something of importance to be learned here. Interpreting an empirical test as a type of consistency test has advantages as well as disadvantages.

The advantages of interpreting empirical tests as a subset of consistency tests are that the interpretative overtones of "fact" become more readily apparent, and the logical structure of assessing theories against data is made explicit and hence more amenable to analysis. Gardin used this tool well in his analysis of theory structure and theoretical reasoning in archaeology. His most detailed account is in *Archaeological Constructs: An Aspect of Theoretical Archaeology* (Gardin 1980).

Although acknowledging the advantages, in my view it is usually preferable to distinguish between empirical tests and consistency tests, for the following reasons.

Despite the logical similarity of empirical and consistency tests, discovering an empirical error differs from exposing an inconsistency. Empirical error is revealed by contrasting an explanation with data, those either already available or gathered by further research or fieldwork. Inconsistency is uncovered by analyzing a theory and its associated assumptions *without* reference to empirical data. As already explained, *after* exposing an inconsistency one might decide to search for empirical error, but that is a different task than finding the inconsistency in the first place.

Interpreting empirical tests as a subset of consistency tests is also another ploy used by critics of science to argue for relativism. From the (partially correct) premise that empirical tests are really tests of consistency between statements, relativists like to draw the (incorrect) conclusions that there are no empirical tests, and hence that theories cannot be evaluated empirically. This invalid argument hinges on the mistaken assumption that factual statements do not differ from theoretical statements. To be sure, this assumption is usually worded differently, such as "description and explanation do not differ," or "facts and theories cannot be separated." These mistaken claims are just like those used by Hodder to support his attacks on scientific approaches to theory building in archaeology (Hodder 1991; see also Bell 1987a). Hodder is reluctant to embrace relativism explicitly, but the relativistic line of argument cannot be ignored. Interpreting empirical tests as a subset of consistency tests is one of his relativistic tools.

Avoiding Ad Hoc Adjustments to Theories

It is important that theories are interpreted as testable, and that they be tested empirically and for consistency. It is also important that they remain testable when adjusted. The route to maintaining testability is to avoid ad hoc adjustments—adjustments that decrease testability.

Adjustments are normally made in the face of error. They can be classified into two types: those in which testability is maintained or increased and those in which it is decreased. Hypotheses adjoined to a theory to account for empirical error but that leave a theory open to further testing, that is, those that maintain or increase testability, are called *auxiliary hypotheses*. Adjustments that account for error but that reduce testability are called ad hoc adjustments. In everyday language, to make an ad hoc adjustment to a theory is to "explain away" anomalous evidence.

In practice it is best to think of adjustments as situated on a continuum between those utilizing auxiliary hypotheses to those that are ad hoc. This is another case in which thinking in terms of a continuum is helpful when applying method. Certainly there are adjustments that fall near one extreme or the other, but more often than not an adjustment will be somewhere in between.

The methodological goal when adjusting theories is to preserve or even increase testability as much as possible. Striving for that goal in practice is guided by a methodological rule-of-thumb: Do all that is possible to avoid ad hoc adjustments.

Radiocarbon dates and diffusion theory have been cited so many times already that the reader may feel distraught by the prospect of more. The fact is, however, that examples of both ad hoc adjustments and adjustments with auxiliary hypotheses are conveniently found in the controversies surrounding diffusionist theory and the development of radiocarbon dating. That is why I will turn to them again, with the promise that there will be no more after this section.

Adjustments with Auxiliary Hypotheses

Radiocarbon dating techniques became well enough established by 1970 that radiocarbon dates came to be regarded as relatively uncontroversial. By that time it was possible to determine radiocarbon dates quite accurately by calibrating them with carbon-14 levels determined by tree-ring analysis of the bristlecone pine of California. The calibrated dates had also been tested successfully against reliable historical chronologies. Between Willard F. Libby's report of the first radiocarbon dates in 1949 and the widespread confidence in radiocarbon dating by the late 1960s, however, radiocarbon techniques and hence dates were seriously challenged, and in some cases for good reason.

From our present perspective it is difficult to realize that radiocarbon dating was itself a theoretical construct open to legitimate challenge for almost two decades. It was only *after* the calibration with tree-ring analysis and corroboration against historical chronologies that radiocarbon techniques yielded dates that in everyday idiom are called *facts*, that is, low-level theories that survive so many empirical tests that they become relatively uncontroversial. Even though there are still problems, including some sets of dates within which the correct date must be identified by other means, radiocarbon dates have become well enough established that they have become a reasonably reliable tool.

Here is a methodological caricature of the evolution of radiocarbon dating theory. Radiocarbon dating theory faced significant challenges during its development. Some of those challenges appeared to undermine radiocarbon dating theory, to the point where it could only confidently be used for rather crude approximations. Alterations in radiocarbon theory to meet those challenges were quite successful, however, because they emerged from auxiliary hypotheses that left radiocarbon dating theory open to retesting. Retesting after adjustment was corroborative, leaving an improved radiocarbon theory. A reconstruction of some challenges to radiocarbon dating theory and the alterations in that theory to meet the challenges provides clear examples of how to adjust theories with auxiliary hypotheses.

Before beginning the discussion of the development of radiocarbon dating theory I would like to identify some helpful sources. For a more detailed summary of the radiocarbon revolution I recommend chapters 3 and 4 of Colin Renfrew's *Before Civilization: The Radiocarbon Revolution and Prehistoric Europe* (1973a). For understanding radiocarbon dating and its uses in archaeology, I recommend Joseph W. Michels' *Dating Methods in Archaeology* (1973) and Royal E. Taylor's *Radiocarbon Dating: An Archaeological Perspective* (1987).

Willard Libby's radiocarbon laboratory in Chicago was the first of its kind. For a number of years only a handful of other facilities were established in North America and Europe. Because of that, and because of the time and effort required to do radiocarbon analyses in those early years, only a limited pool of radiocarbon dates became available. Furthermore, some dates of artifactual material in similar archaeological contexts and even stratigraphic locations were found to vary more than was acceptable. Finally, some dates were severely at odds with accepted dates established by reliable historical chronologies, and other radiocarbon dates prior to any comparable chronology—that is, prior to about 3,000 B.C. in the Mediterranean and Middle East and prior to about 1,500 B.C. in Northern Europe and Britain—were at times over a thousand years earlier than the dates accepted by scholarly authorities. In the face of such anomalies, many were less than confident in the dates emerging from radiocarbon laboratories.

A number of the earliest hypotheses auxiliary to radiocarbon dating theory concerned two problems: disparate dates, even within one dating period of an archaeological site, and contamination. The hypotheses used to meet these problems were quite different, but they were auxiliary rather than ad hoc.

One of the most commonly used sources for radiocarbon dating is charcoal. Dating from charcoal provides an example, however, of how disparate dates can arise. A charcoal deposit might consist of charcoal from wood that was long dead before burning as well as charcoal from wood that was cut or died shortly before it was burned. When the same deposit contains charcoal from sources of wood that died at disparate dates, radiocarbon analysis of the charcoal can yield quite disparate dates for an archaeological site. Indeed, it can also yield quite different dates for sites that should be similarly dated according to purely archaeological analysis. To cope with the potential discrepancies, an auxiliary hypothesis was added: Dates that are reliable should be based upon the evidence of a large number of dates and should span an archaeological region. The statistical flow of a large set of such dates can then override the potential anomalies due to discrepancies between wood-death dates. The net result was the production of statistically filtered dates that were more reliable than individual dates.

Contamination of charcoal and other substances used for radiocarbon dating was addressed by two auxiliary hypotheses. The first was that reliable dates should be the statistical product of a large set of dates over an archaeological region, thus overriding the variable effects of contamination in specific artifactual material. The thrust of this auxiliary hypothesis is the same as the one used to override discrepancies in wood-death dates. The second auxiliary hypothesis is that reliable dates can be found if contaminants are removed before radiocarbon analysis. This provided the impetus to develop techniques of identifying and removing contaminants. Finding and eliminating contaminants has been an exciting scientific and technological challenge for radiocarbon laboratories ever since its importance was recognized.

Notice that the auxiliary hypotheses preserved and even increased the testability of radiocarbon dating theory. Because an array of dates is more accurate than just a few dates, radiocarbon dating is put to a more severe empirical test against an array of dates. When the dates were corroborated, there was all the more reason for confidence in radiocarbon dating theory. Because uncontaminated artifactual material provides more accurate dates than contaminated material, radiocarbon dating theory is also put to a more severe empirical test against dates from decontaminated material. When these dates were corroborated, there was again all the more reason for confidence in radiocarbon dating theory.

Perhaps the most interesting of all hypotheses auxiliary to radiocarbon dating theory involved fluctuating concentrations of atmospheric radiocarbon. Radiocarbon dates are determined by measuring the proportion of nondisintegrated radiocarbon remaining in an artifact from the time it stopped carbon absorption from the atmosphere—the time it died—until the time of the measurement. A crucial assumption is that the concentration of radiocarbon in the atmosphere has remained constant through time. Only under that assumption can a given proportion of remaining radiocarbon be directly correlated with the number of years since the death of the object.

In the early years the assumption that the concentration of radiocarbon in the atmosphere remained constant was not a lethal hindrance to the use of radiocarbon dates, for two reasons. First, some of the most interesting early radiocarbon dates were very old, for example, dates for early village farming in Iraq (about 4,700 B.C.) and pre-Biblical Jericho in Palestine (about 6,000 B.C.). Such dates were certainly controversial because they were so much earlier than those proposed (or "guessed") by archaeological authorities. Nevertheless, these dates were so old that deviations due to possible fluctuations in the concentration of atmospheric radiocarbon seemed relatively unimportant. Second, such early dates could not be tested against reliable historical chronologies. The estimated dates of authorities were not reliable and hence could not be used to test radiocarbon dates.

Despite the value of the early radiocarbon dates, a serious question was raised about radiocarbon dates that were tested against early but reliable historical chronologies. Willard Libby himself admitted there was a problem. In his brief 1963 article "The Accuracy of Radiocarbon Dates," Libby acknowledged that the radiocarbon dates for Egypt from about 2,000 B.C. to 3,000 B.C., the earliest reliable historical period, were too recent compared with historical dates (Libby 1963). In short, radiocarbon dating theory was faced with serious anomalous data; it required adjustment and retesting. Radiocarbon dating was again adjusted, and again tested successfully. The background and story are recounted briefly here.

The assumption that radiocarbon concentration in the atmosphere has remained constant over time was seriously questioned in the middle 1950s. In 1956 it was discovered that past fluctuations in the strength of the earth's magnetic field had altered the amount of cosmic radiation reaching the earth from outer space. The magnetic field partially deflects cosmic radiation. Because the concentration of radiocarbon in the atmosphere is related to the amount of cosmic radiation reaching the earth from outer space, the changing magnetic field had also altered the concentration of radiocarbon in the atmosphere.

The upshot was yet another hypothesis auxiliary to radiocarbon dating theory: that radiocarbon dates are accurate after being adjusted to account for the actual concentration of radiocarbon in the atmosphere during the time when a dated object was alive. The challenge was to find a reliable way to measure the varying concentrations of atmospheric radiocarbon in the past.

One approach to estimating changes in the concentration of radiocarbon in the atmosphere is to measure changes in the earth's magnetic field. This approach was developed by using samples of baked clay from archaeological sites (Bucha 1970). The approach showed promise, but the timing was inauspicious, unfortunately. A better method for determining past radiocarbon concentrations was being developed concurrently.

Calibration against the radiocarbon content found in the rings of very old trees proved to be the most effective method. The age of tree rings can be counted by starting from the present and moving into the past; ring overlaps with even earlier dead trees allow the age count to proceed yet further into the past. Because tree rings are composed of wood that dies within a year or so of its growth, the radiocarbon concentration in the atmosphere in the live year of a tree ring can be determined from the (known) age of a given tree ring and the portion of nondisintegrated radiocarbon in that tree ring. This approach does have a limitation, of course: It is only useful as far into the past as reliable tree-ring counts can be made. For very old dates—those greater than about 7,000 years—tree-ring analysis is not feasible.

In brief, the actual concentration of atmospheric carbon-14 for any given year was determined by tree-ring analysis. No longer did radiocarbon dating theory labor under the (false) assumption that the concentration of atmospheric radiocarbon has remained constant through time. The result is that radiocarbon dates can be determined much more accurately after being adjusted for actual radiocarbon concentrations determined by tree-ring analysis. Finally, when calibrated radiocarbon dates were tested against early but reliable historical dates, the correlation was much closer. Instead of anomalous dates leading to the demise of radiocarbon dating theory, then, the theory was adjusted and retested successfully. Because the radiocarbon dates were more precise after calibration, the testing against reliable historical dates was more rigorous than before calibration. That is why one could have even more confidence in radiocarbon dating theory after adjustment and retesting.

Notice that all three examples of auxiliary adjustments to radiocarbon dating theory left the theory exposed to refutation. Adjustment for discrepancies in individual dates, for contamination in dated materials, and for actual atmospheric radiocarbon concentrations did not simply "explain away" anomalous dates, but left radiocarbon dating theory ready for further testing. That is why the hypotheses were auxiliary rather than ad hoc.

Finally, the testability of radiocarbon dating theory was not just preserved by adding auxiliary hypotheses; the testability of that theory was actually increased. Earlier it was pointed out that increasing precision, or increasing the number of testable consequences, will augment the testability of a theory. As seen in the preceding discussion, the three hypothesis auxiliary to radiocarbon dating theory did increase its precision and added more testable consequences. As a matter-of-fact, auxiliary hypotheses often render a theory more precise, or extend its testable consequences into a new area. It is no wonder that confidence in theories adjusted with auxiliary hypotheses grows when those theories pass tests after adjustment.

Ad hoc adjustments

The reader has just been presented with examples of auxiliary adjustments. It is now time to turn to ad hoc adjustments, and to see how they curtail or even eliminate the testability of a theory.

Classical diffusionist theory will be the first discussed. Classical diffusionist theory was at least partially testable. As pointed out earlier, it implied that the dates of artifacts diffused from the ancient world should postdate the artifactual models of the ancient world. When it was discovered that some of the supposedly "diffused" monuments actually predated those of the ancient world, the classical diffusionist theory was refuted. Even the refutation by dating chronology was somewhat lucky, however. The chronology implied by diffusion theories did lead to refutation, but only because of the rather fortuitous fact that some endogenous artifacts in Europe were developed before the Mediterranean models from which they supposedly diffused.

Except for the chronology implied by diffusion theories, however, diffusion theories tend to be virtually untestable. There are two reasons, both of which were outlined earlier. They are briefly summarized here.

First, direct evidence that one object was inspired by cultural diffusion from the other is needed to establish diffusion. While there are certainly examples of such proof, it is not often available in prehistory. Second, *lack* of direct evidence is not sufficient to refute diffusion. The reason is that diffusion *may* have occurred but has not been discovered, or might not even be discoverable. Unless some direct evidence for cultural contact can be found, then, or unless independent dating chronologies can provide refutation, diffusionist theories cannot be tested easily.

One attempt to adjust diffusionist theory when direct evidence of diffusion is lacking was championed by Alfred L. Kroeber. Kroeber argued there could be "stimulus diffusion," that is, diffusion of an idea rather than an actual artifact (Kroeber 1940; for a discussion see Renfrew 1973a:110–11). Analysis shows that this adjustment is ad hoc. Direct evidence of diffusion of an idea or inspiration would be more difficult to establish in prehistory—before the written word— than diffusion of a material artifact, and positive proof of diffusion of material objects is quite rare. Furthermore, lack of evidence of stimulus diffusion would not force one to give up stimulus diffusion as an explanation. It could always be pointed out that the stimulant had not yet been discovered, or that the precise nature of the stimulus had not yet been adequately determined. Finally, even chronologies are difficult to use to test stimulus diffusion. A gap in the time it takes for a supposedly diffused idea to become manifest in artifacts could be explained as the result of an idea laying dormant. Because an idea could lay dormant less time in a receiving culture than in a diffusing culture, one could even speculate that a diffused idea flowered *earlier* in the receiving culture than in the culture from which diffusion supposedly occurred.

In short, the "stimulus" adjustment to diffusion theory rendered a weakly testable theory even less testable. In methodological idiom, the adjustment was ad hoc: It decreased testability rather than preserving or increasing testability.

Interestingly, Kroeber did realize that direct evidence of other types of diffusion would make a case for stimulus diffusion stronger. If direct evidence of other types of diffusion is established, though, the need to invoke stimulus diffusion would seem less pressing. Kroeber was also aware that stimulus diffusion "could easily be invoked for wildly speculative leaps of historic fantasy" (Kroeber 1940:19). From this recognition, however, he did not extrapolate an important methodological conclusion: that the stimulus adjustment to diffusion theory rendered diffusion theory virtually untestable.

Incidentally, criticism of Kroeber on methodological grounds should not be construed as an attack on his very substantial and varied contributions. Those contributions have made him all the more visible, even as a target for criticism. Furthermore, the willingness of Kroeber to go to extremes in defending diffusion theory was helpful in revealing the theory's methodological vulnerability. Finally, methodological weaknesses are like other types of weaknesses: They are almost always identified by someone else who has the advantage of a different perspective. Similar comments can be made about the work of others criticized in this book. My respect for their work is undeterred by the criticism.

Before proceeding with more examples of ad hoc adjustments, it is appropriate to outline the relationship between the testability of theories and the testability of adjustments to those theories. Theories that are initially untestable, or only weakly testable, are more prone to ad hoc adjustments than theories that are initially testable. The reason is that weakly testable or untestable theories have few if any testable implications, and hence little or no testability to preserve. Diffusionist theory provides a typical example. Remember that the only directly testable implication of diffusion (barring direct evidence) is that diffused artifacts should always postdate artifacts from which they emanate. When the stimulus adjustment to diffusion closed off that testable implication, diffusionist theory was rendered untestable. On the contrary, theories that are highly testable in the first place have much greater potential for adjustment with auxiliary hypotheses. The reason is that the more highly testable a theory, the greater the number or the greater the precision of its testable implications. This provides more opportunities for adjustment that maintain or increase testability and hence more potential for severe tests once adjustments are made. Processual explanations are an example. The reasons processual explanations can be highly testable were outlined earlier in this chapter. Radiocarbon dating theory is another example of a highly testable theory. In this section we saw how each of the adjustments to radiocarbon dating actually increased the testability of the theory.

Because untestable and weakly testable theories are so prone to ad hoc adjustment, the former are frequently associated with the latter. Either one, but usually both, are typical of what Sabloff calls pseudoarchaeological explanations (Sabloff 1982). There is no lack of examples. Four mentioned earlier were the lost-race explanation of the origins of the Hopewell culture, the various refuted but resurrected ad hoc explanations for the building of the Stonehenge, the extraterrestrial and other explanations for the desert markings in and near the Nazca Valley of southern Peru, and the plethora of ad hoc explanations of the origins and building of the pyramids. These are all discussed in the introduction and text of *Archaeology: Myth and Reality*, edited by Jeremy Sabloff (ed. 1982). For even more examples, see *Exploring the Unknown: Great Mysteries Reexamined* by Charles Cazeau and Stuart Scott (1979).

In sum, when adjustments are ad hoc, theories become less testable. As theories become less testable and even nontestable via ad hoc adjustment, the lack of empirical support pushes them from conjecture toward dogma. Such theoretical culs-de-sac are as unsurprising as they are common. Nontestable or weakly testable theories finally become boring, at least for most. That is to be expected of theories have little or no potential to render greater understanding much less new insight.

That ad hoc adjustments should be avoided seems a trivial point once the importance of testability is recognized. Unfortunately there are a number of factors that can complicate recognition of ad hoc adjustments.

Anomalous evidence itself might not be clear and hence might not be interpreted as evidence requiring adjustment of a theory. Furthermore, it is not always obvious whether an adjustment is auxiliary or ad hoc. It is not surprising that this point would be emphasized by critics of rational procedures in science (Feyerabend 1978), but it has also been acknowledged by some champions of rational procedures (Hempel 1966; Lakatos 1970). Lakatos goes so far as to argue that adjustments to theories can be judged as auxiliary or ad hoc only in historical retrospect (Lakatos 1970).

A decision to adjust a theory in light of anomalous data is indeed not always easy to make. For example, Earle did interpret Wittfogel's theory as refuted, and hence in need of adjustment. Earle was criticized for interpreting Wittfogel's theory as refuted, a criticism that also questions the need for adjustment (Gandara 1981). Furthermore, some adjustments that retain or increase testability may require testing technology that is not available. Techniques for retesting adjusted radiocarbon dating theory, for example, were not immediately available when the adjustments were first proposed. A number of years were required to develop reliable techniques for determining concentrations of atmospheric radiocarbon. Finally, if techniques for testing an adjusted theory are never developed, an auxiliary adjustment would function much like an ad hoc adjustment. For example, if methods of extracting contamination had not been developed, or methods of determining past concentrations of atmospheric radiocarbon had not been discovered, it would not have been possible to retest radiocarbon dating theory after adjustments to account for contamination or varying concentrations of atmospheric radiocarbon. Certainly there would always be the possibility the adjusted theory could be retested when and if the necessary techniques are devised. In the meantime, however, an auxiliary adjustment could function to explain away anomalous evidence just like an ad hoc adjustment.

Despite the kernels of truth in the cautionary comments of people like Feyerabend, Hempel, and Lakatos, in my view ad hoc adjustments are normally recognizable and avoidable. The challenges can be formidable, however, as will become clear in the following discussion.

First and perhaps foremost, one must *want* to distinguish between auxiliary and ad hoc adjustments. The distinction is of little value to those unconvinced by the importance of testability. Those who lean toward a relativistic view of knowledge certainly question the value much less the possibility of testing. Furthermore, one needs to be familiar with the difference between ad hoc and auxiliary adjustments. I do hope this chapter, especially this section, will help readers recognize the difference. Finally, it is important to understand why adjustments should not be ad hoc and why they should be made with auxiliary hypotheses. The late Alfred L. Kroeber may have been an example of one who at least sensed the difference, but did not understand why it is so important to avoid ad hoc adjustments. An earlier quotation from Kroeber indicates awareness that stimulus diffusion theories could run unchecked, but his willingness to recommend them nonetheless implies he was not fully aware of the consequences of allowing theories to become nontestable.

Even if one wants to recognize the difference between ad hoc and auxiliary adjustments, is familiar with the difference between them, and understands why it is important to avoid the former while exploiting the latter, the task is still not always easy if ones favored theories are brought into question. It is important to be critical of ones own theories as well as those of others.

Incidentally, V. Gordon Childe, the best-known of all defenders of classical diffusion theory, did consider testability important. It is to his credit that he ultimately succumbed to the mounting archaeological and chronological evidence against the classical theory. His last published work included a courageous admission made all the more heart-rending by his impending death: "Now I confess that my whole account may prove to be erroneous; my formulae may prove to be inadequate; my interpretations are perhaps ill-founded; my chronological framework—and without such one cannot speak of conjectures—is frankly shaky" (Childe 1958:74; reference from Renfrew 1973a:106).

As painful as it was, Childe did give up diffusion theory. I do have to wonder if he ever fully recognized the ad hoc nature of the adjustments to classical diffusion theory (see Childe 1962). I like to speculate that giving it up might have been less painful if he had.

Given the desire to make testable adjustments and avoid ad hoc adjustments, enough background to recognize the difference between the two, and an understanding of the importance of the difference, a number of specific guidelines can enhance development of the former while constraining intrusion of the latter. First, avoid the temptation to explain away counterevidence because one is convinced that a favored theory is "right." Such temptation typically leads to ad hoc adjustments like those to the "pseudoarchaeological" explanations mentioned in this section. The temptation can also be strong when an archaeological theory shares assumptions with one's political-social outlook. In the first section of this chapter, it was pointed out that Marxist approaches to archaeological explanation do not permit rejection of Marxist dialectical categories. That tendency is likely related to the temptation of many active Marxists to maintain the principal categories of their political-social outlook by explaining away the counterevidence against it (Popper 1957, 1962). Second, assess the structure of a theory for its testability prior to making an adjustment. The reason is that a weakly testable or untestable theory will likely remain so whenever it is adjusted. Third and finally, pay especial attention to the potential retests that would be needed after an adjustment. If there are feasible tests, even more demanding tests, then testability will be maintained and might even be increased.

Encouragement of Competing Theories

Limitations of time and energy, along with other professional commitments, confine most archaeologists to a short list of theoretical pursuits. For the advancement of theory, however, it is crucial to have multiple and incompatible explanations contending for the limelight. There are three reasons for this. First, it is not obvious which among testable but competing theories will lead to the most understanding and insight. With hindsight one can know why some theories have prevailed. At the knife-edge of theoretical development, however, the potential of different theories is not known. Second, weaknesses in one theory are often discovered through the perspective of another theory, especially a competing theory. Certainly errors can be found by empirical and consistency testing, but many potential errors are not even apparent except through the light of another theory. Third, theories tend not to be abandoned, regardless of the evidence against them, unless there are alternatives with which they can be replaced. That requires that other theories be available.

Dominant theories in scientific and other intellectual pursuits normally occupy an elevated status in historical reconstructions. Most histories are not only focused on the "winners," but also tend to portray successful theories as if they were destined to prevail from the outset. Theories that have fallen by the wayside are usually accorded far less attention or are even ignored (Agassi 1963). Such historiographic prejudices yield misleading portraits of actual theory development. There are normally a number and sometimes a multitude of alternative theories competing against each other. Provided the theories are reasonably testable, there is no certainty as to which might bear the most fruit. That is the first reason it is important that numerous theories be pursued.

The second reason for deployment of multiple theories is that revelation of weaknesses and strengths in any given theory is dependent upon the perspective of competing theories. Weaknesses in a given theory are seldom revealed simply by tracing and testing the implications in isolation from the challenge of other theories. Error is often not even perceived much less clarified except from another perspective. Similarly, strengths in any given theory also come into clearer focus when viewed from alternative theoretical perspectives. Finally, the challenge from competing theories encourages more careful, and more thorough, argumentation in support of one's favored theories. If successful, those theories become all the more credible.

An example of how competing theories can bring out strengths and weaknesses in each other is offered next. The example also shows that empirical testing alone is not always sufficient for evaluating a theory.

As already discussed, dates established by radiocarbon testing challenged the classical diffusionist theory, and was crucial to its eventual demise. Competing theories were already playing a role *before* radiocarbon testing, however. Processual explanations had been advanced prior to the establishment of radiocarbon dates, and those explanations had already been instrumental in revealing weaknesses in the diffusionist theory (Renfrew 1973a). Remember also a fortuitous element in the demise of the classical diffusionist theory: If the European monuments and cultures were endogenous but had developed a few hundred years after those in the Classical World, the radiocarbon dates would not have refuted the classical diffusionist theory. In all likelihood, the test results would have been interpreted as evidence in support of the classical diffusionist theory.

A third reason for alternative theories is that established theories tend to prevail, even in the face of counterevidence, *unless* there are promising theories to replace them (Lakatos 1970). Availability of alternative theories is all the more important if a given theory has been established for a long while. The tendency for a received theory to prevail in the face of counterevidence seems to increase with the length of time it has been embraced. Two examples follow.

Newtonian mechanics and dynamics continued to dominate theoretical physics until the relativity theories became available in the early decades of the twentieth century. The fact is that there had been numerous pieces of empirical evidence that posed serious challenges to Newtonian physics long before the relativity theories. The results of the Michelson-Morley experiment on relative light speeds, often cited as *the* empirical shot that downed Newtonian physics, was initially carried out in 1881. That was nearly twenty-five years prior to the advent of the special theory of relativity (1905) and nearly thirty-five years before the introduction of the general theory of relativity (1915). Despite the empirical evidence, Newtonian physics continued to dominate. It was not replaced until the relativity theories had been developed (Lakatos 1970).

The second example has a hypothetical element but will make the point again. It is difficult to imagine the well-established classical diffusionist theory being rejected in light of radiocarbon dating alone. As a matter of fact, we have seen that some prominent anthropologists and archaeologists stood by diffusion theory even after radiocarbon dating techniques were refined (Renfrew 1973a). The availability of processual theories played a major role in the demise of the classical diffusionist theory. Without them, or some other promising alternatives, the classical diffusionist theory might still dominate today.

Incidentally, the importance of multiple theories competing against each other almost always necessitates there be different scholars pursuing alternative theories. Tracing the implications of one theory is more than enough to occupy the time and energy of a group of scholars; the work on alternatives normally must be undertaken by others. This is one reason "schools" of thought cannot be entirely avoided. Furthermore, it is not easy for theoreticians to encourage the generation of theories other than their own. The reason is all too human. Most people fail to find pleasure when competing theories are argued against their favored theory. That confrontation with competing theories stimulates the search for more compelling support for a favored theory would be acknowledged by nearly everyone. Nevertheless, many do not particularly relish a confrontation that might reveal weaknesses as well as strengths.

Despite the understandable dislike most have for alternative theories, confronting the challenge of a competing theory provides an opportunity for personal and intellectual enlightenment. When faced with alternative theories, battling one's own ego can be as exciting a personal drama as the intellectual battle of theories. How one handles that personal challenge is likely to be crucial for inner happiness. It will also have a direct bearing on the enjoyment, or lack thereof, in one's relationships with others in the field. Applying good method, I hope is now evident, challenges much more than one's intellect. It also challenges one's soul.

I now turn once more to a discussion of relativism. Relativists like to believe there are no reliable criteria by which to judge theories. That belief entails that a multiplicity of theories is acceptable. It has been argued in this section that a multiplicity of theories is not only acceptable, but is absolutely crucial. Does this common ground mean that a first step has been taken down the slippery slope to relativism? The answer is no. It is important to clarify the reason.

As just argued, multiple theories facilitate the exposure of strengths and weaknesses in each other. Relativists tend to ignore strengths and weaknesses because they believe there is no way to assess them. Furthermore, encouraging the generation of multiple theories does not imply that they are all "equal," or even that their potential is "equal." The hope is that the better theories will more quickly become apparent, and the less promising ones more quickly exposed. For relativists, there is no way to determine which are "better" or "worse;" they are all "equal." For relativists, then, there is no sense in hoping that better ones will prevail or that lesser ones will fall by the wayside. Furthermore, instead of meeting criticism generated from competing theories, relativists can dismiss criticism on the grounds that all theories are subjective. That is a reason why relativists often assume criticism is little more than a power play by those espousing different views.

Encouraging multiple theories, then, does not lead to relativism. *Not* to encourage competing theories, on the other hand, is likely to leave the impression that a power game is being played. That is a situation attractive to relativists. It confirms their suspicions that in intellectual matters as in everything else, politics—a euphemism for power—is all that counts. It can and does justify, at least in their own eyes, intentional use of politics and power to support their own favored theories.

Making Theoretical Decisions

Methodological considerations become crucial when making decisions about theories, such as whether to support them, modify them, or abandon them. *Guidelines* are simply method instantiated for making such decisions.

Constructing a definitive list of decision-types would be impossible, but the following would be included: choosing broad theoretical goals, setting specific goal(s) for a particular theory, determining which implication(s) of a theory can be tested, deciding how to test a theory, choosing how to utilize criticism of a theory, and deciding whether to adjust or reject a theory. Sub-decisions can be enumerated under these as well. For example, if a theory is adjusted, one will need to stipulate the source of error and determine which auxiliary hypotheses to add. If a theory is abandoned, one must decide whether to maintain the same theoretical goal but approach it by different means, to throw one's energy behind a competing theory, or to follow a novel theoretical route. The list of decision-types could be extended almost indefinitely. In all cases, methodological considerations can and indeed should play a role.

The *methodological realm*—an expression coined for this book—incorporates all areas within which decisions can be made about explanations. The vast majority of methodological decisions are made in the middle range, but some decisions involve controlling models at the higher level or empirical information at the lower level. The methodological realm is large, much larger than many imagine. A thorough study of method increases it even further by revealing more options and more types of decisions.

In practice, various decisions about theories are intertwined to the point where making one decision will by default foreclose other decisions. To decide to adjust a theory in light of criticism, for example, implies that one has decided not to abandon it. In general it is not necessary to identify which decisions are being made by default when another decision is being made. The default decisions are normally obvious, or unimportant. In other words, so long as theoretical pursuits are potentially fruitful, it is not crucial to separate and analyze every decision.

What is important, however, is to be *able* to separate the various decisions, even if some were made by default. The reason is that *when a theoretical impasse is encountered, breaking down the theoretical problem-situation into the series of decisions that led to it often reveals overlooked alternatives.* Careful consideration of those hidden alternatives can suggest routes out of an impasse. More specifically, method can help reveal hidden alternatives out of a theoretical impasse in precisely the broad ways outlined in Chapter 1, and reviewed again here.

First, new goals might be available that had not be considered, or had been considered but excluded because of other decisions. For example, a theory that seems to have exhausted its potential might be reinterpreted for pursuit in another direction.

Second, methodological guidelines can suggest new approaches to old goals. For example, the limitations encountered in processual explanations that exclude human agency may create an impasse. It might be broken by incorporating individual decision making as an explanatory component.

Third, method can help break an impasse by revealing constraints on theories. Recognizing that further development of a theory will be limited because there will be no more test points, for example, could provide the impetus to consider an entirely different type of theory.

It goes without saying that method also provides a rationale for each theoretical decision. It suggests reasons why one would want to choose certain options while avoiding others. If the chosen options are not as fruitful as hoped, one is in a better position to analyze what has gone awry, and why. That, in turn, increases the chances that new choices will lead to more productive results.

In sum, then, method provides tools for making the many decisions required when developing and assessing explanations. The more methodological tools at one's disposal, and the more thoroughly they are understood, the more effectively they can be employed and the more likely that theoretical work will bear fruit.

What Method Cannot Do

It has just been argued that a thorough grasp of method should be an aid to archaeologists. For most decisions concerning theory it can be helpful, and for some decisions it is crucial. Nevertheless, theory development certainly draws on other important resources besides method, and method is not infallible even when used well.

Method cannot *generate* theories any more than carpentry tools can make the wood upon which they are used. Theory conception depends upon intuition, imagination, and so many other factors that attempts to understand it may be little more definitive than exposing the secret of creativity in painting or poetry.

Incidentally, the intractability of understanding theory generation is a major reason why it is seldom addressed in philosophical circles. Hans Reichenbach was the first to make a clear distinction between "the context of discovery," which covers factors involved in theory generation, and the "context of justification," which covers factors involved with the legitimation of theory. He exhorted philosophers to focus their attention on the context of justification (Reichenbach 1938, 1951).

Reichenbach's exhortation is quite sensible so long as it does not become dogma. What can be done with theories once created is much more within the realm of human deliberation and decision than is the creation of theories. If Reichenbach's "context of justification" were broadened to include all facets of theory development involving human deliberation and decisions, then it would become the methodological realm. Even without such broadening, many methodological considerations in this book fall within the context of justification. It can be added that almost all methodological discussions in the philosophy of science fall within the context of justification. Even Karl Popper, the most prominent critic of the inductive methodological tradition with which Reichenbach is associated, concentrates his methodological recommendations on the context of justification (Popper 1962).

As a dogma in philosophical circles, on the other hand, the distinction between the context of discovery and the context of justification has had deleterious consequences. First, it unwittingly can be used to buttress "law and order" imposition of method—using scientific standards, or supposed scientific standards, primarily to distinguish "scientific," or "legitimate," or "justified," theories from others (Gellner 1974). The reason is that overemphasis on justification can encourage the mistaken view that method functions primarily to demarcate scientific theories from nonscientific theories, a matter addressed in the previous chapter. Second, exclusive emphasis on justification has led to projecting method *onto* discovery processes, thus interpreting creative processes as a function of method. Seldom, if ever, can the mechanisms of discovery be made to fit within the tidy strictures of method. Such projection hides important dynamics of theoretical development (Feyerabend 1978), and also leads to questionable historiography (Agassi 1963). Feyerabend argues that the heart of theoretical development lies in the discovery process. Attempts at justification are actually harmful to the development of theory. Agassi shows that a historian of science's beliefs about method inform how he or she will write the history. Projecting a particular view of method onto history typically excludes historical interpretations from other methodological perspectives. I might add that no methodological perspective can account for the numerous nonmethodological factors in science or its history. That is the main point in this section.

Methodological guidelines are not infallible. They will *not* always guarantee the most fruitful decision about theory. Even well-made decisions within the confines of available options might, in retrospect, appear ill-chosen. The reason is that new and unforeseen developments, either in one's favored theory or in competing theories, can intervene to change a theoretical context. For the same reason, following a hunch that might seem less than optimal methodologically can sometimes turn out to be fruitful.

It is clear, then, that method does not guarantee "success." Methodological decisions are within human control, but other factors on the theoretical landscape, such as theory creation and unforeseen developments in theories, are not, or at least much less so. When they intervene, and they certainly will at times, little is to be gained by puzzling over why those factors did not allow theory to develop in a preconceived fashion. Energy can better be spent by using methodological tools to make further decisions in the newly evolved theoretical context.

Guidelines: A Complete Set?

The question addressed in this section is more purely philosophical; that is, the answer will have little if any direct bearing on the application of method. Readers who choose to bypass this section can thus do so without sacrificing anything of importance for archaeology. The reason for including the section, however, is that I do wonder if the future will bring major new methodological ideas important for application. There is no doubt that philosophers will continue to turn up new puzzles, paradoxes, inconsistencies or other problems within the different views of science and method. They will also continue to elaborate and refine views of science and method. But is it likely that such work will add anything of significant value to the bag of tools necessary for archaeologists or others to do their work?

It was pointed out in Chapter 1 that the four views of science —inductive, paradigmatic, refutationist, and anarchic—contrast sharply with each other: They assume different goals, and imply contrasting formula for the generation of knowledge and incompatible criteria for assessing knowledge. Hence the method implied by and the guidelines forged from each view differ markedly. An issue to consider is whether the methodological tools from these four views provide a complete set. That they differ is important; a variety of tools is better than just a few. But is there also reason to believe the methodological tools from these four will suffice?

There is a quick answer to the above question: One could never be confident that a bag of methodological tools is complete. There is, nevertheless, some reason to suggest that the methodological tools forged in this book will be reasonably adequate for addressing the issues outlined in this chapter.

The views of science are themselves interdependent, both thematically and historically. How the interconnections help produce a useful variety of methodological tools is explained here.

The inductive view established the empirical orientation of science. It provided medicine for the subjective proclivities of the medieval Aristotelian view. In turn, however, the paradigmatic view offers intellectual and sociological insights into theory development for which the inductive view does not provide an adequate account. The refutationist view offers a detailed rationale for theoretical development suggested by the paradigmatic view, and also provides a more thorough account of shortcomings in the inductive view. The anarchic view focuses on lacunae in the refutationist position, and throws light on the limitations of any methodological approaches to science and knowledge.

The upshot of the thematic interrelations among the different views is that many important methodological issues are addressed effectively by one or more of the different views. That is because the strengths of some answer to weaknesses in others, and vice versa.

The interrelationship among the views is not just thematic. The views are woven together historically as well, and are interpreted as evolving thematically because of historical contexts. That is the major reason why this book contains historical reconstructions of views of science. Though it is hoped that they are interesting and even entertaining, the histories are much more than anecdotal: They are used to identify and explain strengths and weaknesses of each view.

Viewed collectively, then, the thematic and historical relationships of views of science have coaxed out important issues in method and the tools to deal with them. Perhaps, then, the important tools for application are already at hand, even if they are crude and in need of further refinement.

Method in the Physical Sciences and Other Disciplines

Exrapolated to areas outside the physical sciences, views of science become views of knowledge. As explained in Chapter 1, that is why methods in science permeate other intellectual disciplines. The social sciences, theology, the humanities, and other disciplines often reflect method that can be traced back to methodological roots in the physical sciences.

That methods originally developed for the physical sciences can be adapted for use in other fields by no means implies that there are no differences between the physical sciences and other fields. The data base used in physical science, for example, is more tidy than for most other disciplines (although not nearly as uncontroversial as sometimes assumed). The goals and types of theories differ from field to field, and within a discipline as well. The oft-proclaimed gulf between the physical sciences and other disciplines like archaeology, however, is mostly created by identifying science with a questionable conception of method and then reacting against the misconception. In my view, *the methodological differences between the physical sciences and other fields are far less significant than the similarities.* This is an obvious assumption in this book, but it does need to be made explicit for a number of reasons.

First, the physical sciences were picked as a model for method because testability seems most apparent in the physical sciences. Indeed, the very notion of testability has been developed from studies of the physical sciences. On the other hand, there is no inherent reason why the biological sciences could not be used for the same purpose. After all, testability has been critical in the development of biological theory as well. If methodological views were traditionally associated with biological rather than physical science, the biological sciences would almost certainly have been chosen as the model rather than the physical sciences.

Second, the most significant methodological similarity between the physical sciences and other fields is testability. Testability underlies most of the six issues crucial for theory development identified in this chapter. Furthermore, one can speculate that a similar list could be identified for other fields in which theory development is to be guided by empirical considerations. Economics and psychology are two that come readily to mind. In other words, testability and its associated concepts are what I have in mind when stating that the methodological differences between the physical sciences and other fields are far less significant than the similarities.

Suggested Readings

The six issues discussed in this chapter will be addressed further in other chapters. Annotated suggestions relevant to those issues will be offered at the ends of chapters in which the issues are revisited. The four readings below are more appropriate for this chapter than any other.

1. Dorothy H. Hosler, Jeremy A. Sabloff, and Dale Runge, 1977, "Simulation Model Development: A Case Study of the Classic Maya Collapse."
Pertinent to discussions of theory formulation, empirical and consistency tests, and ad hoc adjustments to theories.

The systemic model of the collapse of the Classic Maya civilization in this study was rigorously tested during development, and was modified as a result. The testability of the model along with the attitudes and decisions of the investigators provide a fine case study.

2. Imre Lakatos, 1970, "Falsification and the Methodology of Scientific Research Programmes."

Pertinent to discussions of searching for theories, ad hoc adjustment to theories, and theoretical decision making.

In this lengthy essay Lakatos outlines a methodological approach to making decisions about theories. The essay is recommended for three reasons. First, Lakatos orients his methodological views much more toward application than is normally found among philosophers of science. Second, and perhaps because of the first reason, his position is considerably more eclectic than usual in the philosophy of science. Third, his notion of "theoretical progress" underlies my concept of "greater understanding," and his notion of "empirical progress" led to my concept of "new insight." For further annotation see the suggested readings for Chapters 3 and 6.

3. Jeremy A. Sabloff, ed., 1982, *Archaeology: Myth and Reality.*

Pertinent to discussions about searching for theories and formulation of testable theories.

The editor's introduction to these essays discusses an array of theories he calls "pseudoarchaeological." Included are theories about the Hopewell culture, Stonehenge, the Peruvian desert markings, and the pyramids. He recounts how they have given way in the face of scientific archaeology, and explains why they have been replaced by alternative theories that can be empirically evaluated. The essays themselves explore the archaeological theories, both pseudoarchaeological and otherwise, in much greater detail.

4. Stephen Shennan, 1988, *Quantifying Archaeology.*

Pertinent to discussion of formulation of testable theories.

This is a fine work on implicative reasoning, with the special advantage of being designed for archaeologists. The numerous ways in which quantification can enhance archaeological work are not only discussed, but are also demonstrated with archaeological applications. Unlike the "cook book" approach of some manuals, Steve Shennan walks the reader carefully through problem situations, forcing him or her to think clearly about what is being quantified, why it would be beneficial to have it quantified, what quantification techniques are available for different tasks, how to use those techniques, and how to exploit advantages while avoiding pitfalls when applying the techniques. Applications range from the empirical through the theoretical sides of archaeology.

Chapter 3   Testability

The degree to which a theory is testable is the most important single indicator of its potential to contribute to the advance of archaeological theory. That statement is repeated here because the concept of testability is central to the methodological prescriptions that enhance theory development. Four of the six issues identified in the last chapter are either directly or indirectly concerned with testability or assume testability: searching for theories that increase understanding and insight, formulating testable theories, exploiting empirical and consistency tests, and avoiding ad hoc adjustments to theories.

In this chapter the concept of testability is further developed, with examples illustrating the concept. One example is discussed in considerable detail: the hydraulic theory of Karl Wittfogel and the research program that it generated.

According to Wittfogel's hydraulic theory, the need to develop and maintain water resources is the cause for the development of state structure. Hydraulic theory and the research program that grew from it are unusually appropriate for illustrating many facets of testability and the methodological prescriptions with which they are associated. Following are a number of further comments on hydraulic theory and why is has been chosen as a pivotal example.

Irrigation was identified as an important element in prehistoric social organization in the 1920s. Wittfogel himself was particularly interested in its significance (Goldfrank 1978:157). Controversies over the role of water resources, especially over the hydraulic theory of Wittfogel, reached a crescendo shortly before and then after publication of his book *Oriental Despotism* in 1957. Much of the understanding and insight provided by hydraulic theory arose from those controversies, which took place from about the middle 1950s until about 1980.

Although hydraulic theory is no longer a centerpiece of theoretical discussion in archaeology, the methodological strategies employed by Wittfogel and others in the development of hydraulic theory are far from outdated. In my view those strategies were, are, and will continue to be fruitful in other theoretical pursuits. Indeed, that the high tide of Wittfogelian debate is now past makes those strategies and their benefits all the easier to ascertain. Furthermore, it should be noted that hydraulic theory is far from dead even though it is no longer undergoing active development. Various versions of hydraulic theory continue to be employed, a fact that bears witness to the success of the hydraulic research program. Finally, I suggest that the productive methodological strategies used in the development of hydraulic theory are a crucial reason why it continues to bear fruit.

Karl Wittfogel and the Hydraulic Theory

Karl August Wittfogel had barely crossed the threshold of the door when he asked "What about irrigation in the pueblos?" This is the description given by Esther Goldfrank when she first met Wittfogel. If the significance of hydraulic theory in Wittfogel's life is not underscored enough by that scenario, here is what followed that first meeting: "After a week of exchanges on this all-important subject, as well as others, needless to say, Karl August Wittfogel and I decided to marry—a step we took on March 8, 1940." (Goldfrank 1978:146).

Interestingly, the rudiments of the "all-important subject"—hydraulic theory—were not foreign to Esther Goldfrank. In the late 1920s she became interested in larger structures and economic problems, especially as they might apply to her work in the pueblos at Isleta. These interests had led her to consider the importance of irrigation, fully fifteen years before she had even heard the name Karl August Wittfogel (Goldfrank 1978:31).

Wittfogel's interest in water resources

It is helpful here to trace the life-long interest of Wittfogel in water resources, especially the impact of water resources on social and economic structure. This will provide at least some clues as to why it was Wittfogel and not someone else who galvanized various ideas into a far-reaching theory about the relationship between water resources and the formation of state structure.

Wittfogel was born and raised in Germany, and eventually received his doctorate from the University of Frankfurt. His thesis was on Chinese economics and society. Goldfrank points out that beginning in the 1920s the effect of water control on societal structure had been the fundamental question for him. In her own words: "His investigations had convinced him that the introduction and management of large-scale waterworks for purposes of irrigation or flood control demanded large-scale cooperation, which in turn necessitated the establishment of directing centers of authority—tribal, regional or national—and the institutionalization of communal discipline" (Goldfrank 1978:157).

Wittfogel's earlier works espousing hydraulic views were not readily accessible to readers in the English-speaking world. Goldfrank (1978:157) identifies them as *Wirtschaft und Gesellschaft Chinas* (Wittfogel 1931), "The Foundations and Stages of Chinese Economic History" in *Zeitschrift for Socialforschung* (1935: IV, 26–60), and *Die Theorie der orientalischen Gesellschaft* (1938). [Note that Goldfrank must be referring to *Zeitschrift für Sozialforschung*. Also, "Die Theorie der orientalischen Gesellschaft" was not a book but an article that appeared in 1938 in *Zeitschrift für Sozialforschung* 7(½).] These works on social organization were the product of Wittfogel's many years of research in China. He left China after the outbreak of the Sino-Japanese war in 1937.

In addition to his interest in the influence of water resources, there are at least two other facets of Wittfogel's background that helped shape his sweeping hydraulic theory. One was the Teutonic intellectual climate in Germany, especially in German academia. A central theme was that change in the human sphere is the product of conflict, and conflict is controlled by authority (for example, see Dahrendorf 1959). The influence of this Teutonic idea is traceable to the nineteenth century, especially to the work of Georg Wilhelm Friedrich Hegel (Popper 1945, and Chapter 8 of this book). The other facet was the crude version of Marxist philosophy that informed the communist movement. According to this view economic forces are not only the unique cause of social and political organization, but also fully determine the structure of social and political organization. Wittfogel himself joined the Communist party in the early 1920s, but broke with it immediately after Hitler and Stalin's nonaggression pact of September 1939 (Goldfrank 1978:155–56).

The importance of conflict in human progress and the significance of economic forces in social and political organization were part of the bedrock of Wittfogel's intellectual and personal life. These beliefs must have informed his hydraulic theory. They can also explain the boldness that is so noticeable in Wittfogel's claims for his hydraulic theory. Before delving further into these matters, however, two other areas need to covered briefly: (1) the types of theories about the origins of the state and, more specifically, (2) the types of hydraulic theories about social organization.

Origins of the state

Defining "state" is difficult. For the purposes here, however, Ronald Cohen's characterization will be satisfactory. Cohen notes that states have an enormous ability to carry out public policy, at least compared to other social-political forms. Furthermore, in order to carry out policy "states evolve a 'ruling class' or, in structural terms, a governing bureaucracy" (Cohen 1978:4). Notice that size is not a necessary defining characteristic. Obviously there must be some minimum number of people, but state structure can be formed in a vast range of societal sizes, from small to enormous.

Cohen also identifies two classic but opposed theories about the origins of the state. First are the conflict theories. They stress the importance of conflict and the need to control conflict. In conflict theories the tendency toward disintegration is held in check by the coercive forces of social control provided by the state. The need for social control of conflict also explains why state structure tends to persist even if conditions that led to the formation of state structure were to change. Social stratification is typically attributed to conflict over resources; like conflict, stratification predates state organization, although the latter tends to ossify the stratification. Second are the integration theories. They assume all societies to be generally stable (relatively unchanging) systems of structural parts. Those parts are integrated into functioning wholes based on widespread consensus of values. Integration theories require neither conflict nor the need for coercion to control conflict to explain the origin of state structure. Furthermore, state structure can disintegrate. If state structure does not function well, or exists after the conditions for its formation have changed, inertia may keep it together for awhile but there is no more reason why it should persist than there would be reason for it to form under the new conditions. In integration theories stratification does not exist prior to the state, but social stratification can be generated by the state (Cohen 1978).

In terminology already adopted for this book, conflict theories and integration theories about the origins of state structure are high-level theories that inform the generation of more specific theories at the middle range. It does not require a lengthy analysis to realize that the qualities of the middle-range theories generated under each of these high-level theories will be quite different. More specifically, conflict theories about the formation of state structure focus on one or a very few scarce but necessary resources as the root of conflict, and state organization must inevitably follow if the conflict is to be controlled. Integration theories about the formation of states, on the other hand, can include multiple and different causes to explain the origins of state structure. The variability of conditions that can lead to state structure do not typically work with inevitability, either. Depending upon contingent factors, certain conditions may sometimes lead to state structure and sometimes may not.

The synopses of these two theories about state formation are just caricatures. Nevertheless, they suffice to make a crucial methodological point: Conflict theories are typically much more testable than integration theories. The reasons are summarized here.

Conflict theories identify one or a very few elements as causes, and imply that the existence of those causes will inevitably lead to state structure. In other words, conflict theories more readily fit the format "whenever X exists, Y is sure to follow." This is a universalized claim, and universalized claims imply more points where they potentially may be shown correct or incorrect than less universalized claims. In less arcane terminology, the more predictions made by a theory, and the more definite those predictions, the more testable becomes the theory. By way of contrast, integration theories tend to be much less testable. The variety and multiplicity of causes in integration theories, along with the lack of inevitability about where they may lead, discourages or even forecloses universalization. In everyday terminology, a theory with fewer and more complicated predictions or less definite predictions will be less testable.

Incidentally, an integration theory for the formation of state structure *for a particular society* can be testable. The systemic models that typically underlie integration theories can be tested against the artifactual record relevant to a particular case, and improved in light of the testing (see Bell 1981). The problem is universalizing such models for testing in contexts beyond that for which they are developed. Because the dynamic elements that lead to state formation can be variable for integration theories, the same model might not even be appropriate for another case. For an account of an interesting but sometimes frustrating attempt to use a systemic model beyond the particular case for which it was originally designed, see Zubrow 1981.

Hydraulic theories about social organization

The distinction between conflict and integration theories about the formation of state structure is certainly appropriate when applied to hydraulic theories about the origins of state structure. Wittfogel's hydraulic theory is a conflict theory par excellence. In his theory, the need to develop and manage water resources in the face of conflicting claims on this essential and sometimes scarce resource leads inevitably to state structure. Furthermore, force will be necessary to control the conflict, so the state structure will be authoritarian. Typical of a conflict theory, Wittfogel's hydraulic theory was universalizable: Whenever competing needs lead to conflict over water resources, authoritarian state structures will form.

Wittfogel did add qualifications that were not sufficiently specified, and these did lower the universality and hence the testability of his claims. He asserted that state society is not likely to form when the scale of the society, the scale of the irrigation system, or other historical conditions are not met. Eva and Robert Hunt (1974) provide a discussion of these shortcomings in Wittfogel's theory. Even Goldfrank notes that Wittfogel believed that "irrigation agriculture in China had its beginnings in areas, and probably hilly areas, where irrigation was beneficial but not necessary, and where the population might have engaged in little or no hydraulic activities" (Goldfrank 1978:188). Despite the well-deserved criticism of Wittfogel's theory because of these vague conditions, his theoretical claims were still considerably more universal and testable than the hydraulic theories developed under the integration model.

A few parenthetical comments are in order. One can now see how closely is the fit between Wittfogel's hydraulic theory and other ideas that informed his thinking. Two were discussed earlier. One was the Teutonic view that change in the human sphere is the product of conflict, and that conflict is controlled by authority. The other was the crude Marxist view that economic forces—forces underpinning agriculture in this case—are not only the unique cause of social and political organization, but also fully determine the structure of social and political organization. Even more interesting, in my view, is that these background ideas can also explain Wittfogel's confidence that his hydraulic theory must have been right. The firmness of one's intellectual convictions is reinforced when they are consistent with ideas in one's personal and social outlook. The conviction becomes even stronger when ideas seem to be directly implied by one's personal and social outlook.

A final comment should be added. Wittfogel's resignation from the Communist party in 1939 and his later anti-communist activities eventually resulted in a Soviet campaign to discredit him. Wittfogel's involvement in these events has raised both sympathy and antipathy, although this is not the place to discuss such matters (for such discussions, see Ulmen 1978 and Newman 1992). What is important here is that the Marxist underpinnings of his hydraulic theory were not altered even though his communist political views changed. One reason is that these political events in Wittfogel's life took place after the foundations of his hydraulic theory had been firmly set in place. Another reason is that a Marxist intellectual outlook is not necessarily associated with a communist political orientation. Many who find a Marxist perspective fruitful in their intellectual endeavors never did embrace communism, and some were active critics of this political ideology long before its recent collapse.

Hydraulic theories generated from the integration model are much more diverse and difficult to classify than those generated from the conflict model. This is not surprising in light of the multiplicity and variety of explanations that can be informed by integration models. In "Historic Patterns of Mesopotamian Irrigation Agriculture," for example, Robert McC. Adams (1974) refers to political conditions, population, and a great number of other factors in the Mesopotamian environment that seemed significant in the formation of Mesopotamian irrigation agriculture. Also typical of integration models, McC. Adams' patterns do not inevitably form, and they can disintegrate after they have formed. A multiplicity and variety of factors also enter the theories proposed by Eva and Robert Hunt in their study "Irrigation, Conflict, and Politics: A Mexican Case" (Hunt and Hunt 1974). As will soon be seen, similar comments could also be made about Timothy Earle's study of irrigation and social organization in Hawaii.

Testability: The key to Wittfogel's theory

That the various hydraulic theories informed by integration models are less universalizable and testable does not detract from their value as platforms from which to criticize, or even refute, Wittfogel's theory. It also does not imply that they are mere speculation, or fantasy. Indeed, a great deal of careful research and thought has gone into the formation of many integration theories. It has already been noted that integration theories for particular societies can be improved by testing against the artifactual record. Nevertheless, when it is not appropriate to universalize a theory beyond its particular context, its testability is not extended and hence it becomes more difficult to know where, in general, such theories are strong and where they are weak. That is why it also becomes more difficult to build modified or even new theories in light of the weaknesses.

To sum up, Wittfogel's hydraulic theory provided the most universalizable and testable explanation for the origins of state structure. That is why it was so exposed to many criticisms and even refutations. In numerous instances its weaknesses provided the impetus for the generation of alternative hydraulic theories. In addition to the understanding and insight that it itself provided, then, Wittfogel's hydraulic theory also served as a stepping-stone to further understanding and insight into the relationship between water resources and social structure. Its testability was absolutely crucial for its role as a stepping-stone. Despite all the criticisms and refutations, that is why Wittfogel's hydraulic theory has been so productive. It is also why it is exemplary.

Testability in Action: The Wittfogelian Research Program

There is no shortage of literature on the hydraulic theory of Wittfogel, or on the criticisms, studies, and alternative theories that followed from it. An excellent historical review of the Wittfogelian research program is included in Hunt and Hunt's 1974 paper "Irrigation, Conflict, and Politics: A Mexican Case." (reprinted in Cohen and Service 1978). By 1974 much of the Wittfogelian research program had run its course. One exception was the work of Timothy Earle, who was at that time a graduate student at the University of Michigan.

In 1974 Earle had just completed his Ph.D. dissertation on the traditional irrigation economy and control hierarchies of the Halelea District on Kauai, Hawaii (Earle 1973). Earle's later studies, which incorporated his dissertation work, included a reflective paper (1977) and a book (1978).

It should be noted that the research incorporated into Earle's theoretical work was not just directed at testing Wittfogel's hydraulic theory, but at testing two other theories about the origins of complexity in social organization as well: redistribution requirements resulting from community specialization and trade (Service 1962, 1975) and warfare (Carneiro 1970). Discussion of Earle's testing and assessment of the latter two theories in Hawaii was not as central to his book as was his discussion of hydraulic theory, and they are not pertinent here anyway. Interestingly, though, all three theories are logically similar in that an initial increase in population density results in a specific cultural adaptation, which in turn results in the centralization of decision making. Like the hydraulic theory, Earle found the latter two theories inadequate.

Earle concluded that Wittfogel's theory was refuted. To be sure, this was not new. The work of people such as Robert McC. Adams and Eva and Robert Hunt had already refuted Wittfogel's theory (McC. Adams 1974; Hunt and Hunt 1974). Nevertheless, Earle's work on Wittfogel's hydraulic theory was different in two ways. First, his dissertation research was explicitly designed to test Wittfogel's hydraulic theory. Others had certainly tested Wittfogel's theory indirectly via their own studies into the relationship between irrigation and social organization, but no one had designed a very major research project specifically to test Wittfogel's theory. Second, Earle very systematically exploited his refutation of Wittfogel's theory. He attempted to identify precisely where Wittfogel's theory was weak and where it was strong, and then he used both in developing his own theory.

In sum, Earle's contributions to the Wittfogelian research program provide a particularly auspicious example of how testability can be used productively in theory development. That is why his contributions are the primary focus of discussion here.

In his 1957 book *Oriental Despotism*, Karl Wittfogel presented and supported his hydraulic theory for the emergence of centralized authority. His pivotal thesis was that centralized authority evolved because of need to manage the technology and organization of irrigation. The underlying assumption was that human intervention to provide anything more than very simple water supply would require mass labor, and that control of mass labor would necessitate centralized management and hence authority. More specifically, Wittfogel's theory stipulated that centralized management of an irrigation system is required at all stages of irrigation development: construction, maintenance, reconstruction following natural disasters or warfare, the allocation of water supplies from the system, and the mediation of disputes over the allocation of water supplies. The corollary thesis is that the various functions of central authority over irrigation turn it into political authority (Wittfogel 1957; Earle 1978).

Restated in the terminology of logic, the need for management of irrigation systems is not just a necessary condition for the development of state structure, but a sufficient condition as well. In a nutshell, centralized state authority is the inevitable product of irrigation development.

Wittfogel did not limit his theory to explaining the development of central authority in regions in need of water, or regions with particular cultural characteristics. Instead, he universalized his hydraulic theory: In all cases where the challenges of irrigation technology are met, central state authority will emerge. The areas in China studied by Wittfogel were relatively arid and hence would seem to provide an auspicious context for irrigation development. With that in mind it is especially noteworthy that Wittfogel generalized his theory beyond the bounds of its arid origins to damp regions as well, including Hawaii.

Wittfogel's hydraulic theory had captured the attention of archaeologists and anthropologists before publication of *Oriental Despotism* in 1957. As Earle points out in his 1978 book, Wittfogel's investigations were introduced to a broader audience through a symposium volume published in 1955. Presented in that volume were studies of the relationship of irrigation and central authority in ancient civilizations such as those in Peru, Mesoamerica, Egypt, Mesopotamia, and India (Steward 1955). The significance of irrigation was recognized in these different areas but the relationship of irrigation to central authority was not clear. Although empirical evidence was brought to bear on Wittfogel's theory, one could not be sure if the empirical evidence in those contexts exonerated or discredited the theory. In refutationist terminology, one could not be sure if the empirical evidence corroborated or refuted the theory.

The controversy surrounding Wittfogel's theory continued after publication of his 1957 book. It centered on causality, that is, whether irrigation was the cause of the formation of central state authority or not. In Earle's view (1978) the ethnological and archaeological studies were still not conclusive. Some ethnological studies tended to support Wittfogel's theory (Gray 1963), but most of them raised questions about Wittfogel's theories (Leach 1961; Millon et al. 1961; Sahlins 1962; Lees 1973). Archaeological studies before and after 1957 concluded that irrigation is better understood as the result rather than the cause of state formation (Wolf and Palerm 1955; Adams 1966; Lanning 1967). A few archaeologists did, however, cautiously conclude that irrigation was crucial in the development of central authority (Sanders and Price 1968; Price 1971).

Earle's reformulation of hydraulic theory

Earle hoped to provide a more definitive test for Wittfogel's theory in Hawaii, an area that is decidedly not arid. He reasoned that irrigation would tend to be less important in an area with adequate rainfall, and if irrigation were less significant for subsistence, then it is more likely that central authority could develop independent of irrigation need. For that reason Wittfogel's theory would face a particularly risky test in Hawaii.

Earle also increased the testability of hydraulic theory by stipulating in explicit detail the purported causal links between irrigation technology and centralized authority. By breaking down hydraulic theory into its many constituent causal connections, Earle clarified the specific implications of Wittfogel's hydraulic theory. Furthermore, he explicitly formulated the causal connections so that they would be testable (Earle 1978:38–47).

From the literature of Wittfogel and others Earle outlined the various factors that would influence the relationship between irrigation technology and centralized authority. Five factors were identified: (1) construction of irrigation systems, (2) maintenance of irrigation systems, (3) reconstruction following natural disasters, (4) defense and reconstruction following warfare, and (5) allocation of water and settlement of disputes (Earle 1978:39). He then analyzed each of these five factors in considerable detail, with the goal of specifying even more precisely the relationships of the constituents of each of the five factors and centralized management. He also identified the numerous factors that could complicate these relationships. Finally, he devised archaeological tests of the relationships. Not surprisingly, his report and assessment of the testing constitute a sizable portion of his 1978 book.

Recounting Earle's analyses of each of the five factors would be prohibitive. Fortunately, what he did and how it increased testability can be understood from an account of his analysis of one factor—the construction of irrigation systems.

Wittfogel discusses the significance of construction early in *Oriental Despotism* (1957:23–29). Irrigation requires heavy initial capital investment, including dams, ditches, and protective dikes. Furthermore, Wittfogel believed large-scale hydraulic technology would necessitate assembling and centrally directing large labor crews.

Earle recognized that because scale is usually measured by the organization of production, Wittfogel's relationship between large-scale hydraulic technology and large labor crews is tautologous. A tautologous relationship is not testable, so Earle suggests instead that measurements of physical size should be the basis for defining the scale of the hydraulic system. The reason is that projected measurements of physical size can be tested against the artifactual record. Earle then rephrased the argument for the relationship between construction and central authority so that it was testable: The scale of an irrigation system (I) determines the man-days of work required for construction (Wc); in turn, this work affects the size of the requisite labor crews (L). Furthermore, as the size of labor crews increases, the need for centralized management (M) should also increase. Simply put, management should be a function (f) of the size of an irrigation system (Earle 1978:39).

Earle then put the argument into two schematic forms: *I* determines *Wc*, which determines *L*, which determines *M*. In other words,

Wc = f(I)

L = f(Wc)

M = f(L)

In sum, M = f(I).

Earle realized that the simple chain of relationships outlined here is complicated by numerous exogenous factors. For example, the first relationship—scale of an irrigation system determines the man-days of work required—assumes that construction technology is constant. This may or may not be true. The introduction of metal tools would increase the efficiency of labor, for example, and the introduction of mechanized equipment would dramatically alter the relationship (Earle 1978:39–40).

Earle goes on to identify exogenous factors that might influence the other relationships in his chain, and accounts for those factors in his discussion. Despite these complicating exogenous facts, Earle still concludes that "Archaeologically, it is possible to test a simplified version of the construction-managerial hypothesis by examining the relationship between construction work per unit time and centralization of authority. If technology is held constant, work may be estimated by the volume of earth moved during construction. Because time is a critical factor, a reliable measure of the time span of construction is necessary" (Earle 1978:40–41).

Earle's modified theory

A discussion of Earle's empirical tests of Wittfogel's hydraulic theory lies beyond the scope of this book and the competency of its author. Fortunately, what is relevant here are his findings along with his conclusions concerning hydraulic theory. Both were used in the formulation of Earle's modified theory.

After an elaborate series of tests of many implications of hydraulic theory, Earle concluded that it was refuted. Earle found in the Halelea district that irrigation systems were small scale. Instead of being associated with a particular type of sociopolitical organization, they were instead found in a full range of sociopolitical types, from acephalous tribes to chiefdoms to peasant communities incorporated into states. Earle thus concluded that there was "virtually no evidence that Hawaiian irrigation would have required centralized management for construction, maintenance, or water distribution" (Earle 1978: 193–94). On the other hand, there was evidence that regional organization was necessary for reconstructing irrigation systems following destruction by natural disaster or warfare, and for protecting irrigation systems from external threat. Nevertheless, the reconstruction and protection of irrigation systems are "insufficient cause for the evolution of a *centralized* regional organization" (Earle 1978:194).

Having concluded that Wittfogel's theory was refuted, Earle outlined a modified theory about the relationship between irrigation and central authority. He argued that central authority in Hawaii developed for reasons other than management of irrigation systems. Having developed, however, regional organization was invoked for the reconstruction and protection of irrigation systems. More important, the increased production of staples from irrigation was used to finance political activities and thus helped stabilize the role of chiefs and their dependents. In addition, the staples formed the capital used to expand productive capacities and thus further increased the influence of central authority (Earle 1978:195).

To sum up, Earle concluded that the development of irrigation systems was neither a necessary nor a sufficient condition for the evolution of centralized authority. Irrigation systems did, however, provide a means by which centralized authority stabilized its control and increased its influence.

In closing this section, I would like to share one methodological concern about Earle's modified theory. It is the same as a concern expressed earlier about the theories of McC. Adams and the Hunts. Earle's modified theory grew from his refutation of Wittfogel's hydraulic theory. Furthermore, Earle does attempt to incorporate the strengths of Wittfogel's theory into his modified theory while eliminating the weaknesses of Wittfogel's theory. Finally, Earle's theory was tested successfully against his artifactual data in Hawaii. In that sense his theory was testable in a localized context. Yet I am not convinced that Earle's modified theory is universalizable and clearly testable beyond the particular context in Hawaii within which and for which it was formulated. This matter will be discussed further in Chapter 6.

Earle's interest in the evolution of social organization continued unabated, to be sure. He even coauthored a later book entitled *The Evolution of Human Societies: From Foraging Groups to Agrarian State* (Johnson and Earle 1987). It is not easy to see how the evolutionary stages are testable, however, even if some or all of the stages may characterize the development of social organization in certain locales. For that reason one also has to wonder if the postulation of evolutionary stages will provide as productive a stepping stone for further theoretical development as a highly testable theory like that of Wittfogel.

Finally, perhaps ironically, in the 1987 book Earle and his co-author Allen Johnson emphasize that the causes, mechanisms, and patters of the evolution of social organization are explainable in terms of a single coherent theory. Unfortunately, a universal theory is not *necessarily* highly testable or even testable at all. Yet universalization is crucial for testability. The reasons for both these statements are explored in the next section.

The Testability of Theories

The core of testability is that theories be refutable, or falsifiable; that is, that they be vulnerable to error. As a matter-of-fact, *refutability*, *falsifiability*, and *testability* and the locutions of these words can be used interchangeably. Two outcomes are possible when a theory is actually tested at a vulnerable point. The theory can be corroborated, that is, found correct at a point where it ran the risk of being incorrect. Or the theory can be *refuted*, or found incorrect.

That theories should be vulnerable to error is the central concept in the refutationist (or falsificationist) view of science. The terminology in the above paragraph comes from the refutationist camp. The focus in this chapter is on testability: on factors that help increase the vulnerability of theories to error. Other important themes in the refutationist view are discussed in Chapter 6.

A testable theory is one that *must exclude some state-of-affairs* from occurring. For example, a theory that explains everything would not be refutable. Outlined here are some of the most common ways of compromising testability.

Some theories are nonrefutable in principle. *Tautologies* are statements that are true in all conceivable instances. "All squares have four sides," or "no circles are triangles," are examples.

Less extreme than tautologies are theories formulated in such a way that all relevant empirical evidence is consistent with them. Earlier in this chapter was an example. Earle stated that Wittfogel's characterization of the relationship between large-scale hydraulic technology and large labor crews is tautologous (Earle 1978:39). Because large-scale hydraulic technology and large labor crews were assumed by Wittfogel to be co-determinant, no empirical evidence could ever falsify the relationship between them. That is why Earle decided to use measurements of physical size as the basis for defining the scale of a hydraulic system. Projected measurements of physical size of a hydraulic system could be tested against the artifactual record.

Strictly speaking, statements consistent with all relevant data are not tautologies. The reason is that such statements do at least make empirical reference, while tautologies do not. Logicians and philosophers reserve the word "tautology" for statements that are a priori true. A priori true means true prior to experience; in other words, it is true without empirical reference. In the broader intellectual world, however, it is also common to use the word tautology for statements that are consistent with all empirical evidence. If one wishes to distinguish between the two meanings, the strict type can be called a *formal tautology* and the broader type can be called an *empirical tautol-*

ogy. As a philosopher I must say that the latter seems oxymoronic. On the other hand, there is no inherent reason why everyone should feel obliged to use terms the same way as those in my professional group.

Vagueness is another culprit that can compromise testability. The more vague a theory the easier it is for it to explain any factual statement. This is particularly deceptive because the more factual statements that can be explained by a theory, the more universal it becomes. That is why a vague statement can be construed as one that increases universality but not testability.

Here is an example. A vague interpretation of two important concepts in Wittfogelian theory—irrigation need and central authority—can allow one to stretch the meaning of one, the other, or both. The relationship between the two can then become so malleable that it is not be clear what if any evidence would refute a claim about the relationship between them. Such vagueness did cause difficulty in Wittfogel's hydraulic theory (Earle 1978).

Vague theories are preferable to formal tautologies. Like empirical tautologies, vague theories can at least be reinterpreted so that they become testable. Earle did reformulate the components of irrigation need and central authority so that Wittfogel's claim about the relationship between the two became testable. (Earle 1973, 1977, 1978). Earle's decision to use measurements of physical size as the basis for defining the scale of a hydraulic system was one of the numerous links in a chain of reformulations that rendered testable Wittfogel's theory about the relationship between irrigation need and central authority.

Another way to compromise the testability of theories is to constrain them with *boundary conditions*: to stipulate a *range* within which theories do apply or beyond which they do not. In everyday language, to set boundary conditions is to add "qualifications" to a theory.

Wittfogel was guilty of adding qualifications. As mentioned earlier, he asserted that state society is not likely to form when the scale of the society, the scale of the irrigation system, or other historical conditions are not met.

Like tautologies and vagueness, qualifications lessen testability.

The reason is that qualifications lessen the universality of a theory. That is also why setting boundary conditions can be understood as the contrary of universalization. Boundary conditions contract the potential number of testable points in a theory whereas universalization increases the potential number of testable points in a theory. At this juncture it would seem that Wittfogel's hydraulic theory is less than a paragon of testability. After all, his theory incorporated three of the compromising maneuvers identified earlier: empirical tautologies, vague theoretical components, and qualifications. We have seen that Wittfogel's theories have rightfully been criticized for such maneuvers (Earle 1978 and see Hunt and Hunt 1974). One can be particularly thankful to Earle for his work in counteracting these compromising maneuvers. Earle did not rest content with criticizing Wittfogel's theory. As we have seen, he reformulated compromising components in Wittfogel's theory so that it became more testable.

Despite the help from Earle, Wittfogel himself should also receive credit for increasing the testability of his hydraulic theory. Even though his hydraulic theory was formulated in the arid regions of the Far East, he did not limit his explanation for the origins of state structure to the Far East, or to arid areas. Neither did he confine his theory to a particular time period. Instead, Wittfogel universalized his theory to explain the formation of state structure anywhere, at any time, and in any climatic conditions. It is particularly impressive, in my view, that Wittfogel explicitly universalized his theory to explain the formation of state structure in damper climates like that in Hawaii (Wittfogel 1957). As pointed out earlier, his theory faced particularly risky tests in damper regions, where the need for irrigation would normally be less pressing and hence the formation of state structure without irrigation development would be all the more likely. He also set the stage for Earle's testing of hydraulic theory in Hawaii.

Universalization and Testability

By this point it should be clear that universalization is critical for increasing testability. Universalization has already been discussed in numerous contexts, but tracing its role in more detail should help one gain a better understanding of how universalization increases testability.

Universal explanations

Compromising the refutability of theories is undesirable: It limits the points at which theories are vulnerable to error. Increasing the refutability of theories is desirable: It yields more points vulnerable to error. Generalizing a theory increases the number of potential points at which it is vulnerable to error. Generalizing a theory thus increases refutability.

The most generalized theories are those that are universal: those that apply in all cases and at all times. Explanations that assume or make universal claims offer the most potential points of error, and hence the most potential points for testing. In short, universalized theories are the most refutable theories.

Universality is embedded in claims such as the following: "All instances of early hierarchical state organization are due to irrigation need"; "if there is insufficient food, then the ruling class will be held responsible"; and "shortage of rain causes settlements to shift toward water sources." Archaeologists sometimes call such universalized claims "general laws" or "covering laws."

Although the grammatical form can vary, all universal statements can be understood as claims about the relationships of events or phenomena that *always* hold without exception. The universality can either be explicit, as in the first example cited, or implicit, as in the second and third examples. The second and third examples are causal assertions. Stipulating a causal connection is the usual convention for making a universal claim. To say that "X causes Y" normally means that "whenever there is X, there is Y."

Some theories hardly need be analyzed to reveal universality. Newton's laws of physics provide a good example. His principle of inertia—that a body in motion will stay in motion unless acted upon by an external force—clearly means that *every* moving body will remain in the same motion unless acted upon by an external force. The universality of Wittfogel's hydraulic theory was proclaimed by

Wittfogel himself. Other theories require closer inspection to uncover the universality embedded within them. For example, consider the following explanation: "Agricultural workers were redeployed to produce religious icons because of the declining prestige of priests, in turn causing a further decrease in agricultural production." This explanation of a singular event can be analyzed into three component statements: (1) "Agricultural workers were redeployed to produce religious icons"; (2) "the prestige of priests was on the decline"; and (3) "whenever agricultural workers are redeployed to alternative types of production, all other factors remaining unchanged, there will be a decrease in agricultural production." The third statement *is* universal: In *all* cases, when agricultural workers are redeployed, other factors remaining unchanged, agricultural production will decrease. This example is an explanation of a singular event—the decrease in agricultural production when the prestige of priests was challenged—yet it contains an implicit universal statement.

An example from physics

Newton's causal explanation of planetary motion rests on two universal statements: (1) A body in motion will stay in motion unless acted upon by an external force (inertial principle); and (2) all masses attract each other (gravitational principle). These two universal statements, used by Newton to explain planetary motion, were also testable by the motion of bodies on an inclined plane, pendulum motion, bodies falling free, and the reaction of bodies upon collision. Such a variety of testable points greatly enhanced the refutability of Newton's theories of motion.

Incidentally, Newton was the first to show convincingly that a causal explanation of heavenly motion could be applied successfully to terrestrial motion. The reason is that his explanation of planetary motion contained universal statements that could be tested by the motion of bodies on an inclined plane, pendulum motion, bodies falling free, and the reaction of bodies upon collision.

Unanticipated understanding and insight

At least some of the understanding and insight provided by theories should be unanticipated, a point discussed in Chapter 2. Indeed, increasing the *variety* of test points is tantamount to directing research into unforeseen realms, the upshot of which is more potential for unanticipated understanding and insight.

The reason that testability is enhanced by the variety of test points becomes clear with a little reflection. Although Newton's laws were tested by the motion of numerous planets, corroborating his laws repeatedly in similar contexts (all with the motion of planets) did not yield as much new understanding and insight as corroborating his laws in different contexts (with the motion of bodies on an incline plane, pendulum motion, free-fall motion, and the reaction of bodies upon collision). Likewise, the universalization of Wittfogel's explanation for formation of central authority increased the variety of test points by explaining the formation of central authority in different societies under different conditions. That is why it led to unanticipated understanding and insight in other contexts.

In short, universalizing theories not only increases the number of test points but also the variety of test points. Increasing the variety of test points directs research into unforeseen realms. It leads archaeologists to search for test points in different societies, under different conditions. The upshot is that universalization can lead to unanticipated understanding and insight into societies distant from that or those that gave rise to a theory.

A cascade of methodological benefits

An entire cascade of methodological benefits has been described: increased refutability, increased variety of test points, research directed into unforeseen realms, and unanticipated understanding and insight. It cannot be emphasized enough that *the key to setting off this cascade of methodological benefits is the universalization of theories*. It makes little difference whether the universalization is implicit within a causal explanation or is explicitly articulated.

An example from archaeology

The benefits of universalization have already been traced in the Wittfogelian research program. Bill Keegan's study of the evolution of the Tainos provides another archaeological example of the benefits that cascade from universalization. Keegan also includes a helpful discussion of the methodological assumptions that guide his work. Those methodological ideas are illuminating in themselves, in addition to being useful for understanding his work.

Keegan's approach falls within the research program associated with Marvin Harris' cultural materialism. This is not the place to plunge into a discussion of the similarities and differences among high-level models, but a few words are needed. *Cultural materialism* is the view that all cultural phenomena are the epiphenomena of the economic orientation of mankind. *Marxist approaches* to explaining social organization and culture place ideational elements in dialectical relationship with economic factors. Some Marxist approaches incorporate cultural materialism because they give priority to the role of economic factors in the dialectic. Other Marxist approaches do not assume cultural materialism because they give priority to ideational elements in the dialectic (Trigger 1989b:341). *Processual approaches* explain change, and assume that change—social, economic, and cultural—is primarily the function of internal dynamics ("processes"). Processual approaches are quite distinct from the others discussed. They do not assume just two categories (economic and ideational) to explain change, they do not assume that any one particular category always takes priority in explaining change, and—unlike some others—processual approaches are closely associated with the methodological guidelines developed and recommended in this book.

In short, cultural materialism sometimes shares common ground with Marxist approaches, and it is not often associated with processual approaches. Given this information one might not expect to find important processual elements in the work of those espousing cultural materialism. Bill Keegan not only identifies processual elements in cultural materialism, but finds them crucial.

There is a parenthetical lesson here: Methodological labels can be misleading. The focus must be on methodological ideas rather than the labels that can shift back and forth over the top of them. Keegan does concentrate on the ideas rather than the slogans, as will be seen later in this discussion.

In a 1991 paper, Bill Keegan highlights a number of significant elements in a processual approach (Keegan 1991). In it, he assessed the role of universalized claims, and his perspective on the confusion about universalization among archaeologists.

Like Marvin Harris in his 1979 book *Cultural Materialism: The Struggle for a Science of Culture*, Keegan advocates formulation of an explicit and integrated research methodology. A central component of that methodology is universal generalizations or laws. As important as the latter may be, Keegan points out that archaeologists are "uncertain, perhaps even uneasy, with regard to laws" (Keegan 1991: 184) and refers to Kent Flannery and Merrilee Salmon as two people who have articulated the uneasiness (Flannery 1982; Salmon 1982). Keegan further notes that neither Carl Hempel nor Thomas Kuhn, the two philosophers who in his view have been the most influential in the New Archaeology, provide an adequate account of the role of universal generalizations. Critics of processual archaeology also misunderstand the role of universalization. This passage from Shanks and Tilley is quoted by Keegan:

> It remains unspecified and unclear what status these generalizations are actually supposed to have and how general a statement must be before it counts as a generalization: two cases? three? fifty? If the generalizations made are not laws they cannot be expected to be applicable in any one particular case so why are these generalizations of use to us? Why must the business of doing science necessarily be equated with the ability, or the will to generalize? This appears to be a procedural rule founded on the basis that generalizing, rather than considering all the particularity of the individual case, is a superior kind of activity. (Shanks and Tilley 1987a:38, in Keegan 1991:185)

Bill Keegan emphasized the importance of universalization in his 1991 paper but was also keenly aware that the role of universalization is not adequately understood in archaeological circles. He illustrated the role of universalization in the development of his theories about the Tainos for both reasons. The highlights of Keegan's theoretical approach and empirical investigations are summarized here. Included are comments on the methodological functions of universalization.

The Tainos are known by many as the people whom Columbus first encountered in the New World. In the 500th year of the anniversary of Columbus' voyage, a well-known student of the Tainos, Irving Rouse, referred to that encounter in the title of his book *The Tainos: Rise & Decline of the People Who Greeted Columbus* (Rouse 1992). The title of Keegan's own 1992 book on the Tainos, *The People Who Discovered Columbus: The Prehistory of the Bahamas,* also refers to the encounter with Columbus (Keegan 1992). Also known as the Arawaks, the Tainos were, along with the Caribs, one of the two principal groups in the Caribbean. How the Tainos arrived in the Caribbean is a fascinating, difficult question (Rouse 1986:106–56).

The problem that captured Bill Keegan's interest dealt with a time period long after the arrival of the Tainos, but not too long before the arrival of Columbus. The Tainos developed complex chiefdoms in the Caribbean Islands, and Keegan studied their evolutionary patterns after A.D. 1200. In particular, he concentrated on the Lucayan Tainos, whose expansion in the Bahamas began about A.D. 700 (Keegan 1991:189).

Keegan assumed that economic dynamics were crucial in the development patterns of the Tainos. The central role of economics is a hallmark of cultural materialism, of course. The assumption is also useful because the artifactual record of economic activity is often rich compared to the artifactual record of other types of activities.

Keegan identified three economic models that would imply different settlement patterns. If Taino economic behavior fit a maximization model, then a steady-state population distribution would be expected. If Taino economic behavior fit a satisficing model, then a weighted distribution of population would be entailed. If the Taino economic behavior were stochastic, then economic behavior would yield a random settlement pattern (Keegan 1991:189–91).

Notice that each of the three models of economic behavior are implicitly universalized, in this case with the familiar "If-then" formula. Each is generalized to the point that regardless of which culture is under investigation, or when it existed, the stipulated model would always entail a characteristic population distribution. It makes no difference that the first two of these universal claims were formulated in other fields—biology and economics—and that the stochastic model of behavior is an alternative that can be considered in nearly any situation. Universalization means that they should apply in archaeological contexts as well. Each of the models has the potential to extend understanding from one context into others.

Testing the models required empirical investigation. Because each of the three models implies a different pattern of population distribution, the latter became the focus of fieldwork. Population distributions were investigated via both subsistence practices and demographic patterns. Using stable isotope analysis, Keegan and DeNiro documented a shift in diet breadth that suggested the marginal-cost pattern typical of maximization (Keegan and DeNiro 1988). Demographic patterns suggested an exponential growth of population, a result that is also consistent with maximization (Keegan 1992: especially Chapter 7). The assessment of population distributions was complicated by a series of interesting geographical and ethnological factors, including the facts that the Bahamas are an archipelago rather than a continuous land area, that the islands varied greatly in size, that social organization favored the pairing of settlements, and that political integration increased over time (Keegan 1991:191–94). The maximization model still prevailed after the data were filtered through these factors.

The Consequences of Not Universalizing

The benefits of universalization have been illustrated by examples from both physics and archaeology. From a counterfactual perspective, look at what might have been lost if there had *not* been universalization. Theories would be limited to providing explanations for only those contexts in which they were developed. Lost would be the understanding and insight into other societies that might be provided by those explanations. Wittfogel's theory would not have been refuted by Earle, and neither would it have provided Earle with *desiderata*—the corroborated and refuted points in Wittfogel's theory—from which to develop a new theory. The maximization model would not have been corroborated by Keegan either, nor would the satisficing and stochastic models have been refuted. In sum, a valuable perspective on the development of the Tainos and similar groups would have been lost.

A methodological argument

The argument for universalization has been methodological. That is, the argument assumes that universalization, like other methodological stratagems, should be evaluated by assessing whether or not it facilitates the expansion of knowledge. Notice that the methodological argument does *not* broach the question as to whether universals exist. There will be comment on that interesting question in Part III of this book.

In my view the methodological argument for universalization is strong enough and clear enough that criticisms are likely based on misunderstanding. The assumptions that lead to misunderstanding are explored below.

Two confusions concerning the role of universalization

Two confusions concerning universalization crop up in methodological debates among archaeologists. One is the mistaken assumption that the goal of archaeological theory should be to establish universals—covering laws—in the sense of verifying them or confirming them, usually by a large number of instances. Shanks and Tilley express this confusion when they ask "how general a statement must be before it counts as a generalization: two cases? three? fifty?"

(Shanks and Tilley 1987a:38). Establishing universals by confirmation was associated with the early ideas of Carl Hempel, and filtered into archaeological discussion principally through the influence of Lewis Binford. The other confusion is the view that universals should have no role in archaeological theory. This position stems from the assumption that cultures are entirely unique, as are the individuals who compose them. The search for universals is thus wasteful because cross-cultural universals do not exist and detrimental because it excludes serious investigation of cultural and individual particularities. This position is most often associated with the postprocessual movement and is expressed forcefully by its most widely known advocates: Ian Hodder, Michael Shanks, and Christopher Tilley.

The two confusions—the goal of establishing universals by confirmation and the outright rejection of universalization—are of course radically different. Strange as it may seem, they are not unrelated. I shall explain why after discussions of each. Some comment on narrative history will start us off.

Narrative history

A conception of scientific history is under investigation here. Because any view of scientific history is quite distinct from narrative history, however, understanding the rudiments of the latter will help bring the former into sharper focus.

Narratives are story-like; they describe and interpret events using a variety of assumptions, sometimes but not always to convey a lesson as well. Among the assumptions informing historical narratives are explanatory generalizations that are "characteristically matters of common knowledge on human dispositions or motivations" (Spaulding 1968:35). The commonality of the implicit explanatory generalizations in historical narratives is the reason that "skillful historical narratives are so immediately satisfying; the historian and the reader possess in common the implicit generalizations that make sense of the narrative" (Spaulding 1968:35). Furthermore, narrative histories typically explain unique events (Goode 1977), which is the reason that they have a "particularizing quality," to use Spaulding's expression (Spaulding 1968:35).

The characterization of narrative history sketched out here is brief, but the methodological point can now be made: Historical narratives are not designed to be testable. There are two related reasons. First, the explanatory generalizations informing the narrative are usually implicit. To be tested they would need to be made explicit. They would also have to be disentangled from a web of other assumed explanatory generalizations, some of which might even be inconsistent with each other. Second, even if the explanatory generalizations were explicit, the goal of a narrative is *not* to test the generalizations. The goal is to use the generalizations to explain something else— typically a unique event—rather than use events to test the generalizations.

Establishing universals by confirmation

In a classic 1942 paper Carl Hempel set out a research program for history: to unveil the "covering laws" that, according to him, would explain historical phenomena (Hempel 1942). The method used to uncover the universals would be scientific in the positivistic sense embraced by Hempel at that point in his career: Universal laws would be confirmed by finding evidence of them in numerous contexts. That 1942 paper and the research program for scientific history proposed in it have been widely discussed by philosophers through the decades.

Incidentally, Hempel's 1942 paper did not become well-known among archaeologists, perhaps because it focused on history and Binford wanted to disassociate archaeological explanation from historical narrative. Hempel advocated scientific history rather narrative history, however, and for that reason the 1942 paper could have been included in the canon of the New Archaeology. In any case, aspects of Hempel's views on general laws in history and the goal of confirming them were discussed in later papers (Hempel 1962, for example) and by many other philosophers as well (Brodbeck 1962 and Kaplan 1964, for example). That Hempel's 1942 paper did not become widely known among archaeologists has thus not kept his ideas from playing a central role in the methodological discussions of the New Archaeology.

Lewis Binford first introduced Hempel's ideas on scientific history into the archaeological literature. Works cited by Binford have included Hempel's 1965 book *Aspects of Scientific Explanation and Other Essays in the Philosophy of Science*, his 1966 book *Philosophy of Natural Science*, and Hempel and Oppenheim's 1948 paper "Studies in the Logic of Explanation."

Binford's influence is surely a major reason why theoretical archaeologists have become so familiar with Hempel's work, or at least his early work. For more background on how others adopted Hempel's ideas and the adoption of those ideas in archaeology, see Watson's, LeBlanc's, and Redman's 1970 book *Explanation in Archaeology: An Explicitly Scientific Approach*, their 1984 version of that book called *Archaeological Explanation: The Scientific Method in Archaeology*, and Fritz's and Plog's 1970 seminal article "The Nature of Archaeological Explanation."

Incidentally, another important aspect of Hempel's proposed method—the "hypothetical-deductive" (H-D) model for tracing the implications of a theory—is not being questioned here. According to the H-D model an explanatory hypothesis should be proposed and its implications carefully deduced for testing. Although there has been considerable debate about the details of the H-D model, there is little question that the H-D model, at least broadly understood, is crucial in science. In a recent article Richard Watson clarifies the function of the H-D model in science and provides an historical perspective on its use (Watson 1991).

In short, then, Hempel's recommendation of the H-D model and its adoption by archaeologists is not the focus of criticism here. What is being called into question is the positivistic slant in Hempel's early philosophy of science and its adoption into the New Archaeology, especially the New Archaeology of Lewis Binford.

"Positivism" is a word with various meanings, so here I focus specifically on the thesis that creates confusion for those trying to understand the role of universals in explanation. That thesis is that the goal of science is to establish universals by verification or confirmation. From this perspective the goal of physics would be to find and confirm universal explanations that hold always or hold within a high degree of probability, and the goal of archaeology would be to find and confirm cultural universals that apply without exception or at least within a high degree of probability. A number of additional theses are integral to the positivistic view of science. They are not significant for this discussion but will be taken up in Chapter 4.

The role of universalization from a positivistic perspective contrasts sharply with the function of universals outlined in the last section. First, from the positivistic standpoint science should consist of only established explanations that are verifiable in all instances or—in a later development—confirmed by some probabilistic convention or confirmed as more probable than competing explanations. From the largely refutationist perspective expounded in this book, science should consist of testable theories that can serve as stepping stones to better theories. Second, from the positivistic perspective a confirmed explanation should not be mistaken, or at least it should be highly probable. From the refutationist perspective explanations should be potentially mistaken, or refutable. Third, the goal of science and means of attaining that goal are different. The positivistic goal is to establish universals by confirmation, whereas the refutationist goal is to develop better theories by exploiting errors in received theories.

Positivism does provide some valuable insights despite the criticism. For example, science can be viewed as the set of established theories. Such a view cannot account for the dynamic changes that such theories will likely undergo in the future, but a reconstruction of theories already tested successfully can be helpful. Textbooks in science typically present only successful theories. Also, a scientist or intellectual may indeed *want* his or her favored theory to be confirmed in all instances. I assume that was the case with Wittfogel, and with others as well. As a matter-of-fact, Isaac Newton and nearly any other scientist or intellectual would normally want their favored theories to be verified in every instance. The desire to confirm favored theories does motivate many scientists. What *is not* so helpful is to assume that the aim of science—not just the aims of scientists—is to *establish* theories.

From whence comes this mistaken conception of the aim of science? I believe it lies in the long-standing inductive tradition in science, a tradition of which positivism is the most recent outbreak. Induction is the subject of the next chapter, however, so this point will be explained in detail there.

Rejection of universalization

The second confusion over the function of universals can be presented briefly. It stems from the belief that searching for universal laws or generalizations detracts from the appreciation of and study of unique qualities of different cultures. The pursuit of general laws is intrinsically etic; for that reason it is maintained that one cannot both universalize and yet capture human agency in theories. In other words, individualistic factors such as cognition and feelings cannot be part of universalized claims. Shanks and Tilley offer a typical postprocessual criticism when they state that "the will to generalize . . . appears to be a procedural rule founded on the basis that generalizing, rather than considering all the particularity of the individual case, is a superior kind of activity" (Shanks and Tilley 1987a: 38).

Criticisms like these cannot simply be dismissed. Deterministic high-level models that exclude human agency, such as biological, evolutionary and ecological models, "do not by themselves provide a sufficient basis for explaining the variability observed in the archaeological record" (Trigger 1989a: 29). It should be pointed out, however, that methodological individualism, a largely refutationist approach to incorporating human agency into theories, is already being utilized for theory building in archaeology (Chapter 8 in this book; Bell 1992a; Renfrew and Zubrow 1993; Gardin and Peebles 1992).

Despite the criticisms, recall again what would be *lost* by not universalizing. Testability would be severely compromised. Weakening or eliminating testability would undermine an important criterion—I believe *the* most important criterion—for deciding where theories are correct and where they are mistaken. Furthermore, without testability to help make judgments about theories archaeologists can be tempted to embrace any theory; that is, they can be tempted by relativism (Chapter 7 of this book; Wylie 1991; Bell 1987a, 1991; Trigger 1989a, 1989c). Finally, to abandon the search for universals would be to abandon the chance to gain understanding and insight beyond the cultural contexts in which universalized explanations are initially formulated.

The two confusions concerning the role of universalization are certainly different, but they are related. When it is realized that it is not productive or even possible to establish universals in the positivist sense, skeptics are almost invited to conclude that the search for universals is wasteful and that scientific approaches are unnecessary or even harmful. In short, the confusions are co-dependents, to use terminology from contemporary psychology.

Reformulating and Interpreting Theories as Refutable

Reformulating theories so that they are refutable and interpreting theories so that they are refutable are often interdependent strategies. Reformulating and interpreting theories so that they are refutable is also related to a number of other methodological strategies developed earlier.

The testability of theories is dependent upon how those theories are formulated. It has already been shown that the structure of formal tautologies renders them nonrefutable. Formal tautologies are not vulnerable to error because counterinstances are not even conceivable. Except for formal tautologies, however, nontestable theories can often be reformulated so that they become refutable. Remember how Earle reformulated empirically tautological components and vague components in hydraulic theory so that they became testable.

The testability of theories is also dependent upon interpretation. On the negative side, a refutable theory can be interpreted so that it becomes nonrefutable. Remember how the dialectic of cultural and material categories so central to Marxist interpretations can be stretched to the point where no phenomenon would serve as counterevidence. On the positive side, interpretation *is* within human control. This means that interpretation hinges upon methodological decision and the guidelines that direct methodological decision. Furthermore, a broad rule for interpreting theories can be spelled out. Following it will be a number of specific suggestions for increasing, or at least not decreasing, the refutability of theories.

The broad methodological rule is to interpret theories so that they are as refutable as possible. The broad rule can be broken into three parts. First, if theories are not refutable, try to interpret them so that they are refutable. Second, if theories are refutable, try to interpret them so that they become more refutable. Third, guard carefully against interpreting theories so that they become less refutable. A number of specific guidelines follow from the broad rule.

First, interpret explanations so that they are applicable in specific contexts. In methodological jargon, to "instantiate a theory," or to "make a theory operational," is to stipulate precisely in what type of contexts it should apply. Instantiating a theory requires describing the conditions of its application in detail, and specifying the observational expectations. Earle increased the refutability of Wittfogel's theory by specifying more carefully what was meant by irrigation need and state structure.

Second, increase the range of an explanation as much as possible. Wittfogel did just this by generalizing his explanation of the formation of state society beyond the arid, oriental context of his studies. The more general the better, so try to make a theory universal.

Third, break down a broad explanation into its specific causal components. That will not only increase the array of implications that are potentially testable, but will render them more precise as well. Earle did this by carefully reducing the development and maintenance of irrigation projects into a greater number of components than had Wittfogel.

Fourth, increase the precision of testable implications by using quantifying or formal techniques whenever possible. Remember that the refutability of theories is increased not only by increasing the number and variety of testable points, but also by making those points as precise as possible.

Fifth, avoid quantitative interpretations of theories that do not enhance testability. As explained in Chapter 2, quantifying explanatory elements not amenable to quantification can lead to tests that seem more severe than warranted. It can also tempt one to "smooth out" quantitative test results, thus making it appear as if a theory has passed a more severe test than it actually has. Also, avoid attempts to measure the epistemological probability of theories. Remember that attempting to measure the confidence deserved by a theory via epistemological probabilities is not possible. Furthermore, attempts to assess theories with epistemological probabilities can tempt one to accept improbable but possible refutations in theories rather than exploit such refutations for further theory development.

Sixth and finally, avoid placing boundary conditions on theories. Adding qualifications to theories is probably the most common way of reducing testability.

Interpretation is also important for another broad methodological rule: to regard theories as refuted when they seem to have failed test(s). This rule is important because it provides the impetus to try to improve theories by adjustment or to explore new theories.

By the way, regarding theories as refuted does *not* entail that they should be rejected by everyone. Those who defend a theory under attack might improve it, a matter to be addressed in the next section. It *does* entail that some theoreticians should reject theories when they are interpreted as refuted. Rejecting refuted theories allows alternative theories to play a role in theory development. If Earle had not rejected Wittfogel's theory, he might not have been motivated to develop his own theory.

Incidentally, Earle has been criticized by Manuel Gandara for being dogmatic in rejecting the original Wittfogelian theory (Gandara 1981). Gandara points out that Earle's method is akin to the dogmatic falsificationism criticized by Lakatos (1970). According to Lakatos, dogmatic falsification of a theory leads to definitive rejection of the theory. Lakatos correctly criticizes dogmatic falsificationism. More specifically, he argues that a theory can only be interpreted as refuted, and such an interpretation might be mistaken.

Furthermore, even if the interpretation is correct, a theory might still bear more fruit. The upshot is that one should be careful about rejecting a theory just because it seems to be refuted.

Gandara is certainly correct in recognizing the interpretative side of Earle's refutation of Wittfogelian theory. Nevertheless, Earle's approach should be defended. As has been explained, his reformulation and testing of hydraulic theory yielded a better assessment of the strengths and weaknesses in Wittfogel's explanation of the origins of state structure. Furthermore, Earle's modified theory provided further understanding and insight. These desirable results might not have been realized had Earle not interpreted Wittfogel's theory as refuted and had not "dogmatically" rejected it.

It is not quite fair for Gandara to label a fruitful methodological strategy "dogmatic," even though the terminology comes from Lakatos' analysis. On the other hand, it is to Gandara's credit that at the very end of his analysis he acknowledges the importance of Earle's rejection of Wittfogel's explanation in stimulating further theory development (Gandara 1981).

By the way, Lakatos' discussion of dogmatic falsificationism does not include an assessment of its benefits. There seem to be a number of reasons. First, his discussion focused on logical misconceptions within dogmatic falsificationism rather than an appraisal of the benefits (and detriments) of applied dogmatic falsificationism. Second, his reconstruction of "dogmatic" falsificationism was used mainly as a stepping-stone to more elaborate versions of refutationism. I hope that the discussion above illustrates why a "dogmatic" approach to rejecting refuted theories can also be a sound methodological strategy.

Refutability in Testing Theories

Vigilance in maintaining refutability must continue beyond interpreting explanations. It is important not to compromise refutability when theories are tested. Guidelines for maintaining refutability when testing theories is the subject of this section.

The artifactual side of archaeology lies beyond the scope of this book, but some commentary on testing is appropriate. Testing, after all, brings together the artifactual and theoretical aspects of archaeology. Two issues are addressed: the need to focus on testable implications of theories and the need to guard against compromising refutability when devising and executing tests.

The most important implications of theories are those that are testable, that is, those that are vulnerable to error. That may be an obvious point, but do remember that theories can have multiple implications that are not readily testable. The general theory of relativity, for example, is a massive web of conjecture with assumptions and implications that have not been tested and may never be. To Eddington's test of the curvature of space can be added three other tests: the rotation of the perihelion of the planets, the infrared shift in the electromagnetic emissions of receding masses, and the convertibility of mass and energy. Beyond the successful tests of these four refutable implications of the general theory, however, its empirical corroboration is quite slim. In archaeological theory there will certainly be copious assumptions and implications that are not testable. Attention should be focused on those that are.

On the artifactual side, one should search for data relevant to a refutable point of a theory. It is not important whether the data is available from completed fieldwork or must be made the object of fieldwork.

It is important to remember that statements about data—not the data themselves—are used in testing a theory. The interpretative bridge between the data and statements about the data can lead to confusion. For example, the data can be "fudged:" interpreted so that an affirmative "test" result is guaranteed. The trouble is that fudging data lowers or eliminates the potential of a test to refute a theory.

Incidentally, fudging need not be intentional. The occasional spectacular cases of deliberate tampering with data have gained wide publicity, but in most cases fudging is simply the unintentional product of the all-too-human tendency to interpret data favorably in light of ones theories (Broad and Wade 1983). There is, however, a refutationist safeguard: Assume that data that might be anomalous *is* anomalous, at least until convinced otherwise. A theoretician may fail to find pleasure in using this safeguard when his or her own theories are at stake, but it does offset the tendency to interpret data in favor of ones theories.

Searching Out the Source of Error

Admitting that data are anomalous means that a tested theory is interpreted as *refuted*. Refuting a theory does not, however, entail that it should automatically be rejected. Instead, it is best to search for the source(s) of the error and, if found, to modify the theory with auxiliary hypotheses. The search for error is discussed in this section and the adjustment of theory with auxiliary hypotheses will be the topic of the following section.

There are a number of reasons it is desirable to search for the source of error before rejecting a theory outright. If the source of error is found and isolated, only it need be rejected while other elements in the theory can be retained. To reject an entire theory prematurely can have the unfortunate consequence of closing off further opportunity for it to contribute to understanding and insight. Furthermore, by isolating the source of error one can adjust a theory to account for the error. An adjusted theory may have new implications and hence new possibilities for testing. Finally, if a theory is ultimately rejected in toto after repeated adjustments and refutations, one can have more confidence that the right decision has been made.

Locating the source of error is a challenge that can require intuition and even sheer luck. Despite these subjective elements, a number of guidelines can be helpful.

A few preliminary comments are in order. First, remember that words such as "theory" and "explanation" do not refer to one statement. It is preferable to conceive of a theory or explanation as a "theoretical web" or "explanatory network." Second, a theoretical web can be conceived as a set of conjoined statements that include implicit assumptions as well as explicit propositions.

In the search for error, the initial task is to break down a theoretical web into at least some of its component statements. Wittfogel's analysis of hydraulic theory for the emergence of centralized authority revealed numerous components in the management of an irrigation system. Included were its construction, maintenance, reconstruction following natural disasters or warfare, the allocation of water supplies from the system, and the mediation of disputes over the allocation of water supplies. Earle broke those components down even further. He stipulated in explicit detail the many causal links between irrigation technology, irrigation management, and centralized authority in all of the facets of hydraulic development. The result was an explicit and detailed array of the components of hydraulic theory. Within such an array Earle was more easily able to identify suspect components.

In sum, disaggregating the statements in a theoretical web is important in searching for the source of error. A theory broken into components is always more likely to reveal its weak link(s) than a less explicit or less precise theory.

If a source of error is not eventually found after reviewing the components in a theoretical web, then one might finally decide to reject the theory in toto and direct energy onto another theoretical path. There is no guarantee that an abandoned theory will not include worthwhile components, but inability to find a specific source of error normally indicates that the theoretical impasse might have to be resolved from a quite different theoretical perspective.

If a potential source of error is found, the next task is to test that source of error. With luck, there just might be report(s) of such a test already available in the literature. In other instances it will be necessary to undertake the time-consuming task of gathering artifactual data to test a potential source of error. Earle did both in his research on Wittfogelian theory.

When testing reveals error(s) in a theory, one might be able to eliminate one or a few components without abandoning the remainder of the theory. This is often possible when mistaken component(s) are independent of others in a theoretical web. For example, Earle was able to reject those components of Wittfogelian theory that required irrigation for the formation of centralized authority. On the other hand, he was able to retain those components of Wittfogelian theory that related irrigation management to political authority.

If an erroneous component is not readily separable from the remainder of the theory, then it is time to adjust the theory with auxiliary hypotheses. Of the three possible outcomes—abandoning a theory entirely, abandoning independent component(s) of a theory, or adjusting a theory with erroneous component(s) that are not independent of the remainder of a theory—the last may be the most common. It is crucial that the adjustment be done with care.

Adjusting Theories

When adjusting theories, refutability should be preserved or increased rather than decreased or closed off. The former—adjustment with auxiliary hypotheses—and the latter—ad hoc adjustment—were discussed and illustrated with archaeological examples in Chapter 2. A re-reading of that chapter may be in order if one needs to recapture the details. The discussion here begins with an example from physics.

Newtonians were disturbed that Newton's dynamic theories did not account for a perturbation, an unexplained variation in planetary motion. His gravitational law and principle of inertia could not account for the small but detectable anomaly in the movement of Uranus. In face of that anomaly Urbain Leverrier (1811–1877) offered a hypothesis: He predicted that the perturbation must be caused by an undetected mass interacting with the planet. The position and size of the undetected mass were calculated by Leverrier. Eventually, when telescopes had improved, a planet—Neptune—was located just as predicted. Instead of the anomaly leading to rejection of Newton's dynamic theories, it provided the impetus to adjust the theories and test them further.

Leverrier's adjustment was made with an *auxiliary hypothesis*: a hypothesis added to a theory to account for anomaly in such a way that the theory remains open to testing. The crucial characteristic of an auxiliary hypothesis is that it not decrease the refutability of the theory to which it is added. Some auxiliary hypotheses, as in the example cited, actually increase refutability by adding point(s) where theories can be tested. It goes without saying that adding auxiliary hypotheses to adjust theories is methodologically desirable.

The Wittfogelian research program provides an example from archaeology. After refuting Wittfogel's claim that the development of state structure was inevitably the result of irrigation need, Earle added a number of auxiliary hypotheses to the remaining components of hydraulic theory. Among those auxiliary hypotheses were the following: (1) that regional organization, though already developed, was used for the reconstruction and protection of irrigation systems, (2) that increased production of staples from irrigation was used to finance political activities and thus helped stabilize the role of chiefs and their dependents, and (3) that the staples formed the capital used to expand productive capacities, which in turn increased the influence of central authority even more. These hypotheses enabled further testing of Earle's modified hydraulic theory (Earle 1978).

The opposite of using auxiliary hypotheses to adjust theories is to make ad hoc adjustments: adjustments that explain anomaly but that diminish rather than maintain or increase refutability. In popular idiom, an ad hoc adjustment "explains away" an anomaly. For example, if Newton had explained the perturbation by appeal to some untestable factor exogenous to his theories—such as the anger of the gods, or an astrological emanation, or as a "deflection" from the normal gravitational attraction—the theory would have been preserved at the expense of closing off its refutability. Instead of continuing to be testable, or even more testable, it would have become less so. The contribution that Newton's theory could have made to further understanding and insight would have been compromised. Perhaps worse, energy spent defending it by ad hoc means is energy that might have been more profitably employed in other theoretical pursuits.

The hypothetical example of an ad hoc adjustment that was just cited is caricatured. Many adjustments are not clearly ad hoc, however, at least initially (Lakatos 1970). Even if an adjustment is made with auxiliary hypotheses the testing might be difficult or inaccessible. Newton's adjusted theory was not tested, for example, until better telescopes became available.

Rather obvious cases of ad hoc adjustments should be avoided without hesitation. The subtle cases are more difficult, however, as explained in Chapter 2. It is not always clear when an adjusted theory should be abandoned, or if it should be abandoned. The key is to ask, continually if necessary, is whether, in the light of anomaly, adjustments are leading to further tests of the theory, or whether they are functioning principally to ward off anomaly. With time, and a bit of intellectual agony, an answer to the question will usually emerge.

Incidentally, tenacity in maintaining a theory is methodologically sound when adjusting with auxiliary hypotheses. To reject a theory when continuing to explore its potential could result in missed understanding and insight, a point made earlier. If adjustments are ad hoc, however, then an adjusted theory loses refutability. In that case tenaciously held theories become dogma.

A Series of Decisions Made with Guidelines

Creating, maintaining, or increasing testability involves a series of decisions about theories. The underlying rule is to generate, preserve, and enhance refutability. The specific guidelines for decisions can be summarized as follows: Formulate explanations that are vulnerable to error, regard anomalies as potential refutations, search for source(s) of error before rejecting theories, use auxiliary hypotheses and avoid ad hoc adjustments when modifying theories, be cautious about rejecting theories before adjustments and tests lead to further refutation, and do abandon theories when they continue to fail tests after adjustment.

Remember that guidelines provide no algorithm to guarantee the most productive decisions. At times the most appropriate methodological decision will, in retrospect, look less productive than if the guidelines had been disregarded. There are a number of reasons for this. The theoretical landscape is constantly changing: an unanticipated competing theory with more promise may emerge, for example, or a well-known competing explanation may provide an unexpected theoretical breakthrough. Sheer luck can also intervene: A theory may provide more understanding and insight than could possibly have been imagined when originally proposed. All of these factors lie beyond the control of any theoretician.

Despite the difficulties, using methodological guidelines to direct theoretical hunches is preferable to using blind intuition. The guidelines recommended in this chapter should increase the chance that decisions about theories will contribute to theory development. If a given theory bears corroborative fruit, the reasons will be more apparent. If it is refuted but is still providing further understanding or insight, then it should be explored further by at least some. If it is refuted and is producing little if any further understanding or insight, there is good reason to reject the theory and turn ones theoretical energies elsewhere. The guidelines for these decisions are all informed by testability. That is why the decisions cannot be made as effectively if theories are not testable.

Suggested Readings

Testability is the most important concept in this book. The theory of testability used here emerges largely from the refutationist view of science. The selections by Popper and Lakatos present and expound upon testability in the refutationist tradition. The principal example of refutationist archaeology in this chapter featured the hydraulic theory as developed and modified by Karl Wittfogel and Timothy Earle. Their works are discussed here.

1. Timothy Earle, 1978, *Economic and Social Organization of a Complex Chiefdom: The Halelea District, Kauai, Hawaii.*
Pertinent to discussions of hydraulic theory and theory refutation.
This book contains Earle's most definitive analysis of hydraulic theory, especially that of Wittfogel. The clarity and flow of Earle's thoughts are par-

ticularly impressive in light of the rather complicated chains of argument necessary for his criticism and then modification of Wittfogel's theory.

2. Imre Lakatos, 1970, "Falsification and the Methodology of Scientific Research Programmes."
Pertinent to discussions on universalization and testability, refutation, adjustment, and decision making.
This essay recounts some misinterpretations as well as criticisms of the refutationist view. It also outlines a number of different interpretations and elaborations of the refutationist view.

3. Karl R. Popper, 1959, *The Logic of Scientific Discovery*.
Pertinent to discussions on theory testability, universalization, refutation, and adjustment.
Karl Popper's systematic formulation of the refutationist view of science is contained in this book, a translation of the German original of 1933. The arguments are sometimes quite complicated, but they are clear and so is the logical flow. Most issues are addressed in a manner more suited to professional philosophers than other scholars. Nevertheless, the implications of Popper's ideas for the practice of science are quite apparent and are frequently drawn out explicitly.

4. Karl R. Popper, 1962, *Conjectures and Refutations: The Growth of Scientific Knowledge*.
Pertinent for general background and to discussion on testability of theories.
The essays in this collection highlight major themes in the refutationist view of science and explore its political and social implications. There are many arguments, but most are not overburdened with detail. These essays are preferable to *The Logic of Scientific Discovery* as an introduction to Popper's refutationist view, and to sample its intellectual ramifications for science and society.

5. Karl Wittfogel, 1957, *Oriental Despotism*.
Pertinent to entire chapter.
In this book Wittfogel presents his hydraulic theory systematically and in detail. Despite the intricacies of the exposition, the organization and writing style make the book quite accessible.

Part II   The Philosophical and
Methodological Roots

Chapter 4   Induction

Franz Boas (1858–1942) was a central figure in American anthropology at the turn of this century. Among his numerous recommendations was one that fit his period as much as it does the present: He exhorted ethnologists to do their fieldwork as soon as possible. Theoretical speculation could wait until later. The rationale was to salvage the unexplored cultural record before contact with the new world and economic development diluted it beyond recognition.

Interestingly, the pleas of Boas and his followers such as Kroeber (1876–1960) for ethnologists to do their fieldwork first and their theorizing later harmonized with the *inductive view* of science, the view that science grows by collecting data and then generalizing—inducing—ideas from the data. The upshot is that the exhortation to save the record first and theorize about it later was also a methodological prescription for an inductive approach to science. It is one of those happy coincidences when a task of necessity—to save the record—harmonizes with intellectual duty—to be scientific. The inductive view was probably no small factor in rallying anthropologists and archaeologists to concentrate their energies on fieldwork.

Gathering the facts and from them inducing ideas is the standard formula for producing science—and hence knowledge—in the English-speaking world. It is a formula presented to school children in the introductory sections of science textbooks. It is also the formula, albeit in more esoteric garb, espoused in texts for advanced research students in the physical, biological, and social sciences. Inductive habits and attitudes permeate the United Kingdom, the United States, English-speaking Canada, Australia, New Zealand, and a sizable portion of other countries in the British sphere of influence. The prominent position of the English language in the contemporary world has allowed the inductive view to ride its coattails into circles beyond the bounds of the English cultural heritage.

How did induction become the dominant view of science? What variations and nuances of induction have evolved into present use? Exploring these questions will help answer others. Why has induction figured so largely in the New Archaeology (external version)? Most importantly, what are the contributions and limitations of the inductive view for theoretical archaeology? All these questions are addressed in this chapter.

Historical Roots of Induction

The history of induction is traced in considerably more detail than that of the other scientific views for a number of reasons. The shear dominance of the inductive view of science allows more opportunity for abuse. Another reason is that a number of powerful religious and political forces lay behind its establishment. They can still lend an ideological tone to the intellectual acceptance of induction. Breaking through the ideological grip is facilitated by an understanding how those forces infiltrated the intellectual rationale for adopting induction. Finally, weaknesses in the inductive view were an impetus for the development of the paradigmatic and refutationist views of science. Familiarity with how those weaknesses were revealed historically is also helpful for gaining a perspective on the advantages and disadvantages of induction.

The historical reconstruction of the inductive view can be divided into three major stages, each of which still has a direct bearing on the utilization of inductive method. First was the formulation of classical induction by Francis Bacon in the early seventeenth century, along with its establishment in the late seventeenth century. Second was the transformation of classical induction into probabilistic induction in the middle eighteenth century. Third was the further modification of induction into positivism in the early twentieth century.

Francis Bacon's Revolution in Scientific Method

Francis Bacon (1561–1626) was a productive thinker and scholar in fields as diverse as law, literature, philosophy, and political theory. Most know of him as Lord Chancellor under James I of England. Among his many intellectual and public contributions, a new theory of how to seek and advance knowledge was to be the most far-reaching and lasting.

Universities and monasteries were the primary centers of learning during Bacon's era, and both were strongholds of Catholic thought. Even though the Anglican Church had already been formed, both Cambridge and Oxford still thrived as Catholic centers. At a time when the ruling house of England encouraged condemnation of the Catholic Church, Bacon became the intellectual battering ram. He blamed Catholic theology in general, and its Aristotelian underpinnings in particular, for stifling innovation and the growth of knowledge.

Henry VIII (1491–1547; reigned from 1509–1547) had further polarized a centuries-old religious and political feud by establishing the Anglican Church. The Anglican Church provided fertile grounds for the reception of new ideas in natural philosophy. That paved the way for one of the most significant intellectual events of the seventeenth century: Bacon's formulation of classical inductive theory. Henry VIII's actions, though tragic to many, especially those closest to him, jarred the entrenched institutions of Aristotelian science. Bacon knocked them down, and Bacon's ideas were the bricks for building new institutions over the rubble.

In such works as *Advancement of Learning* (1605) and *Novum Organum* (1620), Bacon scolded natural philosophy—science—for stagnating. In his view, knowledge had not advanced since ancient times. Natural philosophy had become speculative philosophy, in which squabbles about the definitions of words had come to replace the observational and mathematical approaches of Classical Greece. Bacon even thought that natural philosophy had regressed; in some respects modern thinkers knew less than the Greeks. Yet Bacon admired discoveries and inventions. He marveled at the explorations of Marco Polo and Magellan, for example, and was fascinated by inventions such as the printing press and gun powder.

Two questions arose from Bacon's analysis of the ills of natural philosophy and his admiration of discovery and invention: What demarcates speculative thinking from progressive thinking, and how can progressive thinking be nurtured? The answers can be summarized in two parts.

First, paucity of progress within the Catholic tradition was due to Aristotelian speculation about essences. Second, progress could be made if attention were instead turned to careful observation and recording of the facts.

Aristotle and the essentialist view of knowledge

Bacon focused his criticism on the *essentialist* view of knowledge—the view that everything has an essence, and that knowledge is based on correct descriptions of those essences. There are a number of versions of the essentialist view, but the one with which Bacon grappled had its roots in the work of Aristotle, who lived in the fourth century B.C.

Aristotle (384–322 B.C.), arguably the most prolific philosopher of all time, lived after the Greek Classical period (480–399 B.C.) had passed. That most revered epoch was followed by the invasion of the Macedonians under Alexander the Great, who had been tutored in his early years by Aristotle. With a reputation for being more eclectic than original, Aristotle investigated and wrote on such diverse subjects as the flora and fauna, physics, cosmology, the history of ideas, political and moral theory, aesthetics, and logic. His cosmological views included the theory that everything was made of earth, air, fire, and water. His theory of motion had two principles: that objects of each element would move toward the natural home of that element, and that all other motion is the result of pushes.

Despite the diversity of subjects that caught Aristotle's attention, he approached all subjects with a method suggested by his essentialist view of knowledge. Aristotle adopted the view that everything has an *eidos*—"essence," or "idea" or "form." The essence of being human, for example, is to be rational. To gain knowledge of anything required correct understanding of its *eidos*. Certain knowledge—*episteme* in Greek—was the fruit of describing essences correctly.

Aristotle assumed that essences were located within material objects. That is why the search for truth should begin with observation of objects, and is also why the early Aristotelian tradition had an empirical thrust. Aristotle's numerous studies of living things, for example, included painstaking observation and detailed categorization. That is why Aristotle is often given the laurels for being the father of empirical biology.

What happened to the empirical thrust of the Aristotelian tradition so that Francis Bacon could later heap criticism on it for being too speculative? Aristotle's essentialist view of knowledge, along with many other cosmological and moral ideas, became the foundation of Catholic theology and thought. It also became the methodological underpinning of medieval science. How his essentialist view evolved from observation to speculation can be understood by outlining the two specific methodological steps developed by Aristoteleans for gaining knowledge.

The first step was to describe essences. The subject term of a statement is a label for an essence. An essence was thus described by defining the subject term. For example, "all humans are rational" describes the essence of being human as being rational. Establishing *episteme*, then, began with correct definition. The central role of definition in the Aristotelian approach to knowledge became a distinguishing mark of medieval thought. It also degenerated into *scholasticism*, in which thought is marked by compulsive concern for the meaning of words.

The second step in Aristotelian method was to derive further true statements. The tool was logic: deductive reasoning from premise(s) to a conclusion. By generating chains of logical inference, further statements about essences were established. It is not surprising that the study of logic figured prominently in medieval education.

In sum, then, the Aristotelian approach to gaining knowledge had two steps: (1) to define the words that were labels for essences and (2) to use deductive logic for deriving further statements about essences. The principles of logic were well-established, so the deductive steps in gaining knowledge were not overly controversial. Confidence in the truth of a conclusion could only be assumed if the truth of the premises were assured, however, and the truth of the premises depended on correct definition. There *was* tremendous controversy about how to establish true definitions, and hence wide disagreement about which definitions of essences were true. It is there that Bacon focused his criticism. Bacon argued that lack of progress in the Catholic tradition was due to speculation about essences. Statements about essences were subjective claims and not objective descriptions. Natural philosophy had thus been reduced to scholastic debates about the definitions of words, with no clear standards by which to arbitrate among different meanings.

Baconian science: The classical inductive view

Bacon reasoned that progress would be reintroduced into natural philosophy if the starting point of knowledge—facts—were carefully observed. Unlike Aristotelian definitions, which in Bacon's view were subjective intuitions, facts were indubitable. To guarantee objectivity, one should carefully avoid thinking, or the "prejudices of the mind" in Bacon's idiom.

Thinking does have a role in Baconian method. After the fact-gathering task comes the job of extracting ideas. The latter is *induction*—extrapolating general ideas from particular facts. The Baconian formula for generating knowledge can now be summed up: Gather the facts first, and then induce ideas from those facts. Baconian induction is also called *classical induction*.

Like all views of knowledge, classical induction implies a legitimation criterion for determining which ideas are scientific and which are not. Because all scientific ideas must be inductions from facts, all scientific ideas must be reducible to facts. Ideas not reducible to facts are not legitimate. Ever since Bacon's time, *methods that assume that general ideas are generated from facts or are reducible to facts have been called inductivist methods.* That is the case for classical induction as well as the probabilistic and positivistic versions of induction that are introduced later in this chapter.

The goal of classical induction was to discover and establish absolute truth. Indeed, Baconian method was designed as a tool to guarantee that absolute truth—not just man-made truth—would be revealed. Bacon reasoned that if facts are indubitable, and scientific ideas are induced correctly from facts, it follows that scientific ideas must also be indubitable—that is, they must be truth.

Strengths and weaknesses of classical induction

Classical induction contains a number of strengths and weaknesses. For the most part those strengths and weaknesses carry into its probabilistic and positivistic variations.

Notable strengths of classical induction are the following. First, Baconian method turns the external world—the world of facts—into the source and arbiter of truth. It throws up a warning flag around speculation not based on fact. Second, Baconian method raises the hope that knowledge can be shared by and agreed to by all. The reason is that the "facts" are considered indubitable, and would reveal themselves to anyone looking carefully. This point underlies the principle that tests of scientific theories should be the same for everyone: The facts used to test theories are the same for everyone, and can be observed by anyone.

Each advantage also contains the seeds of a disadvantage. If the arbiter of truth (facts) lies outside humans, confidence in novel or bold ideas can be compromised. Science would not advance without new and penetrating ideas. Turning attention to external facts can inhibit the creative thinking important for generating such ideas. Furthermore, the beliefs that facts are indubitable, and that they will reveal themselves to everyone, are mistaken. These beliefs assume that facts are not tainted by interpretation, and hence are beyond challenge. "Facts" do have interpretative elements, of course, and are open to challenge.

Despite its drawbacks, classical induction was certainly an important step forward in the development of method. The focus on the empirical world, and suspicion of theories not accountable to it, was an advance over the scholastic tendencies of the medieval Aristotelian approach.

The demonstration format

Classical induction provided a formula for the discovery of knowledge: Obtain the facts first, and then generalize ideas from the facts. That formula was not immediately utilized as a format for the presentation of ideas in manuscripts and books, however. Instead, continued use was made of the *demonstration* format, in which fundamental principles and axioms are put forth as the premises for deductions to other ideas. A salient example of the demonstration format is the *Elements* of Euclid. Euclid put forth his axioms and rules of inference, and then deduced the postulates and corollaries from the axioms by use of the inference rules.

The demonstration format for the presentation of scientific theory is sharply at odds with Baconian method for the discovery of ideas. The former necessitates that the most general statements be presented first, with less general statements to be derived from them. The latter entails that general statements should appear after particular ones.

In spite of the differences between the demonstration format and inductive method, the demonstration format persisted for the presentation of ideas. One reason is that the goal of induction—discovery of absolute truth—fit the purpose of the demonstration format, which was to "prove" (demonstrate) the absolute truth. Another reason is that the demonstration format was the accepted format for presenting "high science." High science was abstract and theoretical; deductive mathematics and geometry were prime examples. "Low science" was concrete and empirical; it included practical knowledge such as engineering, technology, and finite mathematics. High science was indeed so closely associated with the demonstration format that the status of the former could not be had without use of the latter.

Incidentally, when the goal of induction was reduced from the revelation of absolute truth to the discovery of probable truth, the *inductive* format came into vogue. In the inductive format, "facts" are presented first and ideas afterwards. Change to the inductive format also signaled the increasing prestige of low science, to the point where the distinction between high and low science blurred and even dissipated in some cases. That did not occur until later, however, when Hume's penetrating criticism of classical induction showed that it could not produce the absolute truth.

Hume's criticism and its consequences on classical induction are presented later in this chapter. Before discussing Hume, however, it would be helpful to see how induction permeated scientific circles, and why it spread rapidly into the intellectual and even common culture beyond science.

The Establishment of induction

A number of factors led to the establishment of classical induction. The first was sociological: Inductive method was an important weapon in the arsenal of the Anglicans in their political and religious battles against Catholicism. The association of classical induction with the rise of Newtonian physics is another reason for the establishment of induction. Intermingled with that reason was another factor: the founding of the Royal Society and its adoption of Baconian method.

The anti-Catholic thrust of classical induction

The anti-Catholic movement in England was encouraged by the royal houses, and anti-Catholicism was crucial in the spread of classical induction. As already noted, classical induction was born amidst criticism of the Aristotelian view of science that underlay Catholic theology and thought. Bacon's exhortations in support of induction were given side-by-side with his criticisms of Aristotelian method, and were not an overly subtle way to criticize Catholicism at the same time.

Newton's mathematical principles

Sixty-one years after Bacon died, Isaac Newton published his *Mathematical Principles of Natural Philosophy* (1687). It outlined a system of dynamic principles and celestial mechanics, along with mathematical formulations for each. Newton's physics was corroborated on nearly every front. Furthermore, Newton's success was attributed to *his adherence to inductive method*. The promised result—absolute truth—seemed to have been delivered. What more could be asked of method?

Newton employed the demonstration format in his *Mathematical Principles*. Structured very much like the *Elements* of Euclid, it begins with his famous laws of motion. From those "axioms" are deduced his explanations of phenomena such as the motion of terrestrial objects, the movement of celestial bodies, fluid flow, and the transmission of sound. If Newton did not use an inductive format for the presentation of his physics, then, why was it believed the he had utilized inductive method? The answer to this question is to be found in the establishment of the Royal Society of London.

The Royal Society

A significant force in the wide acceptance of Baconian method was the Royal Society of London for the Improving of Natural Knowledge, or simply the Royal Society. Even before publication of Newton's *Mathematical Principles*, the Royal Society had adopted Baconian method as the official formula for advancing knowledge.

The Royal Society, one of the first modern scientific institutes, had been founded independent of university influence. An institution free of Catholic domination was believed crucial for the advancement of knowledge, so it was not associated with the universities at Cambridge or Oxford. As a fledgling group organized by such men as Robert Boyle, it passed through infancy in the unsettled times of the Civil War, spent adolescence in the Protectorate under the Cromwells, and reached maturity during the Restoration under Charles II to become one of the most prestigious scientific institutes in the world.

Thomas Sprat's early history of the Royal Society (1667) was pregnant with eulogies to Francis Bacon (Sprat 1966). His history was commissioned by the Royal Society, which recognized Bacon as its intellectual mentor. The frontispiece of Sprat's history shows Francis Bacon seated beside a bust of Charles II. This should be no surprise. Bacon's view of science and method were adopted by the Royal Society as the official method for the advancement of learning.

Not only had the Royal Society adopted Baconian method as the proper approach to scientific investigation, but it also was granted authority over publication of works in science. Anyone who wished their theories to be disseminated would have to give at least the impression that Bacon's approach was the guiding light for discovery.

Despite raging controversies over the atom-empty space metaphysical view of Newton, by the turn of the eighteenth century his physics had received near unanimous acclaim in the fledgling scientific communities of Europe. Newton became one of the most famous and revered members of the Royal Society. The Royal Society, having adopted Baconian method and basking in the success of Newton, hardly had motive to question the belief that Newton had employed induction. In short, adoption of Newton's physics carried with it confidence in the validity of inductive method.

Lessons about the development of method

There are a number of lessons in the tale of the establishment of Baconian induction. One is that new views of science, just like new scientific theories, spring from perceived weaknesses in established views. The Baconian view of science arose from difficulties in the

Aristotelian view. That is why strengths of new views are found at weak points in criticized views. In the case of induction, its strength—emphasis on the empirical side of theory—developed out of the empirical weakness of the Aristotelian view.

A second point is that the weaknesses of a new methodological view are seldom widely recognized. The initial advantages of the strengths of a new view are one reason. Another is its association with a successful research program, such as that of Newton. There are always weaknesses in methodological views, but they normally do not come to light until later.

A third point is that the association of a successful research program with a methodological view makes it difficult for criticism of method to be heard. As unfortunate as it may be, this is understandable: To question the method is to question the very criteria that legitimates a scientific research program.

The third point suggests a fourth: The relationship between a scientific research program and a methodological view is a tenuous one, whereas it is commonly believed that there is a necessary relationship. This point yields a valuable methodological lesson: *Method cannot be justified by historical association with a scientific research program*. There are a number of reasons why.

Scientific method can function to legitimate a research program, usually by those who want to justify a program as "scientific." (Feyerabend 1978, 1982). As argued earlier, however, attempts to legitimate theories are not helpful. Attempts to legitimate an entire research program can serve no better purpose. Furthermore, reversing the order of justification by attempting to use a research program to legitimate a methodological approach is no less barren. The reason is that different methodological views can be used to interpret the success of a research program. In addition to the inductive view, the paradigmatic and refutationist views can and have been used to explain the rise of Newtonianism (Popper 1962; Kuhn 1962). The anarchist view could be used as well, for example by pointing out that gravitation was a mysterious and "unscientific" theory as measured by the inductive standards of the day. Finally, the historical development of methodological views is intermingled with sociological forces that can be even more important than intellectual factors in the establishment of method (Feyerabend 1978).

I argued earlier that research programs do not justify any particular methodological approach. This is one component of Feyerabend's attack on method in science, but the similarity ends here. Feyerabend concludes that science develops best when unconstrained by method; that is, that science develops best in an anarchic context (Feyerabend 1978; also see Chapter 7). The historical reconstruction of induction in this chapter is not used to argue against the importance of method for the development of science, but to expose *misconceptions* about the function of method in the development of science.

Hume's Attack on Classical Induction

Some critics of induction did publish their views during the height of Newtonian science. Two of the most significant were David Hume (1711–1760) and William Whewell (1794–1866). Hume's attack on the logic of induction initially fell on deaf ears, but was celebrated when his criticism led to a modification of classical induction. Whewell's reservations about the historical viability and psychological accuracy of induction were similar to those raised by Thomas Kuhn in the 1960s. The view of science developed by Whewell was also somewhat like the paradigmatic view of Kuhn. For these reasons a discussion of Whewell's attacks will be postponed until the upcoming chapter on the paradigmatic view.

David Hume's contemporaries assumed Newton's dynamics and celestial mechanics were truth. Most also assumed that inductive method was the reason truth had been delivered. Upon comparing these two assumptions, however, Hume found them inconsistent. Intellectuals gave Hume's *A Treatise of Human Nature* a decidedly chilly reception when it was published in 1739 (Hume 1958). The reason is that his attack threw doubt on two cherished beliefs: the certain truth of Newtonian physics and the validity of inductive method.

Hume argued that physics presupposes a universal law of causality: For every event there is a cause. But it cannot be assumed that the same causes will in the future lead to the same effects. Hence physical theory cannot be known with certainty. At best it can be inferred with a degree of probability. The upshot is either that Newtonian physics, if it arose through and is legitimated by inductive method, cannot be absolute truth, that inductive method is not valid, or that both conclusions are true. It is little wonder that Hume's book was less than a best seller when it emerged from the press.

Incidentally, Hume found no reliable way to choose between the truth of physics and the validity of induction. Regardless, he did make a hesitant choice by putting his faith in inductive method and, at the same time, declaring physics to be probable at best.

One need not feel badly that Hume's *Treatise* fell stillborn from the press. It soon gained considerable acclaim. Hume eventually was encouraged enough to rework the *Treatise* into another volume called *An Enquiry Concerning Human Understanding* (Hume 1907). The *Enquiry* was introduced with a eulogistic letter from none other than Adam Smith. It was first published in 1777, the year following Hume's death.

How Hume's criticisms were absorbed into inductive theory is spelled out in the next section. Here, however, it would be convenient to make a few comments about the involuted nature of much philosophical work, including some that has had an influence on archaeology. Standard interpretations of Hume's criticisms provide an example.

Standard interpretations of Hume seldom mention Newton's physics. The omission is understandable at one level because Hume does not refer to Newton, or Newton's physics. Instead of Newton's physics he refers to knowledge of "matters of fact." In any case, it is unfortunate that most students of philosophy, including those who pursue their studies through the doctorate, never realize that the supposed certainty of Newton's physics underlies Hume's criticism. Hume also avoids reference to Bacon, or to Baconian method. The method questioned by Hume is clearly classical induction, however, which he concludes is not adequate to generate absolute truth. Of particular interest here is not Hume's reluctance to mention Newton and Bacon, but the reluctance of so many historians of philosophy to mention them in the standard histories. Why has there been such an oversight?

With few exceptions, historians of philosophy reconstruct the past with minimal recognition of the extra-philosophical problems that are the life-blood of philosophical reflection. Standard histories instead assume that philosophy has its own exclusive set of problems and ideas, and hence its own exclusive history (Popper 1962). This *deformation professionelle* functions in various ways. It does direct scholarly attention to minutia that otherwise might be disregarded, and scrutiny of minutia can lead to new understanding. It also buttresses the belief that philosophy is an exclusive field. That belief encourages professional philosophers—those who earn a living by teaching and writing philosophy—to work on problems that are disassociated from the roots from which many philosophical texts have sprung.

The impulse toward professional introversion in philosophy is not discussed here just to explain the differences between the reconstruction of Hume's criticism of classical induction in this section and those in standard historical texts. It is also here to shed more light on why some philosophical recommendations for method in archaeology—namely, the external approach to method—can be vacuous. Philosophers are seldom trained to use their ideas for problem-situations outside the field. Many are not even inclined to do so. When some do make the attempt, the tendency is to project introverted problems of the profession onto extra-philosophical contexts.

In short, professional introversion works against attempts to make academic philosophy relevant to other disciplines. Another tendency in the profession—to defend a "pure" view (see Chapter 1)—also works against making academic philosophy relevant to other disciplines. It is no wonder that many outside the field of professional philosophy are puzzled about what we do, especially when the goal is to be helpful to those in other disciplines.

The Birth of Probabilistic Induction

What led to acclaim for Hume's arguments when they had initially fallen upon unwilling ears? It was realized that induction could be saved if classical induction were altered in light of Hume's criticisms. Hume had argued that induction could yield probable truth at best, and classical induction was malleable enough to be modified into probabilistic induction.

Probabilistic induction can be characterized as follows: Induction from facts can generate knowledge that is probable but not certain, and knowledge is legitimate—scientific—if it is reducible to the facts within an acceptable range of probability. In a nutshell, knowledge progresses by inducing or justifying theories from the facts within a prescribed range of probability. Since the birth of probabilistic induction, probability theory and inductive theory have been so closely related that induction really means probabilistic induction.

A far-reaching if unintended consequence of the new probabilistic twist to induction was the spur it gave to the study of probability theory. The Royal Society gave especial attention to the best papers on probability. Numerous talented minds in the English-speaking world were motivated to take up the study of finite mathematics. The contributions of Thomas Bayes (1702–1761) were and continue to be particularly celebrated by inductivists (Bayes 1963).

Bayesian method

Use of probability theory emerged largely on the Continent, for the most part to solve practical problems (Hacking 1975). The initial foundations of probability also came from across the Channel. Books such as Jacques Bernoulli's *Ars Conjectandi*, written in 1713 (Bernoulli 1969) and Abraham de Moivre's *The Doctrine of Chances*, written in 1718 (Moivre 1967) laid out the principles for determining the probability of a sequence given the probability of a single event, but tools for measuring the probability of an outcome in light of prior knowledge were not available. To make such tools was the goal of Thomas

Bayes in his famous "Essay Towards Solving a Problem in the Doctrine of Chances," which was originally published in 1763 (Bayes 1963).

To calculate the probability of a given outcome based on prior knowledge, one needs to know—or at least assign—the *prior probabilities*. A prior probability is the probability of a given phenomenon occurring before trials are made. Bayes outlined how formulas can be generated to use prior probabilities in combination with *posterior probabilities*. A posterior probability is the probability, given the evidence *and* prior knowledge, that a certain phenomenon would be observed. To this day the label "Bayesian" implies the use of prior and posterior probabilities in the calculation of probabilistic statements.

Bayes' formulas allow adjustment of the prior probabilities in light of the posterior probabilities. Furthermore, successive use of Bayes' formulas "wash out" or "swamp" any arbitrariness in the assignment of prior probabilities by modifying the calculated outcome in light of the posterior probabilities. The upshot is that the calculated probabilities of outcomes approach the actual probabilities of outcomes.

Because Bayes' approaches allow posterior probabilities to override prior probabilities, Bayes' formulas do provide a link between the estimated probability of outcomes and the actual probability of the outcomes. That is why they did and still do fuel the inductive hope that calculations of the probability of theories can be made in light of empirical evidence.

Unfortunately, the inductive hope was not and will not be realized. To calculate the probability of interesting scientific theories—such as calculating the probability that Newton's theory of gravitation is true—requires designating the constituent elements of the outcome. Included would be the gravitational attraction of the moon to the earth, the sun to mars, and the fingernail of ones left hand to the fin of fish off the coast of Japan. Bayesians recognize that the prior probabilities of these elements would have to be assigned arbitrarily. The arbitrariness is not significant mathematically. It is mathematically demonstrable that the prior probabilities will be washed out with repeated uses of Bayes' formulas. The trouble is that there is no reliable empirical way to determine the posterior probabilities necessary to wash them out. For example, one cannot devise an empirical test to determine the posterior probability of gravitational attraction between objects.

In sum, Bayes' formulas will not fulfill the hope that theories can be inductively legitimated. They have nevertheless been profoundly important theoretically, and useful in unanticipated ways.

Thomas Bayes became a celebrated member of the Royal Society. His interesting techniques for calculating the probabilities of outcomes were associated with the lingering (but unfounded) hope that such calculations could provide a probabilistic measure of theories. The association of Bayesian techniques with inductive theory is implied in the label *Bayesian method*, an expression so closely identified with probabilistic induction that the two are sometimes used synonymously.

A Bayesian attempt to verify theories in archaeology

J. E. Doran and F. R. Hodson suggested the possibility of using Bayesian tools in archaeology, and outlined the mathematical principles of Bayesian theory for archaeologists (Doran and Hodson 1975). A number of years later Merrilee Salmon actually attempted to apply Bayesian method to theory assessment in archaeology. Doran and Hodson wished to give archaeologists mathematical and computing tools that might be helpful in their work. Salmon, on the other hand, was committed to recommending Bayesian method in archaeology by her inductive philosophical position. That is why her proposed use of Bayesian tools for assessing archaeological theory was a pivotal theme in her book *Philosophy and Archaeology* (Salmon 1982).

In *Philosophy and Archaeology*, Salmon encouraged archaeologists to raise questions about the difference between *guessing* and *knowing*. To distinguish between them, Salmon intends "to seek in works of philosophy of science, fairly specific guidelines for ways to make their discipline [archaeology] more scientific, that is, to ensure that archaeological claims embody knowledge rather than guesswork" (Salmon 1982:2). Not only did Salmon assume the traditional inductive goal of confirming knowledge (confirmation would differentiate "knowledge" from "guesswork"), but it soon became clear that she would use inductive tools to attempt reaching that goal. Those tools were Bayesian.

Crucial elements in Salmon's model of confirmation are the assignment of prior probabilities and then use of Bayesian techniques for confirming hypotheses as well as for weighing competing hypotheses. A hypothesis is "any statement subjected to evidential testing" (Salmon 1982:32). Hypotheses can never be absolutely confirmed, except in trivial cases, so Salmon turns to inductive tools. In her own words, "Inductive logic is concerned with the support some statements [empirical or factual statements] can provide for others [hypotheses] when they are not conclusively related to each other" (Salmon 1982:33). Salmon then introduces the reader to Bayesian techniques, and recommends them for confirming theories in archaeology.

The reason that Bayesian attempts to calculate the probability of theories are futile has already been stated: There is no reliable empirical way to determine the posterior probabilities that would swamp arbitrarily assigned prior probabilities. Such would be the case in physics, archaeology, or any other field. There is only one other route by which Bayesian techniques could become reliable for confirmatory purposes, and that is by establishing accurate prior probabilities. Salmon thus spends considerable time expounding upon ways to assign prior probabilities.

Establishing prior probabilities of the type Salmon desires is impossible despite all the attention received in her book and in reams of philosophical and mathematical literature. I repeat, priors simply *cannot* be established with confidence except in trivial cases (such as the prior possibility that a coin will turn up heads on one toss is one-half). Salmon knows this and says as much. In discussing formal criteria for assigning prior probabilities, she states, "in actual practice, these formal criteria for assigning priors are seldom applicable in archaeology" (Salmon 1982:43). I would add that I cannot imagine any nontrivial case where they are applicable. In addition to formal criteria for assigning priors, Salmon also explores other criteria for assigning prior probabilities. Her discussion is superb, but she admits that other criteria will not enable one to obtain more than a "subjective degree of belief," to use her own terminology.

In short, the "swamping" of arbitrarily assigned priors through continued use of Bayesian techniques, while demonstrable mathematically, provides no good reason to have more confidence in the successively calculated probabilities of hypotheses. Furthermore, assigning the priors can at best be done with a "subjective degree of belief." In short, the Bayesian techniques fail to provide a measure of the confirmation of hypotheses.

Even though Bayesian techniques are not applicable, Salmon states the following: "Even though the formal methods for calculating probabilities may not be applicable in many cases, the inductive relations that hold between hypotheses are extremely important" (Salmon 1982:44–45). I simply cannot agree. Nothing is lost by not knowing, or thinking one knows, the inductive probability of hypotheses. Statistical regularities in nature (not to be confused with the inductive probabilities of hypotheses) can still be exploited fully. Furthermore, anomalous data can still be used to improve hypotheses. Indeed, they can be better exploited because one would not be tempted to accept improbable but possible anomalies in hypotheses. Finally, attempts to measure the confirmation of theories, whether by probabilistic or other means, only makes sense after a theory has been developed and tested with at least some success. By that point, however, the interesting theoretical action is likely to be over. In my view, methodological guidelines should be designed to help one caught up in the theoretical fray—in the generation, testing, adjusting, retesting, and sometimes rejection of theories—rather than designed for use after the theoretical battles have subsided.

My assessment of Salmon's recommendation of inductive goals and methods, especially Bayesian techniques, has been quite critical. Nevertheless, Salmon's book makes numerous other contributions that are quite valuable. This is not the place to recount them because they are not related to her inductive recommendations. I have had the opportunity to discuss the contributions elsewhere (Bell 1984).

Bayesian tools for comparing assumptions and data

Although use of Bayesian method for inductive assessment of theories is not feasible, I want to point out that Bayesian tools can be useful for other purposes, even in theoretical archaeology. Here is an example.

Clive Ruggles is also critical of attempts to use Bayesian method for inductive assessment (Ruggles 1986). He does not recommend Bayesian method for the purpose of eliminating any among competing theories or establishing the probable truth of any of them. He does, however, recommend Bayesian analyses as one among a combination of ways to compare the plausibility of different cultural assumptions underlying archaeological theories with the data that is relevant to the assumptions (Ruggles 1986).

Because Ruggles does not propose using Bayesian tools for assessing or comparing hypotheses, he calls his use a "semi-Bayesian approach." The gist of Ruggles' approach is as follows: (1) Define a model to describe data informed by various parameters; (2) use background knowledge and beliefs to assign prior probability distributions of the values of the parameters; and (3) use the prior distribution and the data at hand to calculate the corresponding posterior probability distributions of the parameters (Ruggles 1986:12). Ruggles proposes using such Bayesian analysis on as many models as one wishes, reflecting different beliefs about our cultural background knowledge. In each case one can see how the prior model is altered by the data at hand.

Ruggles' semi-Bayesian approach allows one to examine and re-examine a given set of data as often as one pleases in light of models informed by different background knowledge and beliefs. In his own words, "this sort of approach seems very much in tune with the continual examination and re-examination of our data in the light of different ideas and models" (Ruggles 1986:12).

Each set of results from Ruggles' semi-Bayesian analyses can be presented graphically. That is why Ruggles' approach provides a clear presentation of the various models and how the data are related to them. On the other hand, the purpose is not to make decisions about any of the models. In Ruggles' words, "the lack of any means to 'decide' upon particular courses of action is surely no restriction in a subject whose aim is actually to describe material data, and whose interpretations will necessarily have subjective elements" (Ruggles 1986:12).

Ruggles then goes on to show how one could use his semi-Bayesian approach to analyze different explanatory models of the Nazca line azimuths (Ruggles 1986:8, 12–13). The assumption in one model is that no background knowledge of any culture is relevant to a study of the Nazca lines. Another model assumes that, because the direction of water flow is of great importance in the Nazca culture, lines are inherently more likely to be oriented parallel to the directions of local water flow across the Nazca pampa. Yet another model includes both the assumption that the direction of water flow is of great importance and the assumption that particular astronomical targets known to have been important in other South American radial line systems (such as the *ceque* system at Cuzco) were also of great importance to those who constructed the Nazca lines. Each of the three models would yield a prior distribution, and would be presented graphically. The prior convictions expressed in the models above are then combined with actual measurements of the Nazca line azimuths to yield posterior distributions. Each of the three models with posterior distributions would also be presented in graphic form. Finally, the prior and posterior graphs of each model could be compared with each other, and with those of the other models, to see how see how the assumptions in each model are related to the data.

Ruggles' proposal to use Bayesian tools to specify the relationship between the assumptions informing theories and the data relevant to the theories does indeed clarify that relationship. By using the tools on various theories it also provides another criterion for assessing the pros and cons of theories, and another way of comparing theories as well. I might add that Ruggles' proposal of a semi-Bayesian approach to theory analysis and comparison seems quite promising in archaeology. It is also original as far as I know.

Ruggles' proposed use of Bayesian tools is certainly different from attempts to use Bayesian method to assess theories inductively. The crucial difference is that the posterior probabilities in Ruggles' approach *are* determined empirically: they are associated with the prior probabilities, of course, but they are also are an outgrowth of the relevant data.

Confirmation by statistical relevance

One route to probabilistic confirmation of theories is through use of Bayesian tools. Another route to probabilistic confirmation is through statistical relevance: a probabilistic measure of the relationship between an explanation and the relevant data. The model normally proposed is the Statistical-Relevance (S-R) model. Wesley Salmon has been the central figure in the development of the S-R model (see especially W. Salmon et al. 1971). Among others, Merrilee Salmon (1982) and Kelley and Hanen (1988) have found the S-R model helpful for their views on archaeological theory.

The extensive amount of literature concerning the S-R model in both philosophy and archaeology may be at least partly due to its perceived potential for use in Hempel's covering-law program. More specifically, covering-laws—universalized explanations—are unlikely to be confirmed in every instance, but might (some hope) be confirmed within some probabilistic range. Albert Spaulding expresses this hope very well: "Explanations may be deductive, in which case the covering law admits of no exceptions, or they may be probabilistic-statistical (or inductive, if you prefer), in which case the covering law has the form of a frequency distribution" (Spaulding 1968:34).

The attempt to confirm universals, whether absolutely or probabilistically, was criticized in the last chapter. The gist of the criticism was that confirming universalized explanations is not productive for further development of theory. If the goal is theory development, which I believe is a worthwhile goal, universalized explanations should be vulnerable to error, and thus more able to serve as stepping stones to better theories. Confirming them would not be particularly helpful, if helpful at all, for that purpose. Here is another criticism: Theories cannot be inductively confirmed anyway.

The heart of the S-R model is that an event is explained when all the factors relevant to its occurring or not occurring are identified, and the probability of its occurrence in light of those factors has been determined. In order to use the S-R model, then, one must first identify all the factors relevant to an event occurring or not occurring, and then determine the probability of its occurrence in light of those factors. The last requirement is particularly bothersome. Consider a universalized theory such as Newton's law of gravitation. Any two bodies of mass would have a gravitational attraction: the sun to the earth, the earth to the moon, the book on a shelf to the automobile in the garage, and so forth, ad infinitum. But one could never assign prior probabilities to each of those constituents, much less calculate a probability from them. Attempting to calculate the inductive probability of any universalized explanation would face the same difficulty, in archaeology or elsewhere. I might add that Wesley Salmon's statistical relevance model, unlike Hempel's model, should hold even when a statistical explanation has a low probability. That difference still would not enable the model to overcome the difficulties already discussed. For an analysis, see Turner 1982.

Incidentally, there are inductive attempts to meet criticism that I have presented here. I do not find those attempts to be satisfactory. I do not believe that archaeologists would, either. They are part of my own profession, however, so at least a very brief review might be informative.

One attempt to meet the criticism is to turn discussion to explanations with probabilistic components that can be empirically determined or tested against regularities in nature. Examples are probabilistic explanations of radioactive decay, the probabilities of events occurring in game theory, and probabilities of social correlations ("X percent of teenage boys will become felons"). Certainly probabilistic components such as these would be appropriate; they can be empirically determined or tested against regularities. But attempts to calculate the probabilities of theories *without* probabilistic components that can be empirically determined or tested against regularities in nature are quite different indeed. As argued earlier, calculations of the latter are simply not possible.

Criticism is also deflected by turning to a discussion of the theory of probability, which really means a discussion of the theory of the logic of probability. A brief example was the discussion of Bayesian theory earlier in this chapter, prior to the criticism. Discussions of the theory of the logic of probability, however, no matter how involved and extensive, and no matter how interesting and worthwhile for other purposes they might be, do not overcome the practical difficulties in applying the logic of probability to confirm theories inductively. That is a sweeping claim, but I at least have never found such discussions sufficient to show how theories can actually (not hypothetically) be confirmed inductively. That is why I am convinced that a discussion of theory of the logic of probability would only be a distraction, and quite an involved distraction at that. It would not deflect the point being made here: that universalized theories cannot be inductively confirmed. Neither would it meet the criticism launched earlier: that the inductive confirmation of theories, even if it could be done, would not likely help further theory development.

It has become clear that there are crucial differences between probabilistic statements that can be empirically determined or tested and probabilistic statements that cannot. In the next section is a more detailed discussion of those two types of probabilistic statement and the differences between them.

Stochastic Regularities versus Epistemological Probabilities

The modification of classical induction into probabilistic induction has been set within the history of inductive theory. Yet more needs to be said about the roots of probability theory *before* it merged with inductive theory. The reason is not only that inductive theory changed forever after Hume's assault on induction, but that conceptions of probability also changed dramatically. In brief, probability was adopted for a task it could not fulfill when it merged with inductive theory. The merger did and still does lead to confusion in the use of statistics and statistical inference.

Roots of probability theory

Probability had its own rather unique history, which began before and is separate from the development of classical inductive theory. Its roots were in Continental Europe. These are simple facts, but ones important to remember because it is so customary to conflate probability with induction.

Probability began to gain a foothold on Continental Europe during the middle of the seventeenth century. Influential work was done by Blaise Pascal (1623–1662) and his associates at the monastery in Port Royal near Paris, by Gottfried Leibniz (1646–1716) in Prussia, and by Christiaan Huygens (1629–1695) in the Netherlands (Hacking 1975).

On the practical side, the focus was on such areas as the probability of winning games, of making correct medical diagnoses, and of establishing accurate actuarial tables. Games have probabilistic elements that are crucial for calculating the chances of winning. Leibniz was fascinated with the relationship between diagnosis and treatment in medicine. Medical treatment required diagnoses from symptoms. He thought it crucial to estimate the likelihood that a set of symptoms denote a cause, and hence the "probability" that a treatment would be appropriate. Christiaan Huygens, the Dutchman known for his contributions to light and pneumatic theory, was fascinated by the possibility of structuring reliable actuarial tables for cities in the Netherlands that sold annuities to raise public funds.

Theoretical problems also provoked interest in probability. Pascal, for example, even carried probability into his theological speculations. *Pascal's wager* is his famous "proof" of the reasonableness of betting on God's existence. The proof uses a probabilistic model:

The benefits of believing in God's existence are so enormous that even if there were only a slight probability of God's existence it is still a worthwhile wager. Even though probabilities cannot be stipulated for such a proof, it illustrates Pascal's hope that probabilistic analyses would become central in rational deliberation.

The Art of Thinking (subtitled *Port Royal Logic*) contains an outline of the new ideas. It was written by Antoine Arnauld and Pierre Nicole, associates of Pascal at Port Royal, and was originally published as *La Logique ou L'Art de Penser* in 1662. (Arnauld and Nicole 1964). The *Port Royal Logic* is a clarion call to think differently—to think within a probabilistic framework—about a range of both practical and theoretical problems. Little could its authors have known that probability would be integrated into a foreign view of knowledge in England during the next century.

Stochastic regularities

Notice that the probabilities used to tackle practical problems are rooted in observable regularities. In formal idiom, regularities in nature are called *stochastic regularities*. Because they are observable in nature, *calculations based on stochastic regularities can be tested against the empirical record*. Stochastic regularities are fundamental in calculating the likelihood of outcomes of games, the etiologies of diseases from symptoms, and the likelihood of deaths over a population range.

Utilizing stochastic regularities to make judgments about the likelihood of events is sensible. Following is an elementary example of a probabilistic calculation in game theory. In addition, the example is used to spell out in more detail the roles of constituent events and prior probabilities.

Suppose one wishes to calculate the probability of throwing "heads" on three successive tosses of a coin. In order to calculate the probability of the outcome, all the constituent events must be known and the prior probabilities of each constituent event must be stipulated. The *constituent events*, remember, are the events that comprise the outcome. In the example, each of the three tosses of the coin is a constituent event. There are three constituent events in this particular example, then, and each is the same: tossing heads in one throw of a coin. Remember that a *prior probability*, or *prior* for short, is the probability (of a constituent event) that can be assigned before it occurs. In this example, the prior probability of each constituent event is ½. Analysis of the structure of the coin and how it comes to rest on a surface is sufficient to determine the priors. *But* also notice that the priors in this example could be observed as well, that is, they can be corroborated as stochastic regularities. Throwing a coin repeatedly would reveal that the frequency of tossing heads is ½. Finally, the calculation of the probability of the outcome is made by multiplying the prior probabilities of each of the three constituent events: ½ times ½ times ½ equals ⅛, the probability of tossing heads three straight times.

The details of calculating the probability of an outcome have been presented to clarify a number of points. First, there must be a definitive list of the constituent events in an outcome. Second, the prior probabilities of each constituent event must be stipulated. Third, and most worthy of note, the priors must be stochastic. They might be stipulated analytically, as in the example cited, but they must also be potentially observable.

Epistemological probabilities

Calculating the probabilities of outcomes that can be tested against stochastic regularities must be distinguished from attempts to establish theoretic probabilities that lack stochastic underpinning. The "calculations" in Pascal's wager about believing in God would be an example of the latter. Other examples would be attempts to calculate the probability that Newton's law of gravitation is true, or the probability that Wittfogel's theory that state structure will form whenever there is need to develop large-scale water resources. In all these examples the constituent events cannot be listed, and even if they could the prior probabilities of the constituents would not be known. The probabilities of theories without reliable stochastic roots are called the *epistemological probabilities* of theories.

As pointed out earlier in this section, interest in probability was historically rooted in attempts to solve problems that did have stochastic underpinnings. When probability theory merged with inductive theory, however, the stochastic underpinning was cleaved off.

The goal of classical induction was to establish true theories from the evidence. When probability fused with induction, the goal was modified to calculating the probability of theories relative to the evidence. As just argued, however, calculating the probability of many theories is impossible because the constituents and the priors cannot be determined. Furthermore, such calculations could not be stochastically corroborated even if the calculations could be made. Surprisingly, the epistemological side of probability was and still is embraced despite these insuperable difficulties.

The merger of probability with induction forced probability away from the stochastic roots necessary for its successful use. This is much like knocking away the foundation from under a house. Ironically, the merger of probability with induction also gave probability an intellectual status that was far-and-away more elevated than it received when stochastic insights first drew interest on the Continent nearly one century before the merger with induction. Finite mathematics had been a low science, but it merged with the inductive method that many thought was responsible for generating high science. To be sure, there were also benefits from the merger. It spurred interest in the study of finite mathematics, for example, and expanded the understanding and use of the stochastic side of probability. These consequences are far from negligible. Nevertheless, the inductive view of science, which has been and still is regarded by many as a bastion of the physical and social sciences, continues to be fused with the fruitless epistemological side of probability.

The use of statistical techniques in archaeology

Attempts to use epistemological probabilities to confirm theories is one way to abuse statistical techniques. This abuse is due to confusing epistemological probabilities with stochastic regularities. Although archaeologists are not particularly prone to this type of confusion, some philosophers with an inductive position are vulnerable to it. Attempts to use Bayesian method to confirm theories are based upon the confusion, as are attempts to use statistical-relevance models of confirmation.

Archaeologists would typically only use statistical methods with stochastic roots, that is, statistical methods that are based upon regularities in nature. The methodological reason that statistical methods should be stochastic has already become obvious: Without stochastic roots probabilistic claims are not testable. That is indeed a very important point. Other than that, however, the use of statistical methods in stochastic situations is a subject for applied mathematics in archaeology (for example see Doran and Hodson 1975; Shennan 1988) and is not tied exclusively to any one view of science. In short, it is beyond the scope of this book. Nevertheless, a few brief comments seem appropriate.

One reason for commenting on the use of statistical techniques in stochastic contexts is to make clear that the criticisms of epistemological uses of probability are *not* a generalized attack on the use of statistical methods. Statistical methods can and obviously have been useful in the development of archaeological theory. On the other hand, other misuses of statistical methods—other than those due to confusing stochastic regularities with epistemological probabilities—can and obviously have occurred in archaeology. This leads to another reason for the comments: It would not be fair to blame misuses of statistical methods on the inductive tradition. The high status of probability in the inductive tradition could dull one's critical acumen when using statistical methods. Another possibility, however, is that respect for probability in the inductive tradition could alert one to potential abuse. Indeed, the respect for probability in the inductive tradition could encourage one to consider use of statistical methods in helpful ways that might not even occur to those outside the tradition. The final reason for comments on the use of statistical techniques in stochastic contexts is that familiarity with scientific method as expounded in this book, and particularly with the notion of testability, might help one avoid at least some of the abuses.

Use of statistical techniques in the determination of radiocarbon dates is an example of how such techniques can be used beneficially. Remember that any one particular dating measurement might be misleading for a number of reasons, including the possible mixtures of different aged woods (if charcoal were used as the dating source) and potential contaminants. A series of dating measurements, even after eliminating numerous contaminants, can provide a statistical array of dates that will wash out the influence of measurements that by themselves are misleading. That is why "a radiocarbon date" is a statistical outgrowth of many dating measurements, and is expressed with a standard deviation on both sides.

The title of David Hurst Thomas' 1978 article "The Awful Truth about Statistics in Archaeology" could lead one to believe that all use of statistics in archaeology is suspect. Actually, Thomas wants archaeologists to be well versed in statistical theory so that they can use statistical methods well and avoid abuse of statistical methods (Thomas 1978:231–32). The determination of radiocarbon dates is cited by Thomas as an example of beneficial use of statistics (Thomas 1978:232). Another example is Lewis Binford's use of statistical techniques in his analysis of Kaolin pipe stems (Thomas 1978:232–33). Jean C. Harrington discovered that clay pipe stems underwent a regular reduction in size between 1620 and 1800 (Harrington 1954). Binford realized that the pipe stem reduction is an example of regression. His regression formula enabled archaeologists to estimate the age of a pipe stem from the mean diameter of the pipe stem (Binford 1962). Thomas points out that there was controversy over Harrington's sample as well as Binford's analysis of it (Thomas 1978:232–33). Thomas seems convinced that Binford was on the right track, however, and that "any archaeologist can use *and understand* the regression technique in practical research" (Thomas 1978:232).

Abuses of statistics in archaeology occupy much of Thomas' article. For purposes here, a brief discussion of the types of abuse will suffice. In Thomas' own words, the types of abuse include the following: "(1) a slavish adherence to the 0.05 level of statistical significance, (2) inferring causal relationships from statistical significance, (3) confusing statistical significance with strength of association, (4) modifying a priori hypotheses of levels of significance to account for specific sample data, (5) diddling with contingency tables in order to obtain statistically significant results, (6) testing hypotheses by a "fishing expedition" approach, (7) misinterpreting p as a measure of significance, and (8) misusing or ignoring the assumptions of statistical models" (Thomas 1978:233–40). Thomas then goes on to show how some of these abuses occur in a number of archaeological studies. He also offers his thoughts on why archaeologists can feel pressure to use statistics, reasons that have little to do with the improvement of their theorizing (Thomas 1978:233–43).

One might see links between induction and some of the abuses. For example, the first abuse, slavish adherence to the 0.05 level of statistical inference might, in some cases, be due to slavish faith in inductive method. In probabilistic induction all general theories are interpreted as probable, a convention that requires a statistical convention such as the 0.05 rule. On the other hand, positivistic induction (discussed later in this chapter) explicitly forbids the inference of causal relations from statistical correlations, and hence would prevent the second abuse, inferring causal relationships from statistical significance.

Despite some possible links with induction, then, abuses of statistical techniques in archaeology are not obviously associated with the confusion between epistemological probabilities and stochastic regularities. Thomas attributes them partly to the fashion in using statistics. It should also be added that some of the earliest program packages for computers contained statistical programs. Fascination with computers and the potential uses of computers was associated with use of statistics programs.

Although abuses of statistical techniques are not generally the outgrowth of any one view of science, avoiding abuse of statistics can be helped by an awareness of method. Two specific reasons are outlined next.

First, uses of statistical techniques, like uses of scientific method, should always be understandable. Even when application of statistical techniques becomes complicated, one should always be able to understand in detail what one is doing any why. If not, then one should rethink the situation until it becomes clear, or change the situation so that it becomes clear, or even consider giving it up entirely if clarity is not eventually obtained.

Second, like other components of theories, statistical components should not compromise testability. Indeed, statistical techniques should ideally enhance the testability of theories, as we saw in the discussion of the development of radiocarbon theory in Chapter 3. That central methodological point, which requires that statistical techniques always be grounded in stochastic regularities, should help archaeologists and others avoid at least some potential abuses of statistics. For example, one would avoid confusing causal explanations with statistical correlations because they are not necessarily related. One might indeed search for causal relations behind statistical correlations, but the search would be for testable causal explanations. As another example, one would be skeptical of any statistical conventions that might not enhance testability. The 0.05 convention can allow improbable but possible events, which can lower testability because it can encourage acceptance of anomalies rather than exploitation of anomalies for further theory development. Modifying a priori hypotheses of the levels of significance to account for specific sample data, and diddling with contingency tables in order to obtain statistically significant results would both be interpreted as ad hoc maneuvers that reduce testability. Each maneuver modifies the generalized requirements of a test of a theory in a specific context, but in such a way that the theory simply fits the modified requirements rather than being tested by them.

It is satisfying to point out a few ways in which understanding scientific method, and especially testability, can help one avoid some abuses of statistical techniques. On the whole, however, proper use of statistical techniques and avoiding abuse of statistical techniques are subjects unto themselves. Like all applications of finite mathematics, there is no substitute for a thorough background in the mathematical theory and rather extensive practical experience in applying the theory.

The Collapse of Newtonian Science and the Rise of Positivism

Induction survived Hume's criticisms but was transformed into probabilistic induction as a result. Induction also survived the attacks of William Whewell in the nineteenth century, a matter to be discussed in the next chapter. The vested religious and political interests, along with the association of induction with Newtonian science, were sociological factors that contributed to the prosperity of the inductive view. Additional factors also buttressed the position of induction.

The longevity of induction was partly due to the fact that no viable alternative was available. Immanuel Kant (1724–1804) proposed a new view of knowledge: that knowledge is generated through a conjunction of a priori categories of the mind with input (noumena) from the external world. Kant's view was confined to philosophical circles, however. The density of his arguments and the difficulty of his style did not make it easily accessible to a broad community, either in the past or present (Kant 1934). The only other established alternative was the deductive view of Descartes: the view that knowledge advances by identifying certain true ideas from which are deduced other true ideas. This *Cartesian deductive view* suffered from being rooted in a different culture, and its deductive flow from first principles was uncomfortably similar to the discredited Aristotelian approach. The Aristotelian insistence that empty space is impossible was also identified with Descartes' "plenum" metaphysics—the view that space is always filled. Both the Aristotelian and Cartesian metaphysics were at odds with that of Newton, who postulated that atoms are located in space that is otherwise empty. To argue for theories like those of Aristotle, or unlike those of Newton, was *not* the way to make them credible during the high tide of Newtonian science.

At the turn of the twentieth century, when Newtonian physics began to falter and was finally laid to rest by the new theories in relativity and quantum mechanics, inductive theory could no longer ride the coattails of its mentor. Surprisingly, however, induction survived again after another transformation. It turned out that a modified version of probabilistic induction fit the methodological constraints of a dominant interpretation of subatomic physics.

Subatomic physics was one of two quite revolutionary developments that emerged shortly after the turn of the twentieth century. Relativity theory was the other. A few comments on relativity theory and its methodological implications will set the scene for a discussion of subatomic physics and the methodological debates to which it gave rise.

Relativity theory and induction

Einstein was the principal figure in the development of relativity theories. First came the special theory of relativity in 1905. It contained the revolutionary ideas that parameters such as time and space are relative to velocity, but that the velocity of electromagnetic waves is constant regardless of the position or speed of an observer measuring it. In 1915 the general theory of relativity was proposed. It introduced the effects of mass into special relativity. Specifically, mass changes with velocity (relative to an observer), space curves around mass, and mass is interchangeable with energy.

The special and general theories of relativity were formulated not just metaphysically, but mathematically as well. The mathematics was important. Remember that mathematical formulations of a theory allow its implications to be traced more accurately and make its implications more precise, thus subjecting theories to more rigorous empirical tests.

The special theory was tested and corroborated quickly at many points, and was rapidly accepted in the scientific community. The general theory, on the other hand, was and continues to be much more difficult to test. At the conclusion of World War I, Arthur Eddington finally did organize a test of the general theory. Eddington's expedition went to West Africa in order to be in position for a complete eclipse of the sun. During an eclipse, the angles between stars that lay close to each side of the sun can be measured when the sun passes between the stars. The angles between the same stars can also be easily remeasured at night, when the sun is absent. The general theory predicts that space curves around mass, so that the observed angles between stars should be greater during the day with the sun between the stars than at night when the sun is absent. The difference in the angles between daytime and nighttime measurements were found to be the amount predicted by the general theory. The general theory of relativity was corroborated, at least at one important point. The Eddington eclipse test also challenged Newtonian physics, thus driving another nail—one of the final nails—into the coffin of Newtonianism.

When Einsteinian physics overthrew Newtonian physics, inductive theory could have been overthrown as well. It was not, for a number of reasons.

Einstein himself was reluctant to draw definitive methodological implications from his relativity theories (Schilpp 1951). Karl Popper did recognize difficulties in inductive theory, and did conclude that it should fall. As a matter-of-fact, he developed his refutationist view of science in the aftermath of the Newtonian downfall and establishment of the relativity theories. Popper's refutationist view of science did not appear in systematic form until the early 1930s, however, and did not become widely known until even later. Most important, a new field of theoretical physics stole the limelight. Induction survived because yet another modification, this time a modification of probabilistic induction, emerged with this new field.

Quantum theory, realism, and the Copenhagen interpretation

The other revolutionary developments in theoretical physics occurred at the subatomic level, and especially in quantum mechanics. The context was different than for the development of the relativity theories, in which there existed a dominant view (Newtonian physics) that was ripe for replacement. Subatomic physics in general and quantum mechanics in particular were new on the scientific scene, having no clearly established theories against which new ones could be compared and assessed. The lack of a scientific antecedent affected the debates over method, too. The extraordinarily spirited controversies over method in quantum mechanics were partly due to the fact that there was no established scientific research program from which to "inherit" a view of science.

The need for methodological foundations in quantum mechanics spurred debates that involved nearly all major figures in physics and the philosophy of science, including Bohr, Heisenberg, Einstein, Schroedinger, Popper, and Reichenbach. The inadequacy of the various methodological views to accommodate the new types of theories could have suggested that methodological views are not absolutes, but instead have strengths as well as weaknesses. What happened, however, is that a new modification of inductive theory stole the show.

Probabilistic induction is supposed to deliver probable truth. As with classical induction, however, it was assumed that scientific theories were about "facts." Facts were not generally considered figments of the imagination, but were constituents of the real world. In philosophical terminology, probabilistic induction assumed *realism*: the view that theories are attempts to portray actual structure. Realists insist that ideas are not just tools to help orient mankind or to help solve practical problems, but also are and should be attempts to explain the way the actual world works.

A major challenge to realism was about to explode. The dynamite was manufactured by an interpretation of subatomic physics that emerged not long after the First World War. It was the controversial Copenhagen interpretation of quantum phenomena. Two pivotal components of the Copenhagen interpretation contributed to an attack on realism.

One crucial component was the complementarity principle of Niels Bohr (1885–1962). The reference to Copenhagen is out of deference to Niels Bohr, that charming Dane whose own ideas and inspirational support of those of his colleagues were crucial in the development of subatomic physics. Nevertheless, Bohr was shocked when Erwin Schroedinger (1887–1961) showed that quantum phenomena could be explained by a wave model. Schroedinger's wave interpretation did not require the assumption that energy must come in the discrete packets, as in Bohr's quantum interpretation. Unable to resolve inconsistencies between the wave and quantum interpretations, Bohr formulated the *complementarity principle*. According to the complementarity principle, the wave and quantum interpretations are complements of each other rather than inconsistent with each other.

Particularly disconcerting about the principle of complementarity is its methodological implication: Inconsistent theories are acceptable. Inconsistency indicates error, providing the impetus to search for better theories. To accept inconsistency, much less endorse it, would undermine the role of error in the advance of science and knowledge.

The complementarity principle was buttressed by a second theory with a questionable methodological implication. Werner Heisenberg (1901–1976) worked closely over an extended period with Niels Bohr. Among his contributions was the *uncertainty principle*. The best known instantiation of the uncertainty principle is that the precision with which the position of an electron can be determined is proportional to the imprecision with which its momentum can be known, and vice versa. The reason it seems impossible to be more precise about subatomic structure is that the measuring medium (electromagnetic waves) interferes with the electron, and thus with the parameters to be measured (position and momentum). The uncertainty principle pushed physics into a totally new impasse: It would be impossible to gain knowledge of subatomic structure beyond the limits already encountered. The mathematics associated with the uncertainty principle are still integral to subatomic physics, although numerous particles smaller than electrons have been postulated, such as quarks. Nevertheless, in the eyes of many at the time, the uncertainty principle implied another disconcerting methodological conclusion: There can be no reliable knowledge of structure smaller than that already discovered. This is a methodological faux pas; the purpose of method is to help extend knowledge, not to trip up the attempt.

That inconsistency is unavoidable (from the complementarity principle) and that a limit to knowledge had been reached (from the uncertainty principle) encouraged the conclusion that further theories about underlying structure would be highly speculative and difficult if not impossible to test empirically. In philosophical idiom, *realistic* interpretations of theories could no longer be a reliable part of science. That is why the methodological side of the Copenhagen interpretation reawakened *positivism*: the view that scientific statements should be confined to observable phenomena, and that speculation about unobservable structure—metaphysics—should not be part of science.

Probabilistic induction and positivism merged

The Copenhagen interpretation served to merge positivism with probabilistic induction in the following way. Crucial theories in subatomic physics were stochastic. For example, a statistical array expresses the probability that an electron would be in a given position at given time, even though an exact position at an exact time could not be determined. The positivistic slant of the Copenhagen interpretation was fused with probabilistic induction because the stochastic nature of subatomic theories *seemed to vindicate probabilistic induction as well as positivism*. Unfortunately, the "vindication" of probabilistic induction depended on a confusion that has always plagued inductive theory: Stochastic regularities are used to sanctify epistemological probabilities.

The Copenhagen interpretation not only reawakened the positivistic view of science, then, but solidified the hold of probabilistic induction as well. It fused the two, the product of which is the contemporary version of induction. Contemporary induction is often called *positivism*. Do remember, however, that this use of "positivism" connotes not just an anti-realist interpretation of theory, but probabilistic induction as well. Both elements—anti-realism and probabilism—are outlined in more detail in the next three sections.

Positivism

The positivistic (antirealist) slant of contemporary induction is that scientific theories are not and should not be attempts to describe the real world, but instead are tools to orient us in the world and to help solve practical problems. More specifically, positivistic approaches mandate that scientific statements should be based on correlations of observable phenomena that exclude *metaphysical* statements: statements about underlying structure, such as causal relations. Also excluded are semantic properties of theories, such as truth-value. Claims that a theory is true or false assume that it corresponds or does not correspond to the real world.

Even the terminology of contemporary induction has been modified to accommodate its positivistic side. "Fact," for example, which implies some connection to an element in the real world, is not considered proper idiom. Instead, "data" has become fashionable. "Data" implies mere observational input. In the terminology appropriate to positivism, then, knowledge grows by gathering and then correlating data.

Epistemological probability is the other element in contemporary induction. That is why the goal of contemporary induction is to establish the probable truth of theories. It is also the reason why theories are considered legitimate if they fall within the range of a probabilistic convention. According to the "95 percent" convention, for example, a theory is acceptable if it is verified by at least 95 percent of the relevant data.

Following are a few comments on the history of positivism prior to its fusion with probabilistic induction. They serve to clarify the sometimes confusing terminology associated with positivism.

The word "positivism" comes from the French word *positer*: to posit. It was first employed by Auguste Comte (1798–1857), who argued that the start of all science must be what is posited to our immediate senses. Speculative assertions not reducible to observables must be excluded from science. For that reason positivism came to mean "anti-metaphysics."

Although Comte coined the label "positivism," he was certainly not the first to have exploited its themes. Andreas Osiander, who in the sixteenth century wrote a preface to Copernicus' *De revolutionibus,* claimed that Copernicus' heliocentric (sun-centered) view did not have to be true, or even resemble the truth. It was sufficient, claimed Osiander, that the heliocentric view should produce calculations that match observations. Osiander's ploy had a political and religious advantage: It made the heliocentric view more palatable to Catholic theologians, who were committed to the Aristotelean geocentric (earth-centered) interpretation of the universe (Popper 1962).

Incidentally, a number of other philosophical positions that overlap with positivistic themes are sometimes confused with positivism. The names are even interchanged at times. *Instrumentalism* is one position that overlaps with positivism. According to the instrumentalist view, scientific theories are not and should not be attempts to describe the real structure of the cosmos. Instead, they are and should be tools or *instruments* that help us operate in this world. *Conventionalism* is another position that overlaps with positivism. Conventionalists, like positivists, argue that scientific theories cannot be confidently known as either true or false. The criterion for embracing or rejecting theories, then, is agreement within a scientific community. In other words, scientific theories are *conventions* adopted by scientists. Like other conventions such as protocol, manners, and language, theories are customs adopted by and used within a scientific community.

The label "conventionalism" can cause confusion when referring to positivism. An important reason is that Karl Popper, a staunch defender of the realistic intent of scientific theories, describes his own view of science as "conventionalist." (See Popper 1983 for a discussion of realism and Popper 1959 for a discussion of conventionalism). Popper recommends that scientists use "conventions" to decide either to accept or reject theories (Popper 1959). It is clear that Popper's meaning of conventionalism is far different from the positivistic meaning. Conventions by which to accept or reject theories does not imply that the theories themselves are "mere conventions."

By the way, conventionalism has its own history, in which scientists and philosophers such as Henri Poincare (1854–1912) and Pierre Duhem (1861–1916) figured prominently. Notice that conventionalism, like positivism, is a methodological tradition with roots in France. Both traditions share the thesis that knowledge is only tenuously connected to the real world, if at all. For positivists, scientific theories should exclude assumptions about the real world; for conventionalists scientific theories are the product of agreement rather than tests of correspondence with the real world. The shared cultural roots, ramified by shared skepticism about the connection between theory and reality, explains why positivism and conventionalism are labels that are sometimes interchanged.

Positivism in Scientific and Academic Circles

Positivism, the contemporary version of induction, is still a view of science supported by some professional philosophers. As has been seen, it was influential in the physical sciences; it remains so in the social sciences. It has also been a centerpiece of methodological debates in the external version of the New Archaeology. Familiarity with positivism in each of these areas should be helpful. Seeing its shortcomings in a variety of contexts helps make them all the more clear.

The Philosophy of Science

When the Copenhagen interpretation captured the scientific community many philosophers of science adopted the positivistic method with which it was identified. The "Vienna Circle" was built around contemporary induction. Inspired by thinkers such as Otto Neurath, Julius Kraft, and Moritz Schlicht, the Vienna Circle became well-known by the 1930s. At about the same time in Berlin, Hans Reichenbach, along with protégés including Carl Hempel, independently developed ideas similar to those of the Vienna Circle. Contacts between the groups were initiated, and before long "Vienna Circle" also became a label that referred to those embracing contemporary induction whether as part of the original group in Vienna or not.

In addition to being part of a popular model of method, the positivistic slant of contemporary induction played another role in the field of philosophy. The anti-metaphysical component of contemporary induction was employed to fight the bombastic metaphysics that characterizes the philosophical tradition stemming from Georg Wilhelm Frederich Hegel (1770–1831). There indeed was and still is need for a weapon to fight the murky speculation of the Hegelian tradition, and positivism became the standard of rationality by which to rule it out of court. This helps explain why positivism has continued to be important among academic philosophers even though physicists have abandoned the dubious methodological implications of the Copenhagen interpretation.

Another reason that the influence of positivism continues in academic philosophy is less commendable. Methodological views tend to be held ideologically by many academicians. That has been the tendency with positivism since the 1920s. A leading figure in the years since the First World War, Ludwig Wittgenstein (1889–1951), declared that metaphysical statements were pseudo-knowledge. Most of what had been traditionally known as philosophy was thus disparaged (Wittgenstein 1953, 1961). The effect was to turn philosophical study toward the analysis of concepts rather than using concepts to investigate problems in areas such as science, logic, ethics, and religion. When applied to formal systems such as mathematics, analysis of concepts is usually called *logical positivism*. When applied to less formal systems, such as ordinary languages, it is called *linguistic analysis*. Those offshoots of contemporary induction have dominated academic philosophy in the English-speaking world ever since, both serving as monuments to the desire on the part of some to avoid metaphysics at all cost.

Incidentally, Guy Gibbon's 1989 book *Explanation in Archaeology* contains a lengthy historical and thematic account of positivism in academic philosophy. The explication of recent positivism in philosophy is excellent, and quite detailed. I recommend it to students of philosophy.

Though positivistic trends still wield considerable influence in philosophy departments in the English-speaking world, other schools have also carved a niche. Perhaps the most notable has been the refutationist school that has grown up around the ideas of Karl Popper and his followers. Some refutationists have not escaped the tendency to be ideological in their convictions, either, but cracking the near total dominance of contemporary induction has stimulated fruitful debate about method.

The physical and social sciences

Positivism has had a quite wide following in the physical and social sciences outside theoretical physics. Physical chemistry since World War I and chemical engineering since World War II have had instrumentalist overtones. A tendency in both fields has been to generate equations for incorporating data with little or no conjecture about structural or causal explanations behind the data correlations. Such equations are often called *empirical equations*, an apt label that connotes the absence of metaphysical assumptions.

As with nearly all positivistic approaches, anomalous data can be explained away in one or more of three ways. (1) The equations are altered—the pejorative term is "fudged"—so that the data can be incorporated. (2) "Boundary conditions" are imposed that, in essence, stipulate that some data is not pertinent to an equation. (3) The anomalous data is interpreted as improbable but acceptable within a probabilistic convention of acceptability, such as the "95 percent" convention.

Each of the three types of manipulation are ad hoc: They function to preserve a theory in the face of anomalous data by decreasing its refutability. There are certainly times when these various ad hoc procedures are justifiable, such as when one is only interested in solving a practical problem, for example. The consequences are not beneficial for teaching or for theory development, however.

Because teaching method normally reflects beliefs about scientific method, students are often encouraged by professors and textbooks to plug parameters into empirical equations. Although this approach can be practical for routine work, it can impose limitations on the student, practicing engineer, or chemist when faced with an anomaly or a totally new problem. Without adequate training in generating formulas, which requires understanding the theory behind mathematical equations, it is not easy to discover the cause of an anomaly. Without a foundation in metaphysics (underlying structure and causal relationships), it is only possible to adjust a formula in an ad hoc way and it is nearly impossible to generate an entirely new formula. Perhaps even more important is that theoretical progress can be impeded. The opportunity to use anomalous data as a springboard to search for modified or new theory is lost through use of ad hoc techniques. The possibility of gaining new understanding and insight is lost with it.

Behaviorism can be defined as the application of positivistic method to theory development in psychology. In the stimulus-response (S-R) model, stimuli are correlated with responses. Conjectures about structures in the organism, or "black box," are disallowed. Because inquiry is restricted to correlations of the stimulus data and response data, the only measure of confidence in the correlations is the same as for all applications of positivism: a probabilistic convention.

Behavioristic approaches to psychology have gone far beyond the S-R model. Many psychologists have focused on the "black box," or organism. To use specialized terminology, the "stimulus-organism-response," or S-O-R approach, is more widely employed at present.

Despite the welcome change from the S-R model, positivistic tendencies permeate S-O-R approaches as well. For example, some psychologists still have difficulty incorporating into their theories the possibility that humans, much less animals, can think and make creative decisions. In other words, it is difficult to accept that a response passing through a brain from a stimulus might also be influenced by a "mind." Another difficulty is that positivism continues to be a standard by which to judge the legitimacy of theories. Instead of grappling with theories because they yield new understanding or insight, psychologists can be more interested in assuring that their theories meet behavioristic standards. Legitimating theories as "scientific" is usually wasteful, as discussed in Chapter 1. Legitimating theories with positivistic standards is particularly confining because of the paucity of theories that can satisfactorily meet them. Theories that humans can think and act in creative ways, for example, are suspect.

The probabilistic side of contemporary positivism has also made statistics a centerpiece of behaviorism. Of course, statistical techniques are useful in certain contexts, but they can also become ritualistic without clear benefit. Opportunities provided by statistics can also be compromised. Statistically significant correlations of data can provide a window through which to discover causal relationships, for example, but the window will not be particularly helpful if one feels uneasy about looking through it.

Positivism in Theoretical Archaeology

Different meanings of positivism

Positivism has different meanings, a point that is not surprising when one has become familiar with the various scientific and philosophical influences on its development. In its broadest meaning positivism is identified with any or all methods of science, so that any "scientific approach" is called positivism. Ian Hodder (1991) assumes this meaning in his criticisms of scientific approaches in theoretical archaeology. In its narrowest sense positivism simply means anti-metaphysics. Professional philosophers use this meaning, often (and correctly) employing it as the contrary of realism.

In archaeological discussions the meaning of positivism is usually not the broadest. The narrow meaning—positivism as anti-metaphysics and hence anti-realism—is sometimes part of what archaeologists mean by positivism. Other than the variable position on realism, however, archaeologists often associate positivism with processual or New Archaeology. The following three theses stand out: (1) There are universal "laws" in the structure and transformation of human institutions; (2) Explanations must be empirically verifiable; and (3) Individualistic elements, such as minds, might exist and might be influential in human events but theories that incorporate such elements are not verifiable.

As already discussed, universal laws are ofttimes called "covering laws" by archaeologists. Empirically verifiable explanations are normally testable (refutable), at least in practice. In my view that is extremely important and beneficial. In methodological discussions, however, verifiable often seems to mean inductively confirmable, with the goal of establishing universals. What is put into methodological practice is much more significant than what is preached in methodological sermons. Nevertheless, I do wish more processual archaeologists would preach what they practice. Perhaps this book will be of help for that purpose.

Finally, the inclusion or exclusion of individualistic elements splits processual or new archaeologists into two camps. In the American approach, such elements are strictly excluded. In the British approach they can be included, so long as individualistic elements are very carefully associated with the available artifactual data. Actually, incorporating individualistic elements in theories about the unwritten past should sometimes be done within an inductivist framework. These matters will be discussed in the third part of this book (Chapters 8 and 9).

The inductive tradition continues in archaeology

Inductivist guidelines will prove to be helpful when incorporating some individualistic elements into archaeological explanations. Except for that, however, it has been argued that inductive approaches are quite barren for theory development. Nevertheless, the inductive shadow still lingers in methodological debates.

For example, Ian Hodder still chooses positivism as his principal target of criticism in *Reading the Past* (Hodder 1991; Bell 1987a; also see Chapter 7). Induction has also become ritualized in a scientistic cloak, a fact that is not surprising when one is familiar with its history. In any case, the failure of inductive rituals has been a major source of a relativistic backlash in archaeology on the part of Hodder and others (Hodder 1991; Bell 1987a; also see Chapter 7).

Inductive theory underlies some of the best-known books concerning method in archaeology. The inductive underpinnings and scientistic tendencies of some recommendations in Merrilee Salmon's *Philosophy and Archaeology* have already been discussed (Salmon 1982). The covering-law model received a boost among some archaeologists with the publication of Watson's, LeBlanc's, and Redman's *Explanation in Archaeology* (1971). The covering-law tradition was continued in *Archaeological Explanation* (Watson et al. 1984). Because inductive verification to establish general laws is associated with the covering-law program, however, the drawbacks of the former tend to debilitate the latter.

Another book on method in archaeology, *Archaeology and the Methodology of Science* by Jane Kelley and Marsha Hanen (1988), is more recent. It also has an inductive slant, but with a format expanded to incorporate some quite fruitful recommendations. Kelley and Hanen discuss traditional inductive theory as understood by philosophers of science, along with its more recent nuances. Their detailed presentation is critical as well as expository. That they recognize weaknesses in inductive theory is certainly commendable. Because the views of both Kuhn and Popper are contrary to induction, both are appropriately discussed in the book. On the other hand, the assessment of lacunae in induction could be more forceful and direct. For example, analyses of the unending nuances and modifications in inductive theory do not overcome its basic difficulties, as I hope this chapter is making clear. Also, the critique of traditional inductive theory is used to highlight the benefits of more recent developments in induction rather than to reject the inductive program. Finally, the many references to inductive literature may be of interest to professional philosophers and perhaps to some archaeologists as well, but they seem to me to have only tangential relevance to application in archaeology.

When the authors turn to a more general discussion of explanation and inference in archaeology, they largely adopt the inductive goal of establishing theories. As the reader hardly needs be reminded by this point, a central theme in this book is that advancing theoretical understanding and insight is a better goal than attempting to establish theories. For advancing theory, given explanations should be used as stepping-stones to better explanations. Finally, the authors recommend inductive means to establish theories. Their recommendations largely arise from recent versions of induction discussed in the philosophy of science. A favored model is called "inference to the best explanation," in which competing theories are rigorously compared in order to establish the best one. Comparing theories, rather than analyzing one theory independent of others, is indeed a worthwhile task. Revelation of strengths and weaknesses, at least comparative strengths and weaknesses, is facilitated. On the other hand, the goal is still inductive: to establish a theory, in this case the best theory. That is suspect. The comparison is retrospective—on successes and failures already realized—and is made at a given moment. The greatest potential for further theory development, however, is not necessarily possessed by a theory judged the "best" at any given time. Before dating chronologies improved significantly, for example, diffusionist explanations of culture seemed "best," or at least better than theories about endogenous development.

Despite the criticisms above, *Archaeology and the Methodology of Science* has some most valuable features. There is a lengthy and insightful discussion of archaeological cases, the point of which is to illustrate application of method. I am not convinced that the examples illustrate the value of applying the broad methodological approach outlined by the authors, but the discussion of examples is nevertheless peppered with useful methodological insights. For example, generalization of theories beyond the contexts in which they are formulated, exploring the implications of theories to find test points, searching out strengths and weaknesses of theories by use of risky tests, and exploiting competing theories to reveal weaknesses in other theories are all incorporated in one way or another. Such methodological recommendations are shared by this book. Furthermore, the discussion of the social context of archaeology sheds considerable light on the various nonintellectual forces that can push and pull an archaeologist during his or her career. Finally, the book is well written. The detailed and comprehensive summaries of issues within inductive theory in academic philosophy are among the best I have ever encountered.

Incidentally, Alison Wylie (1982) has put considerable time into a comprehensive criticism of positivism in archaeology. Her focus is on the positivism of Lewis Binford. In my view Binford's actual work in archaeological theory has been fruitful because of its refutationist roots. Wylie is right, however: Systematic attempts to use (not just espouse) positivism are quite barren.

Advantages and Disadvantages of Induction

Comments on inductive theory have been scattered throughout the historical reconstruction. This section provides a more explicit analysis of inductive method. The analysis is organized around two facets of inductive theory: the goal of induction and inductive standards of theory structure.

The goal of induction

The goal of inductive method is to establish theories. That goal has remained the same from the time of Bacon, the only change being from the attempt to establish certain truth to probable truth and then to probable correlation. The goal is often hidden behind different terminology, of course. For example, the goal can be expressed as the attempt to distinguish knowledge from opinion. Establishing knowledge, it turns out, is how knowledge is to be distinguished from opinion (Salmon 1982). Inductive *means* of establishing knowledge can also be stated in different idiom. Attempts to calculate the "statistical relevance" of theories for example, are attempts to establish the epistemological probability of theories (Salmon 1982).

There are a number of difficulties with the goal of attempting to establish truth or probable truth. First, it cannot be done. Second, the attempt can hinder exploitation of anomalous data for theory development. Third, the goal encourages preoccupation with theory legitimation.

The first criticism is that the inductive goal is impossible to reach.

It is clearly not possible to establish certain truth. It is also not possible to establish the probable truth of theories. Calculating epistemological probabilities would require a definitive list of constituent events as well as prior probabilities for each (neither of which is possible). Furthermore, to test epistemological probabilities of theories would necessitate an underlying stochastic regularities. The trouble is that epistemological probabilities are not rooted in stochastic regularities. Bayesian techniques to establish epistemological probabilities fail as well, and for similar reasons, even though repeated uses of Bayesian formulas will mathematically swamp arbitrarily assigned prior probabilities.

It should be pointed out again that attempts to establish the epistemological probabilities of theories are not to be confused with exploiting stochastic regularities for theory development. Furthermore, the impossibility of establishing epistemological probabilities becomes more obvious once the differences between epistemological and stochastic probabilities are understood. It also helps to remember that the epistemological side of probability merged with the inductive theory after Hume's incisive criticism of classical induction, and that epistemological probabilities and induction have been fused ever since. Puncturing the aura of induction can also make it easier to recognize the difference between epistemological probabilities and stochastic regularities.

That it is impossible to reach the inductive goal is not disconcerting in itself. Goals, after all, function heuristically: as tools to guide one in a fruitful direction. Striving for justice, for example, is important even if perfect justice is never obtained. Unfortunately, attempts to reach the inductive goal of establishing the truth or probable truth can be harmful rather than helpful. The second and third criticisms of the inductive goal expose the detrimental consequences of attempting to establish the truth or probable truth of theories.

The second criticism of the inductive goal is that it hinders exploitation of anomalous data for theory development. One reason is attitudinal. Attempts to establish truth or probable truth of theories will, in most cases, be attempts to establish favored theories. Such hardly encourages recognition of anomalous data. Most people fervently hope *not* to find data that conflicts with their theories. The other reason is methodological. Even if establishing the probable truth of a theory were possible, it could encourage one to accept anomalous data that is improbable but possible. For example, data might be interpreted as anomalous, but still be regarded as acceptable if it falls within the boundaries of a statistical convention. The consequence is the same as with an ad hoc adjustment to anomalous data: It encourages the preservation of theory in spite of anomalous data instead of the improvement of theory by exploiting anomalous data.

Unlike attempting to establish probable truth, search for probable data correlations can be productive. Finding a correlation can indicate a stochastic regularity. A stochastic regularity may point to an underlying explanation that, in turn, might lead to new understanding and insight. On the other hand, if one insists on remaining loyal to the positivistic rule that explanations underlying the correlation are "metaphysical" and hence out of court for science, there will be no attempt to find underlying explanations. In brief, the positivistic impulse to correlate data can lead to breakthroughs in developing theory as long as the positivistic prejudice against causal, structural, and other types of "metaphysical" explanation is ignored. The solution is simply to drop the metaphysical restriction on contemporary induction.

The third criticism of the inductive goal is that attempts to establish theories can easily degenerate into attempts to legitimate theory. As argued in Chapter 1, whether a theory is "scientific" or not by any methodological criteria—inductive or otherwise—is of no value in itself. It can only be valuable *if* it would serve to aid theory development. In the case of inductive method, it can detract from theory development. Specifically, a "scientific" theory in the inductive tradition is one that is established certainly or probabilistically. But it has already been argued that it is impossible to determine either (first criticism) and that attempting to do so can be harmful (second criticism). It has also been argued that much if not all of the development of a theory will already be finished before a theory could be established by inductive confirmation.

Incidentally, if the inductive goal of establishing the truth or probable truth of theories is misconceived, how did it take hold in the first place? The historical answer is that Bacon adopted the goal from the Aristotelean tradition. Aristoteleans had assumed that there is certain knowledge—*episteme*—and that it was humanly possible to obtain that knowledge. Bacon did not challenge that goal, but instead formulated a different method by which to attain it.

It must next be asked why the goal of establishing theories is still so entrenched three-and-a-half centuries later. The inertia of induction is one reason. There is another reason, however, and it may be more important: It has been (mistakenly) assumed that abandoning the goal of establishing theories will inevitably lead to relativism. It is feared that if there are no reliable criteria by which to establish theories, any theory is as plausible as any other. As emphasized at a number of points already, the fear of (and sometimes fascination with) irrational approaches and the inevitable relativism they imply is never far from the center of methodological debate.

Most people are suspicious of relativism, perhaps because it might be used as a tool to cast doubt on their favored theories, not to mention the moral, political, or economic views they may hold dear. That fear is not entirely unfounded, but the plausibility of relativism can be magnified rather than reduced by trying to establish theories inductively. The reason is that disappointment in attempts to establish theories can rebound to the conclusion that there are no reliable guidelines for assessing theories (Popper 1962). If there are no reliable guidelines for assessing theories, then any theory can be considered as legitimate as any other.

Inductive standards of theory structure

Ideal inductive theories are generalizations from an empirical base— "inductions from the facts." Reaching the ideal is impossible: All important generalizations incorporate assumptions not reducible to the facts, or data. The ideal plays an important role nevertheless. One significant advantage and one drawback are identified here.

Interpreting theories as generalizations from an empirical base is advantageous because it serves as a reminder that theories must be answerable to an empirical world that transcends our ideas. In archaeology, the artifactual record is the empirical basis for theories. Whatever problem-situation theories may resolve, they must do so in a way that answers to the artifactual record.

The drawback is a misunderstanding about the function of universalized components in theories. By way of review, universalization is seen in claims like "all instances where masks are found in a burial site are instances in which gold is found as well," or "every need for large-scale irrigation will lead to the development of state structure." Generalizations like these are explicit, or at least assumed, in most significant theories. The inductive conception of universals, however, misconceives their function in theory development.

In the inductive view, the goal is to find and establish generalizations that apply in all instances (classical induction), or as many instances as possible (probabilistic induction). A typical example is Hempel's exhortation to establish "covering laws"—universals that apply in all historical instantiations. Another example is Salmon's goal of distinguishing between knowledge and guesswork by use of statistical-relevance models.

The trouble is that universals function differently than as portrayed in the inductive vision. Remember from the last chapter that there are two methodological reasons why theoretical generalizations are so important. First, they direct research from one context into others. For example, a theory about the relationship of burial items to social status might be developed by studying one culture, but if generalized the theory could then lead to understanding and insight into other cultures when used to study the latter. Second, universals can be highly testable: the more generalized a theory, the greater the amount of empirical data that can be called upon to test it. In short, universality is a feature of theories that increases testability. Any increase in testability increases the opportunity to improve theories.

In sum, when the misconception of the function of universals is conflated with the misconstrued goal of establishing theories, the goal of science is interpreted to be the (certain or probabilistic) establishment of generalizations. The upshot is that scholars attempt to confirm "covering laws" in all contexts, or they attempt to use "statistical-relevance" models or Bayesian techniques to confirm theories probabilistically, or they attempt to establish the best among competing explanations. These attempts are typical and even inevitable outgrowths of the inductive vision.

Beyond induction

As a mandate to gather data and to describe it accurately in field reports the inductive view of science has contributed immensely to the growth of empirical archaeology. It is a tribute to induction that archaeologists give so much weight to the artifactual record and the careful fieldwork necessary to gather that record. It will also be argued in the last part of this book that inductive guidelines can be beneficially used when incorporating some individualistic elements into archaeological explanations.

On the other hand, for making decisions about theories (other than those with individualistic elements) the tools forged from inductive method are of minimal value. There are no archaeological examples to illustrate the benefits of inductive method in this chapter because I cannot think of any (see Bell 1984). When induction is ramified to include elements from other methodological views, then meaningful examples can be found (Kelley and Hanen 1988). In the latter cases the benefits flow not from induction, in my view, but from the ideas imported into induction.

By this point it may not be necessary to make the following point explicit: Inductive approaches recommended to archaeologists come not so much from archaeology, but from philosophical models of induction recommended either by philosophers or by archaeologists who have adopted inductive models from philosophers. Those to whom reference has been made are Hempel (1942, 1952, 1962, 1965, 1966, 1988), Salmon (1982), Watson et. al. (1971, 1984), and Kelley and Hanen (1988). I do have to wonder if archaeologists would even think of an inductive framework without the external recommendations. I do not believe an investigation of productive theory development in archaeology would lead to inductive guidelines, at least if the arguments and analyses in this book are reasonably correct.

Finally, disappointment in induction, which is identified by many as *the* method of science, has inadvertently led to skepticism about science and buttressed flirtations with relativism (see Hodder 1991 and Bell 1987a). Better tools for making decisions about theories—and a stronger shield against relativism—are found in the refutationist view of science.

Suggested Readings

Induction has been heavily criticized in this chapter. Nevertheless three books recommend inductive approaches to archaeologists, and all three have captured considerable attention. Annotation is in order even though commentary has already been offered in this and earlier chapters.

1. Jane H. Kelley and Marsha Hanen, 1988, *Archaeology and the Methodology of Science.*
Pertinent to discussions on positivism and induction.
Kelley and Hanen criticize earlier versions of induction in favor of more recent inductive approaches, such as "inference to the best explanation." The discussion of many recent concepts in inductive theory distinguishes this book from (Salmon 1982) and (Watson et al. 1971 and 1984). As in Watson et al.'s books, however, many references and distinctions seem unnecessary for applying method in archaeology. Kelley and Hanen broaden the view of induction in some quite beneficial ways. For example, they recognize the importance of risky testing and generalization beyond a data base. These are desirable methodologically, although they are more clearly associated with the refutationist view than with induction. The exploration of case examples provides numerous methodological insights even if, in my view, they are not closely associated with an inductive framework. The analysis of sociological factors that guide career paths of archaeologists is penetrating and should not be missed.

2. Merrilee Salmon, 1982, *Philosophy and Archaeology*.
Pertinent to discussions of induction, probability theory, and positivism.
Merrilee Salmon recommends statistical-relevance models (S-R models)
for the confirmation of theories. In this chapter I have argued that epistemological calculations of probabilities, of which S-R models are examples,
are not helpful much less possible. The same conclusion was drawn in an
article-length review of the book (Bell 1984). Interestingly, the latter part of
Salmon's book is critical of attempts to apply precast methodological approaches. Salmon's analysis of method in Binford's work makes the crucial
distinction between the method espoused by him and the method evident
in his work. Her criticism is properly directed more to the former than the
latter. This book is well written, and the line of argument is easy to follow.
These qualities are further enhanced by Salmon's willingness to forgo unnecessary references and concepts insignificant for archaeological practice.

3. Patty Jo Watson, Steven LeBlanc, and Charles Redman, 1971, *Explanation in Archaeology: An Explicitly Scientific Approach*. An updated version is
Archaeological Explanation: The Scientific Method in Archaeology, 1984, by the
same authors.
Pertinent to discussions on induction, probability theory, and positivism.
Covering-law models are recommended in these books, but with an inductive slant toward confirmation. Despite the difficulties with induction
and the many references to philosophical literature that seem unnecessary,
there is methodological insight to be gained in some of the detailed discussion of archaeological theorizing.

Criticisms of inductive approaches in archaeology began to appear almost
a soon as induction was recommended. Two sources are annotated here.
4. Jeremy A. Sabloff, Thomas W. Beale, and Anthony J. Kurland, Jr.,
1973, "Recent Developments in Archaeology."
Pertinent to discussion of positivism in theoretical archaeology.
This is a review article of methodological literature on the early New Archaeology. That literature was largely inductive. The presentations are well-
organized and clear, and the authors include helpful explanatory comments.
The overall thrust is quite critical, and appropriately so in my view.

5. Alison Wylie, 1982, *Positivism and the New Archaeology*.
Pertinent to discussions of positivism and induction.
This is Alison Wylie's Ph.D. dissertation. The analysis is critical of at-

tempts to apply positivism. The immediate focus is on positivism in archaeology, but Wylie's arguments are germane to positivism in any context. There are nuances and distinctions that I do not think are important for archaeologists, but remember that this is a dissertation in philosophy rather than archaeology.

Chapter 5   The Paradigmatic View of Science

The early fate of Thomas Kuhn's *The Structure of Scientific Revolutions* was far more auspicious than David Hume's *Treatise of Human Nature*. Instead of emerging unwanted from the press, Kuhn's *Structure* was widely read and hotly debated from the moment it was first published in 1962. It has appealed to intellectuals in diverse fields, including sociology, psychology, history, philosophy, and theology. The influence of Kuhn's book is born out by the fact that the word "paradigm" has been adopted into the lexicons of nearly every academic and intellectual community, not to speak of the public at large. Use of the word "paradigm" to designate any broad outlook or vision has certainly not escaped archaeology (for example, see Dunnell 1986). As a set of theses about how theory changes, the paradigmatic view has also been discussed in the archaeological literature (for example, see Sterud 1973; Meltzer 1979; Binford and Sabloff 1982; Kelley and Hanen 1988). Furthermore, the paradigmatic perspective has been used to interpret the history of archaeology. An illuminating example is Marshall Becker's historical reconstruction of theories about Maya social structure (see Becker 1979).

Despite archaeologists' interest in and familiarity with the paradigmatic view, it has not been central to methodological discussions in the New Archaeology. That is not surprising, for two related reasons. New Archaeologists of all stripes have focused on rational aspects of theory development, whereas the paradigmatic view incorporates irrational elements into its description of theory development. Emphasis on irrational elements also means that rational elements—methodological guidelines—play a considerably less significant role in the paradigmatic view.

Whatever its shortcomings, the paradigmatic view also provides archaeologists a valuable perspective on theory development. Most important is the light it throws on the professional and other nonintellectual pressures that can frame theoretical discussions and influence career paths.

The paradigmatic view grew from two serious lacunae in the inductive view of science: the lack of a role for assumptions (a "paradigm") in theory development and the need to account for the role of irrational elements, such as dogmatism and social pressure, in the dissemination and adoption of theories. The paradigmatic view fills these lacunae, but not without difficulties of its own.

Summary of the Paradigmatic View

According to Kuhn, scientific communities operate within a framework of assumptions called a *paradigm*. Included among the assumptions in a paradigm are an array of problems considered important to investigate, theories about underlying structure and causal relations ("metaphysical theories"), theories that interpret the underlying structure and causal relations empirically ("scientific theories"), methodological guidelines by which theories are legitimated, and empirical techniques regarded as reliable (such as use of measuring instruments and microscopes). Establishing a paradigm by verifying its implications through research is called *normal science*. Broadly speaking, paradigms give direction to normal science by identifying the problems considered important to investigate and by regulating the types of theories considered acceptable as solutions.

During normal science paradigms guide the work of a scientific community. Because the goal of normal science is to establish a paradigm, anomalous research findings and critical commentary tend to be ignored or even dismissed. That is one reason paradigms are not destabilized by criticism during a period of normal science. Another reason paradigms persist during a period of normal science is that they continue to yield theoretical understanding and empirical insight despite anomalies. A number of nonintellectual factors also buttress the stability of paradigms, however, to the point where they become doctrine or even ideology. One is professional training. Standard textbooks are written assuming a paradigm. Another is professional authority. Recognized leaders in a field espouse the paradigm. Furthermore, proposals for research funding must be acceptable within a paradigmatic framework. Finally, professional publications largely screen out articles and reports that breach the pattern of normal science.

Eventually a paradigm begins to exhaust its potential for new discovery, at which point its accumulated anomalies become more noticeable and bothersome. That ushers in a period of *extraordinary science*, or *revolutionary science*. The paradigm itself is finally challenged; anomalies are at last displayed on center stage and criticism is permitted rather than suppressed. In addition to attacks on the received paradigm, extraordinary science is marked by search for alternative paradigms.

Eventually a new paradigm will replace the former one, thus ending the revolutionary period. A new paradigm is accepted partially on rational criteria: It accounts for at least some anomalies in the former paradigm. But irrational factors are also important in its acceptance. Adopting a paradigm is like a religious conversion, with deep emotional overtones and submission to all its tenets rather than just a select few. Another period of normal science begins under the aegis of the new paradigm.

The preceding synopsis of the paradigmatic view of science is given without qualifying comments. Actually, the paradigmatic view is frustratingly ambiguous in a number of important ways: The concept of "paradigm" is unclear, the rational and irrational elements in theory selection are conflated and become confused, and the descriptive portrait of scientific change slips into a prescriptive formula for theory development. These problems will be addressed after a brief historical reconstruction of the paradigmatic view.

William Whewell's Criticism of Induction

Wide-spread use of the word "paradigm" and the theses in the paradigmatic view itself stem mainly from Thomas Kuhn's *The Structure of Scientific Revolutions* (Kuhn 1962). The ideas developed by Kuhn were not entirely new to the intellectual world, however. In the years between 1835 and 1840, William Whewell (1794–1866) analyzed induction and found it wanting as an explanation for the advance of science. Whewell also proposed the rudiments of a new and different view of knowledge. Kuhn, who was not familiar with Whewell's contributions when he wrote *The Structure of Scientific Revolutions*, independently reconstructed Whewell's major arguments and carried out the implications further. In this section Whewell's criticisms of induction is reconstructed, as well as his rudimentary paradigmatic view.

As discussed in Chapter 4, David Hume's logical attack on induction in 1739 led to the transformation of classical induction into probabilistic induction. A bit less than a century later, William Whewell (pronounced "Hew'-ol") put forth historical and psychological arguments against Baconian induction. Like Hume's work, Whewell's major essays—*History of the Inductive Sciences, from the Earliest to the Present Times* (1837) and *The Philosophy of the Inductive Sciences, Founded Upon Their History* (1840)—set forth unpopular theses.

Whewell's studies in the history of science and psychology of discovery revealed that the processes of advancement did not resemble the research and generalization stages prescribed by Bacon. Scientists, Whewell found, made bold guesses and then tested them against facts. Many of the guesses turned out to be mistaken, but some were correct. Even correct ideas, however, could not be proclaimed the truth; they might be found mistaken by later tests. Furthermore, free-ranging thought and vivid imagination were requisites for bold guesses. These qualities of thinking are at odds with the quite constrained role of the mind in the inductive vision.

Although facts seem unimportant for generating knowledge, Whewell maintained that facts were significant for legitimating knowledge. When an idea had helped a scientist understand phenomena, he would then deduce the implications to confirm the idea. If the facts were there as expected, the idea would be legitimate. Unlike in induction, however, legitimate ideas are not entirely reducible to known facts. The reason is that ideas tend to "colligate" (Whewell's expression) into intelligible wholes. Colligated ideas entail facts that have not been foreseen because those ideas do not arise strictly from known facts. Scientists adopt colligated ideas as a package, or psychological unit, and interpret the world through that package.

In short, the inductive view of knowledge gave neither an historically justifiable description of how science develops, nor a psychologically accurate picture of how scientists think. Whewell concluded that neither the history nor the psychology of science fit the inductive formula for the advance of science during the approximately 170 years during which science was supposed to have been inductive.

Despite Whewell's justified criticism of induction, and his recommendation of a paradigmatic replacement, several factors hindered his views from gaining wider attention. One is that his own interpretation had no name despite being penned by one of the greatest nomenclators in the history of science. Another is that Whewell's writing style was rather heavy. Compared to the seminal works of someone like Bacon or even Hume, reading through his volumes was an onerous task that is no less challenging today. Another reason Whewell's criticism received meager attention is that the inductive view was still riding the success of Newtonian science. Inductive theory had been modified to incorporate Hume's criticism. Whewell's analysis, by way of contrast, left no room whatsoever for the modification of induction. Whewell's paradigmatic view was so different that its acceptance would have required rejection of induction.

Overthrowing induction would have been difficult enough, but during the halcyon days of Newtonian science it was nearly impossible. Whewell had, however, planted seeds for the paradigmatic view. Those seeds remained in germination for over a century. Thomas Kuhn finally sprinkled water on them in the early 1960s.

Rational versus Irrational Interpretations of Kuhn

Critics and supporters of Kuhn's views on science take different sides on many issues, but on one point nearly everyone agrees: *The Structure of Scientific Revolutions* is ambiguous. One assessment of

Kuhn's book lists twenty-one different ways in which Kuhn employs the word "paradigm" (Masterman 1970). For the purposes of this section it will suffice to outline two broad interpretations of Kuhn's paradigmatic view. One emphasizes the role of rational factors in scientific development, the other highlights the importance of irrational forces. The methodological implications of the two interpretations are vastly different.

Before discussing the difference between the interpretations, it is interesting to note that they share much in common. Four theses can be identified that are shared by both interpretations: (1) Science requires adoption of imaginative new ideas; (2) facts are revealed by the light of those new ideas and research is directed toward uncovering the facts; (3) scientists inevitably group ideas into units (paradigms) and an individual idea may seem inseparable from the paradigm to which it belongs; and (4) facts are forced to fit the unit of ideas, while anomalous data tends to be ignored. There is a fifth thesis that is both embraced and rejected in Kuhn's book, however. It is (5) that comparisons between competing paradigms can be made by estimating the success of the ideas in explaining facts. The comparison allows a given paradigm to be judged better than another paradigm.

Themes in Kuhn's book that suggest the fifth thesis are the following:

- A paradigm is thrown into doubt when an accumulating number of facts do not justify it.
- A new paradigm must explain crucial facts that are anomalies in the old paradigm.
- A new paradigm explains facts about which its predecessor implies nothing.

But other themes contradict the fifth thesis:

- No paradigm can be compared with another.
- Adoption of one paradigm rather than another is ultimately a leap of faith.
- Acceptance of a new paradigm is an emotional experience, not an intellectual transition.

- Paradigms spread, and are accepted, because of sociological reasons, such as the fame of its inventors or supporters or the popularity of a textbook espousing the paradigm.

In short, there are two conflicting interpretations: Paradigms can be compared and selected by intellectual criteria—the *rational interpretation* as I call it—and paradigms can neither be compared nor selected by intellectual criteria—the *irrational interpretation*.

Incidentally, like other contrasting methodological poles discussed in this book, there is a continuum between the extremes. One would be hard pressed to find anyone who practiced at either the rational or irrational extremes. Most would fall somewhere along the continuum, with an emphasis on either the rational or the irrational elements but with some of each.

By the way, Marshall Becker's 1979 paper on changing views of Maya social structure was not intended to provide a discussion or detailed example of Kuhn's paradigmatic view (Becker 1979). Nevertheless, it provides a Kuhnian mixture of irrational as well as rational tendencies in theory acceptance and preservation. On the irrational side, "Kuhn's (1962:151) observation that paradigms are accepted on faith rather than on the basis of logical argument can be demonstrated to apply quite well to theories about Maya social structure" (Becker 1979:3). Becker (1979:3) points out that the history of theories about Maya social structure demonstrates "how a thesis came into existence, and continues as the model best known to the public, despite the lack of supporting archaeological evidence." Rational elements also play an important role in Becker's history. He recounts how archaeological counterevidence gradually disrupted the spell of ingrained interpretations, the result of which was the emergence of new views to guide research.

The two interpretations of Kuhn's paradigmatic view—the rational interpretation and the irrational interpretation—lie on each side of that central controversy about the nature of science: Is science rational, or is it irrational?

If one asks whether the scientific enterprise is rational or irrational, an answer is not difficult to find: Science has both rational and irrational components. Another question needs to be asked, however: Should science be approached as a rational enterprise? Although Kuhn's *The Structure of Scientific Revolutions* gives no definitive response, the answer in this book is clearly in the affirmative. Not to do so would be to surrender use of empirical data and reasoned argument so important for gaining new understanding and insight. Not to approach science rationally would also amplify the role of the irrational components woven into the fabric of science. At the extreme it would elevate the irrational components to dominate science; that is, it would open another route to relativism.

Incidentally, prior to publishing *The Structure of Scientific Revolutions* Kuhn was intrigued with irrational elements in science. A 1961 paper read at Worcester College, Oxford, for example, had the title "The Function of Dogma in Scientific Research." In that 1961 paper Kuhn emphasized the role of dogmatic attitudes in science (Toulmin 1970). Subsequent to publication of *The Structure of Scientific Revolutions* he tended to embrace the rational interpretation. For example, in 1970 he stated that his view is more similar to the refutationist view of Popper than different from it (Kuhn 1970b). In short, prior to *The Structure of Scientific Revolutions* Kuhn focused principally on the irrational side of science. *The Structure of Scientific Revolutions* contains both rational and an irrational components. After *The Structure of Scientific Revolutions* he gave greater emphasis to the rational elements in science.

Why are both rational and irrational components included in Kuhn's paradigmatic view of science? That is the question explored in the next section.

Description of Science or Prescription for Science?

The picture of science sketched out in *The Structure of Scientific Revolutions* was intended by Kuhn to be a description of science rather than a prescription for science. When, as a young man, Kuhn turned from physics to the study of the history of science, his goal was to understand what had occurred and why—a description—

rather than imposing his own categories on what should have occurred and why (Kuhn 1962).

Like Whewell before him, Kuhn was astonished by the discrepancy between the inductive prescription for scientific progress and how science had actually progressed. He used his description of science to criticize the prescriptive formula of induction, a formula that he found discordant with many events and processes in the history of science (Kuhn 1962).

Although Kuhn avoided prescriptive recommendations, he did think it appropriate as a historian of science to attempt to describe both rational and irrational components of actual science (Kuhn 1977). It seems unfair to find fault with that conception of his role as a historian. It is also unfair to isolate just the irrational components in Kuhn's paradigmatic view and then accuse him of endorsing relativism (for example Popper 1970; Watkins 1970). It is fair, however, to assess the influence of the descriptive insights of the paradigmatic view on the decidedly prescriptive task of applying method. That assessment is the purpose of the next section.

Contributions and Limitations of the Paradigmatic View

Identifying the contributions and limitations of any scientific view is complicated by different interpretations of its goal or its method for reaching the goal. For example, it was argued that interpreting the inductive view broadly—meaning that theories should be empirically grounded—is helpful. It was also argued that interpreting induction positivistically—meaning that theories should be limited to data correlations—is not so helpful. Generally speaking, advantages of a methodological view can be turned into disadvantages by altering its interpretation, or vice versa. Sorting out contributions and limitations of the paradigmatic view is particularly challenging because of an excessive number of ambiguities in its meaning.

Some confusion will be avoided by limiting the interpretative range of the paradigmatic view. Specifically, the purely rational interpretation will be avoided, as will the purely irrational interpretation. Other than sidestepping ambiguity, there are three other reasons for avoiding these extreme interpretations. First, Kuhn includes both rational and irrational elements in his paradigmatic view. To focus on just one or the other would do injustice to his work. Second, if the rational elements are given exclusive attention, the paradigmatic view collapses into a crude refutationist view. In that case the refutationist view is more appropriate. Third, if interpreted irrationally, the paradigmatic view collapses into relativism. In that case relativism could be addressed directly, as it is in numerous contexts in this book.

The paradigmatic view contributes to an understanding of theory development in several ways. It gives insight into the psychology of theory development. It also sheds light on how the sociology of an intellectual community can influence theory development, not to speak of the careers of members in such a community. There is, however, a severe limitation to the paradigmatic view. It does not yield fruitful guidelines for making decisions about theories. Details are spelled out in the three subsections that follow.

The psychology of theory development

Tenacity to a set of ideas is a prominent theme in the paradigmatic views of both Whewell and Kuhn. Tenacity is particularly important when a new set of ideas is being formulated and established. New ideas are likely to be at odds with established ones. For that reason boldness is necessary to persevere through the criticism that certainly will be forthcoming from devotees of approaches that have already enjoyed success.

Tenacity continues to be crucial as a research program develops. When anomalous data are encountered, for example, it is often productive to carry on with the research program rather than stop because of discordant data. Anomalies will have to be faced at some point, but potential understanding and insight might be lost if a research program is rejected too soon.

Of course there are dangers associated with tenacity. Ignoring criticism at the outset of a research program can result in time wasted on ideas not worthy of pursuit. Ignoring anomalous data during an active research program can also be a mistake. Anomalous data can lead to adjustment of a theory with auxiliary hypotheses. Remember that auxiliary hypotheses leave a theory open to further testing and hence provide the opportunity to gain even more understanding and insight. If adjustments to anomalous data can only be made by ad hoc maneuvers, that can also be helpful information. It would indicate that further development of a theory might be limited. If so, one might best begin a serious consideration of other routes to solving a theoretical problem.

Two examples of misplaced tenacity are particularly well known. Alfred L. Kroeber's commitment to diffusionist theory might have been considerably less tenacious he had realized that its adjustments were ad hoc. V. Gordon Childe's allegiance to the classical diffusionist theory in the face of mounting counterevidence and ad hoc adjustments was even more tenacious. His eventual admission that the classical diffusionist theory was highly suspect is all the more impressive in light of the strength of his belief in classical diffusion.

The final drawback to tenacity is a bit more subtle. Tenacious allegiance to a set of ideas makes it difficult if not impossible to separate the more beneficial from the less promising ideas in a set.

A dominant thesis of the paradigmatic view is that research is not directed simply by a "theory," or "explanation," but instead is informed by a rather large set of assumptions—the paradigm. Tenacious allegiance to an entire paradigm means that the individual ideas within the paradigm tend to be adopted or rejected in toto rather than assessed on individual merit. The psychological disposition to accept or reject an entire set of ideas rather than attempting to sort them out individually is detrimental for a number of reasons.

First, not all ideas are equally worthwhile simply because they are gathered together in a unit. Like policy recommendations in the manifesto (platform) of a political party, some ideas are better than others. Not to separate ideas can lead to adoption of less desirable ones along with those that are more promising, and rejection of more fruitful ideas with those less so. The unfortunate consequences can be illustrated with an example from archaeology.

The New Archaeology, it will be recalled, incorporates different ideas. For most the New Archaeology is synonymous with processual archaeology, and connotes the attempt to explain social structure and change using rigorous methodological guidelines. Nevertheless, there are a multiplicity of different and contrasting ideas that come under the umbrella of the New Archaeology. Methodological guidelines can be coaxed from an internal analysis or can be imposed from an external source. Furthermore, within the internal and external approaches are further methodological divergences, such as between positivistic approaches and refutationist approaches. On top of this, in the British approach one might consider narratives appropriate in some instances, as well as the inclusion of individualistic elements. At least historical narrative and human agency would not be ruled out categorically. Neither would be acceptable in the American approach to the New Archaeology, however.

The multitude of ideas within the New Archaeology "paradigm" not only contrast with each other, but are also of different value in different contexts. That point should be quite obvious in this book. Still, some are tempted to endorse the New Archaeology as a whole and without exception, or at least some version of it. More disconcerting, in my view, is that others reject the entire New Archaeology "paradigm" rather than carefully evaluating different components. Ian Hodder, for example, identifies processual approaches with positivistic method, and both of those with the New Archaeology. By pointing out the poverty of positivistic method, he rejects processual theories and the New Archaeology as a package along with positivistic method (Hodder 1991). Treating the New Archaeology as a unit made it more difficult for Hodder to see that positivistic method is *not* operative when processual approaches are fruitful. It also made it easier for him to conflate methodological tools with theories. Throwing out poor method (positivism) does make sense, but it does not make sense to throw out processual goals and approaches along with it (Bell 1987a; Peebles 1991, 1992).

Interpreting the differences between postprocessual and processual approaches as an unbridgeable bifurcation with little if any common ground has been part of the postprocessual "paradigm." In that sense it is appropriate to label the postprocessual approach as the "anti-processual" approach (Renfrew 1989b). Fortunately, that tendency is breaking down. The fruitlessness of continuing to view theoretical archaeology as split between two mutually exclusive approaches with little if any common ground became particularly clear at the 1989 Theoretical Archaeology Group Conference in Newcastle-upon-Tyne. Numerous papers included comments on the importance of stepping across the supposed gap, not to mention the many parenthetical comments accompanying those and other papers. For example, Matthew Johnson, when making introductory comments to his paper "The Englishman's Home and its Study," noted that he largely agreed with the critique of processual archaeology. Nevertheless, he said he was "shocked" to realize that his studies of traditional houses in England revealed variety and change to the point where he was enticed to use processual concepts, such as considering variabilities rather than just similarities and dynamic processes rather than just static structure (Johnson 1989).

John Barrett, in the abstract of his paper "Archaeology in the Age of Uncertainty," recognized that there are differences between the approaches. The reasons are much like those of Kuhn: "We need to belong to a community of practitioners who can agree upon the general aims of our work, the development of a creative program and the grounds for a critical evaluation of what we produce. At base, this is what scientists do" (Barrett 1989). Nevertheless, Barrett (1989) also states that an absolute grounding for theory and chronic relativism are both misguided, and that there is a need for different traditions and room for both as well.

Processualists are also bridging the paradigmatic gap. At the same Theoretical Archaeology Group Conference, Colin Renfrew delivered a paper entitled "Archaeology—Humanity or Science?" In that paper Renfrew pointed out the potential dangers of subjectivity in postprocessual approaches but also emphasized the overlap and potential for mutual benefit. Postprocessual approaches could benefit by the more careful and consistent use of method that characterizes processual archaeology, for example. On the other hand, the processual turn toward cognitive archaeology has been partly inspired by the postprocessual movement (Renfrew 1989b). The shift toward cognitive interests in the processual camp has recently been made even more explicit. In April 1990 a conference on cognitive archaeology was held at Lucy Cavendish College, Cambridge. At that conference Renfrew went so far as to identify two phases of the processual movement: the earlier systemic phase and the emerging cognitive phase.

Interestingly, archaeologists long ago were explicitly warned against the dangers of accepting or rejecting groups of ideas as a whole. That warning came from none less than David Clarke (1968). Nevertheless, as the paradigmatic view has made clear, there is a psychological propensity to adopt, or reject, entire sets of ideas. Awareness of that tendency can help dampen its deleterious effects.

The sociology of scientific communities

The psychological insights of the paradigmatic view are mirrored in the sociological milieu of scientific communities. A community that accepts a framework of ideas can pursue research unhindered by continuous discussion of assumptions. Rather than constantly questioning presuppositions or being questioned about them, attention can instead be focused on exploring the potential of the assumptions. This suggests another benefit.

When difficulties are encountered in research, those who share assumptions not only provide moral support, but can also help resolve difficulties, at least in a way acceptable to those within the community. Mutual support, moral and intellectual, can certainly aid theory development.

Finally, sharing a set of ideas provides common standards for assessing research within a scientific community. Research can be collectively evaluated only if there are shared standards.

Each of the benefits contains potential detriments as well. That an intellectual community tends to shield itself from questions about its assumptions discourages valid criticism and the benefits that criticism can provide. Sharing a common framework can also stifle those within the community who might want to explore alternative assumptions. Furthermore, someone excluded from the community might offer a perspective that could resolve difficulties in a way not apparent to those fully committed to the paradigm. Finally, using common standards for assessing research can exclude innovative approaches that do not meet those standards.

In addition to the impact on use of method, sociological forces also frame the professional lives of archaeologists. In their book *Archaeology and the Methodology of Science*, Jane Kelley and Marsha Hanen show how the sociological structure of archaeology funnels archaeologists into particular career paths (Kelley and Hanen 1988: Chapter 4, especially pp. 123–163). They point to Kuhn's paradigmatic view of science as the catalyst that awakened many to the influence of sociological factors in academic disciplines. An academic position might have been obtained because of dedication—read loyalty—to a certain method, for example, and one's identity among colleagues may be largely the product of one's methodological orientation. From a Kuhnian perspective, then, a processualist or post-processualist might feel particularly uncomfortable with the categories of an opposing paradigm, and disoriented professionally as well as intellectually when incorporating elements from another camp.

The psychological and sociological insights of the paradigmatic view do throw light on dimensions of scientific and intellectual work that are largely ignored in the other views of science. The only other approach in which considerable attention is given to such factors is the anarchic view discussed in Chapter 7. In the anarchic picture of science, however, nonintellectual factors are emphasized to the point where methodological guidelines are declared useless and even harmful for making decisions about theories.

Psychological and sociological dimensions of method application

Method is prescriptive: It provides guidelines that indicate how decisions about theories *ought* to be made. The context for applying method, however, is complicated by numerous factors that can facilitate, hinder, or abort the application of method. Not the least of those factors are the psychological predispositions of an investigator and the sociological milieu in which he or she operates. The goal is to use such extra-methodological elements where they can enhance the application of method but counter those elements where they hinder the application of method. Here is an example.

Suppose a processual archaeologist is attempting to explain a rather sudden change in social organization with systemic approaches, that is, with approaches that highlight internal dynamics rather than exogenous forces. An anomaly appears: The systemic explanation implies conditions that are inconsistent with the artifactual record. Specifically, the artifactual record suggests a more sudden and different type of transformation than can be incorporated within the systemic model. The upshot is that the systemic explanation seems erroneous in some way.

The archaeologist has been working within the North American processual "paradigm" for many years, but is aware that systemic models do not incorporate the potential consequences of new ideas and innovations as sources of change in societies. The archaeologist wants to explore the possibility that a major conceptual transformation led to the anomalous change.

It would be difficult to find fault with the methodological reasoning of this archaeologist. The trouble is that the new type of theory—a theory about cognition—is at odds with the accepted processual paradigm. When the archaeologist suggests the cognitive approach to a processual colleague not sold on the new cognitive phase within the field, the proposal is dismissed as being dangerously close to what the colleague calls the "subjective theoretical mush" that has been gaining ground within the profession. Furthermore, the colleague states that taking such an approach would be more than just fruitless; it would likely put a question mark beside the professional reputation of an archaeologist. Needless to say, the archaeologist feels a bit insecure about exploring a type of theory with which he or she is not familiar and to which associates are hostile. In the face of these sociological pressures and psychological doubts, what should be done?

In this case it would be appropriate to break from at least one bastion of the North American processual paradigm—the allegiance to theories that disallow cognitive and other elements of human agency in explaining change. The processual paradigm need not be discarded as a whole, however. The goal—explaining change—could certainly remain intact. So could the methodological guideline to form theories—in this case a theory incorporating cognition—that can be tested against the artifactual record. In short, the archaeologist need not be imprisoned by the processual "paradigm," nor need he reject it entirely. It would be best to alter some assumptions in the North American processual paradigm while continuing to embrace others.

It is perhaps too easy from a philosophical distance to recommend the theoretical path an archaeologist should follow. Setting out on the path suggested may force him or her into battles against the psychological tendencies and sociological pressures captured in Kuhn's description of science. With sound methodological reasons for following that path, however, the archaeologist should pursue it. If he or she were familiar with the paradigmatic view of science, the psychological and sociological barriers would at least come as no surprise. Breaching them is never easy, but familiarity with them should help.

Incidentally, as more people act on methodological reasoning rather than succumbing to the psychological and sociological pressures, the easier it becomes for others to do likewise. An archaeologist willing to counter pressures that detract from sensible reasoning about theories is also setting conditions that will make it easier for others to do the same. A daring thinker can bring out the courage in others.

Comments on processual approaches to cognition will conclude this example. As pointed out earlier, exploring the thoughts, decisions, and actions of individuals by use of theories testable against the artifactual record is indeed capturing the interest of some processualists. Reconstructing prehistoric cognition within processual constraints was the subject of that conference on cognitive archaeology in Cambridge, England, in April 1990. A forthcoming volume with the papers from that conference has the tentative title, *The Ancient Mind: Elements of Cognitive Archaeology* (Renfrew and Zubrow 1993). Another conference exploring the incorporation of semiotic, symbolic, and structural elements into archaeological theories was held in Bloomington, Indiana, in 1987. Papers from that conference were published in a volume entitled *Representations in Archaeology* (Gardin and Peebles 1992). Finally, methodological individualism provides the philosophical and methodological framework for testable studies of the thoughts, decisions, and actions of people. Methodological individualism is the topic of Chapter 8.

A lack of methodological guidelines

Despite the insights into extra-methodological forces working within an intellectual community, there is an enormous drawback to the paradigmatic view: It does not provide prescriptive guidelines. As argued earlier, method provides guidelines that indicate how decisions ought to be made. The prior example illuminates that point: The archaeologist used sound methodological reasoning to make decisions about a processual theory, but the guidelines for his or her reasoning did *not* stem from the paradigmatic view. As a matter-of-fact, decisions would have to be made *in spite of* the implications of the paradigmatic view. The latter would have encouraged him or her to remain committed to all the tenants of the processual framework or to abandon it in toto. Neither would have been a sound choice. Furthermore, some processualists and postprocessualists are willing to abandon their monolithic "paradigms," a point that became clear at the 1989 Theoretical Archaeology Group Conference. Such daring is to be encouraged on methodological grounds, but it would not be feasible from a paradigmatic perspective.

   That the paradigmatic view does not provide helpful method for making decisions about theories is hardly surprising. Kuhn wanted to describe how theoretical frameworks change, but his historical reconstruction is largely psychological and sociological. Very little if any specific attention was given to method and how it may have been instrumental in the development of science. Even though Kuhn's description does include rational elements, his characterization of the latter is confined to the "macro-level." It does not entail guidelines helpful for making decisions about particular theories in a specific contexts. In short, his goal was not to *prescribe* how theoretic decisions ought to be made. By way of contrast, the refutationist view discussed in the upcoming chapter provides some of the most useful prescriptive guidelines for making decisions about theories.

Suggested Readings

The central book annotated here is Thomas Kuhn's widely read exposition of the paradigmatic view. The remaining three readings include a variety of perspectives on Kuhn. They explore such diverse topics as the difficulties in understanding the paradigmatic view, the deleterious consequences of the paradigmatic vision, the importance of Kuhn's psychological insights into science, the significance of his insights into the sociological forces active in scientific communities, and the impact of the paradigmatic view on the social sciences.

1. Barry Barnes, 1982, *T. S. Kuhn and Social Science.*
Thomas Kuhn has repeatedly asserted that his paradigmatic view developed from his studies of the history of the physical sciences and was not intended to provide a statement about the social sciences. Nevertheless, Kuhn's influence on the social sciences seems to have been considerably greater than on the physical sciences. Barnes traces the many significant implications of Thomas Kuhn's work on the social sciences. It is a short book that is clear and well-organized.

2. Jane H. Kelley and Marsha P. Hanen, 1988, *Archaeology and the Methodology of Science.*
Kelley and Hanen's book contains a well-organized and reasonably brief exposition of Kuhn's view of science. Inspired by Kuhn's insights into the sociology of scientific communities, the authors also make a penetrating analysis of the sociological influences that shape the career paths of archaeologists.

3. Thomas Kuhn, 1962, *The Structure of Scientific Revolutions*.

This is the book that articulates the paradigmatic view of science. It is well-organized and can be read quite quickly. It is also readily available in paperback.

4. Imre Lakatos, and Alan Musgrave, eds., 1970, *Criticism and the Growth of Knowledge*.

The essays in this collection are generally quite critical of the paradigmatic view although some do include commentary on its strengths. A number of essays merit particular attention. In "Normal Science and Its Dangers" Karl Popper discusses the relativistic theses in Kuhn's view of science. In "The Nature of Paradigm," Margaret Masterman explores the ambiguity of the concept "paradigm," confusion about which continues to plague discussions of Kuhn's work. "Reflections on My Critics" is a compilation of Kuhn's rejoinders to numerous interpretations and criticisms of his paradigmatic view. Kuhn's interpretation of his own work in this essay is closer to the rational interpretation than is apparent in *The Structure of Scientific Revolutions*.

Chapter 6   The Refutationist View of Science

Themes from the refutationist view of science dominate the methodological recommendations in this book. Indeed, refutationist ideas so dominate the arguments as to how archaeologists ought make decisions about theories that the entire book can be viewed as a core of refutationist recommendations and refutationist criticisms modified by contributions from other views of science.

Given that the book is largely refutationist, a separate chapter on refutationist method might seem redundant, but this brief chapter is being included for a number of reasons. First, familiarity with at least some of the historical roots of a view of science and its method can help one better understand why they have taken the shape they have. That is as true for the refutationist view as for any other. Second, understanding the problem-situations from which the refutationist view emerged will help one better understand its limitations. The strengths of the refutationist view are touted throughout this book, but its weaknesses have only been mentioned in passing. This chapter will provide opportunity to discuss more directly some of the potential difficulties that can be encountered when applying refutationist method. Third and finally, the story behind the rise of the refutationist view is interesting in itself, at least to me. I hope it might be the same for archaeologists.

Before beginning, I wish to emphasize that the account of the refutationist view in this chapter is no more "purist" than have been the accounts of other views of science and method in this book. "Purist" roughly means "as usually understood by academic philosophers strongly committed to defending a view." Indeed, purist presentations can be less than helpful when the goal is to sharpen ones skills in applying method. Recall some of the reasons discussed earlier in the book. Refutationist or otherwise, methodological views tend to be molded around logical and other abstract problem-situations encountered in academic philosophy rather than around the actual problem-situations faced by practitioners. Purist presentations also ride roughshod over the fact that method is a tool, and that use of productive tools from one tradition should by no means obviate use of worthwhile tools from other traditions as well.

Introduction

When classical induction fell back to probabilistic induction there was no longer hope that science could be justified as absolute truth. If not absolute truth, though, what is science? A different answer is provided by each of the views proposed since classical induction. The most important have been probabilistic induction, positivism, the paradigmatic view, the refutationist view, and the anarchic view. Unique among them is the refutationist view because error, instead of being undesirable, is recognized as the principal vehicle in the search for better theories, or "moving toward the truth."

The principal themes in the refutationist view were formulated by Karl Popper in the early part of the twentieth century. The collapse of Newtonianism left induction particularly vulnerable. The refutationist view became a contender to replace it.

According to the refutationist view, science includes conjectures that are *refutable*—vulnerable to empirical error. Science advances by discovering error and then adjusting theories, or finding new theories, which overcome the error but which themselves remain refutable. Science is not truth, then, but the pursuit of the truth by overcoming mistakes.

The goal of science is to progress: to generate theories that are closer to the empirical truth. The goal of science is *not* to justify theories, as in induction. From the refutationist perspective, inductive attempts to establish the truth or probable truth of theories are dysfunctional. The reasons were given earlier but are summarized here: Truth in the absolute sense cannot be assured, epistemological probabilities cannot be calculated, belief in epistemological probabilities encourages acceptance of possible but improbable anomaly, attempts to establish theories do not necessarily improve theories or aid in the search for better theories, and attempts to establish theories inductively could only be done after important theory development has been completed. The emergence of the refutationist view was intertwined with these difficulties and other factors as well.

The Emergence of the Refutationist View

The historical scene for the emergence of the refutationist view was dominated by developments in physics, inductive theory, and philosophy shortly after the turn of the twentieth century. These important influences were discussed in the historical reconstruction of induction in Chapter 4. Additional props in the historical staging of the refutationist view that were not mentioned in that chapter are depth psychology and Marxist interpretations of history. Proponents of depth psychology and Marxist interpretations of history claimed their fields were "scientific," although Popper was skeptical. To prepare for a discussion of depth psychology and Marxist interpretations of history we need to revisit physics in the early twentieth century.

Physics and inductive theory in the early twentieth century

The establishment of the special and general theories of relativity in the early decades of the twentieth century marked the end of the Newtonian era. It might also have ended the reign of inductive theory, but it did not. Three reasons for the survival of inductive theory were discussed in Chapter 4, namely, the rise of the Copenhagen interpretation in physics, the resultant modification of induction into positivism, and the philosophical drive to banish bombastic metaphysics. Induction also survived Einstein's wariness of probabilism.

Certainly, Einstein respected the empirical foundations of science, but was renowned for his personal distaste for empirical work. His discoveries were made through *thought experiment*, that is, hypothetical experiments in which the implications of theories are traced and assessed. This pattern of discovery is distant from the inductive formula, which consists of doing empirical research and generalizing explanations from the research. In addition, the relativity theories made no appeal to the probabilistic justification that is a hallmark of contemporary induction. Furthermore, Einstein was antagonistic to the probabilistic interpretations emerging in subatomic physics. His exclamation that he could not believe that "God plays dice with the world" is so well-known that it has become popular lore (Frank 1947: 208). In sum, inductive theory survived in spite of, not because of, developments in relativity physics. What buttressed the methodological status of induction were developments in subatomic physics.

Recall that the Copenhagen interpretation underwrote the positivistic modification of induction. A facet of the Copenhagen interpretation not addressed in Chapter 4 can now be conveniently discussed: the correspondence principle.

The first theories in subatomic physics were formulated not long after the First World War. One of the most important was the correspondence principle put forth by the Dane Niels Bohr. The *correspondence principle* entails that a discrete packet of energy—a "quantum" of energy—emitted from or absorbed by an atom "corresponds" (is equal to) a change in the energy level of an electron orbit around the nucleus of an atom. The correspondence principle provided a beacon for studying events within an atom. By linking phenomena observable external to atoms (quanta of energy) to events internal to atoms (changes in orbital energy levels), events occurring inside atoms could be explored by observation of phenomena outside of atoms. Specifically, measuring energy absorption by an atom or energy emission from an atom became the handle for diagnosing what was occurring within an atom.

The correspondence principle was accepted quickly and still survives as one of the pillars of subatomic physics. The trouble is that the correspondence principle is also confused with Bohr's principle of complementarity. A methodological implication of the principle of complementarity was highly undesirable, however: that inconsistent theories are acceptable.

The success of Bohr's correspondence principle, and the tendency to confuse it with one of the pillars of the Copenhagen interpretation, are further reasons (in addition to the reasons cited in Chapter 4) for the popularity of the latter. Remember that the Copenhagen interpretation was a major factor in buttressing inductive theory after the downfall of Newtonianism. Although the methodological assumptions of the Copenhagen interpretation later lost favor, the induction with which it was associated provided Popper with a thriving rather than dying target for criticism.

Karl Popper in Vienna

As a young man in Vienna during and after World War I, three disparate intellectual currents attracted Popper's attention (Popper 1962; Schilpp 1974). First was the general theory of relativity recently proposed by Einstein and corroborated by Arthur Eddington's measurement of spatial curve shortly after the war. These were matters addressed in Chapter 4. Second was the depth psychology of the Freudian school. Popper was himself particularly interested in the theory of complexes of Alfred Adler, with whom he had worked in poorer areas of Vienna. Third was the materialist interpretation of history embraced by Marxists. Marxist theory was raising excitement among intellectuals and provided the inspiration for communist political and social ideology. During the collapse of the old social order in the aftermath of the First World War, Marxist philosophy and communist ideology were being seriously entertained as replacements.

Popper was intrigued that all three sets of ideas—the relativity theories, depth psychology, and Marxist interpretations—were thought to merit scientific status. He believed that the relativity theories were scientific. In Popper's view, some themes in depth psychology and materialist interpretations were contributions to knowledge, but he did not think they should be designated as scientific. Popper thus posed the question: What demarcates the relativity theories from depth psychology and Marxist interpretations? Underlying this question was another: What demarcates science from nonscience?

Popper's answer was that scientific theories are *refutable*—vulnerable to empirical error—whereas nonscientific theories are not vulnerable to empirical error. Specifically, the relativity theories were vulnerable to tests that potentially could have *refuted* or *falsified* them, even though such tests were passed. Theories in depth psychology and Marxism, on the other hand, were either nonrefutable or were refuted and then preserved by ad hoc adjustment.

The theories in depth psychology seemed to explain any human behavior, including behavioral patterns that are inconsistent with each other. For example, inspired and prodigious practice on a piano could be attributed to a person's complex about music, but avoiding the piano entirely could also be explained by the same complex. Far from being refutable, then, Adler's theory could be confirmed by any empirical data. This meant that no empirical data could serve as counterevidence.

Unlike Adler's theory of complexes, Popper believed that dialectical materialism was refutable. It had also been refuted, in Popper's view, because the development of communism had not followed the path predicted by Marx. The best-known example is Marx's prediction that the change to collective socialism would take place in the most industrialized countries first, such as England or Prussia. That the revolution took place in largely agrarian Russia refuted that prediction. Lenin explained away the anomaly with his famous "weak-link" hypothesis: The revolution would occur where differences between classes were most exacerbated. In his view the class antagonisms were greatest between the peasants and aristocracy in Russia. This ad hoc modification of Marxist theory explained the anomaly, but by decreasing the testability of the theory. Remember that explaining away anomaly by ad hoc hypotheses will preserve a theory, but the decrease in testability will lessen or close off the potential for further understanding and insight. That is why ad hoc adjustments can turn theories into dogma.

In short, the relativity theories had been put to risky tests—tests that they could have failed. That they survived those tests made them much more credible than theories that could not run risky tests (such as some in depth psychology) or that failed tests but were modified by ad hoc procedures (such as some in Marxism).

It should be noted that "metaphysical theory" has a different meaning for Popperians. Popper and his followers use the expression *metaphysical theory* to mean a nonrefutable theory. This is a *logical* definition of metaphysical theory: It is based upon the logical property of nonrefutability. As discussed earlier in the book, a "metaphysical theory" ordinarily means a theory about ultimate structure, including causal relations. One example is the Newtonian theory of atoms and empty space, and how those play a role in such theories as gravitation and inertia. Another example is the Freudian theory that the human psyche is composed of id, superego, and ego, and how those components interact. Many theories qualify as metaphysical under both the logical definition and the ordinary definition. The Freudian theory of the psyche is an example: It is both nonrefutable and is a theory about ultimate structure. Others that are metaphysical in the ordinary sense are refutable, and hence not metaphysical in the logical sense. The Newtonian theory of atoms and empty space is an example.

Popper of course exhorts us to formulate and interpret any non-refutable theories as refutable, whether they be metaphysical (in the ordinary sense) or otherwise. Tim Earle did just that. Remember how he reinterpreted some nonrefutable elements in Wittfogel's hydraulic theory so that they became refutable. Popper's exhortation is certainly desirable. On the other hand, potential verbal confusion could be avoided if Popper had not usurped the expression "metaphysical" as a label for any nonrefutable theory. Using Popper's terminology, for example, the nonrefutable components of Wittfogel's hydraulic theory might lead one to call his hydraulic theory "metaphysical." That label for Wittfogel's hydraulic theory would certainly be confusing to anyone not familiar with Popperian terminology.

Popper's refutability criterion for demarcating science from non-science is not in itself valuable. By itself the distinction would only be used to designate what is science and what it is not. It was argued earlier that categorizing theories as scientific or nonscientific is of no intrinsic importance in advancing knowledge. It can actually be harmful by deflecting attention from more significant aspects of theory development. Popper's demarcation criterion between science and nonscience did, however, become a productive tool for work on a multitude of problems concerning the nature of science and knowledge. Actually, the entire *corpus* of Popperian philosophical work can be understood as the product of using the refutability criterion to propose solutions to problems in physical science, biological science, sociology, psychology, social theory, and political philosophy. Next is a brief discussion of how Popper used his demarcation criterion to dissolve the problem of induction. Ideas that emerged in his dissolution of the problem of induction were subsequently used in the formulation of the refutationist view of science.

Dissolving the Problem of Induction

The *problem of induction* is the problem of how to justify the truth of explanations when the latter are interpreted as generalizations from factual statements. The problem of induction has fascinated philosophers since the eighteenth century. It arose from David Hume's convincing argument that ideas induced from facts could not be justified as truth. The problem of induction has been reformulated many times, and in many ways. Even a summary of the proposed solutions would be voluminous. Popper reformulated the problem in a way that does capture its thrust, in my view, and then dissolved it (Popper 1962).

Popper restructured the problem of induction as follows: How can factual statements establish the truth-value of explanations? To answer, he split the question into two parts. First, How can factual statements establish the *truth* of explanations? And second, how can factual statements establish the *falsity* of explanations?

The first question *is* the problem of induction as normally understood. Popper argued that there is no adequate answer to it. However, there is an answer to the second question. The first question cannot be answered adequately because factual statements cannot establish the truth of explanations. The logical step necessary to establish—justify—explanations by factual statements is called the *fallacy of affirming the consequent*. This fallacy has the following structure:

P implies Q

Q————————

Therefore P.

The fallacy of affirming the consequent does not guarantee the truth of the conclusion (P) even if both the premises ("P implies Q" and "Q") were true. Here is an example: If raining implies that the ground is wet, and one observes that the ground is wet, must it be true that it has rained? The answer is no. The ground could be wet without having had rain: A sprinkler system might have been on, for example, or a fire hydrant might have burst open or a river might have flooded. The point is that data cannot be used to establish the truth of the theory.

The answer to the second question is that a factual statement can be used to establish the falsity of explanations. The logical principle is valid and is called *modus tollens*. *Modus tollens* has the following structure:

P implies Q

Not Q————————

Therefore not P.

Unlike with the fallacy of affirming the consequent, the truth of the conclusion does follow if the premises were both true. Here is an example: If raining implies the ground is wet and the ground is not wet, must it be true that there has been no rain? The answer is yes, and in all instances. *Modus tollens* is not a fallacy, but a valid form of reasoning from premises to a conclusion. The point is that data can be used to refute a theory.

In sum, then, the answer to the first question is that *factual statements cannot establish the truth of explanations*, but the answer to the second question is that *factual statements can be used to refute explanations*. The problem of induction—captured in the first question—cannot be solved because its solution would require use of a logical fallacy.

In addition to showing that the problem of induction cannot be solved, Popper also *dissolved* the problem of induction. The problem of induction is dissolved because attempting to establish the truth of theories is unimportant. The route to theory improvement is not to establish the truth of theories, but to find error in theories. Popper's demarcation criterion thus led to his dissolution of the problem of induction, and both provided the seeds that grew into his refutationist view of science.

The Refutationist View of Science

The goal of science is to progress: to discover theories that are better than received theories. Better theories are found by discovery of error in received theories, and exploitation of error to search for theories that supersede the error.

Theories should be tested at points where they are vulnerable to error. Two outcomes are possible. A theory can be found correct at a vulnerable point; that is, it can be *corroborated*. Or a theory can be found mistaken at a point where it is vulnerable; that is, be *refuted*, or *falsified*. Corroboration should generate more confidence in a theory because it has passed test(s) where it might have failed. Like virtue, theories are more valuable after having met challenges. Refuting a theory at a test point is important for several reasons: It indicates where the theory is weak, and also provides a point where a revised or new theory should be corroborated. Science progresses when more highly corroborated theories replace refuted theories.

The brief synopsis of the refutationist view is given here simply to pull together some basic ideas that inform this entire book. The details are much more involved, even when the focus is largely confined to those refutationist themes important for applying refutationist method in practice (as in this book). In the remainder of this chapter I will amplify one refutationist theme only tangentially addressed earlier—the relationship between refutability and realism—and discuss some limitations of the refutationist view, especially when it is applied to a field such as archaeology.

Refutability and Realism

Popper always assumed that scientific explanations were about the real world, even though his more explicit discussions of realism came later (Popper 1959, 1962, 1972, 1983). More specifically, Popper assumed that scientists aim to describe how the world actually works and interpret theories as if they are about the actual world. Over and above the aim of many scientists and how scientists interpret theories, however, there is a quite simple argument as to why scientific theories can yield knowledge of the real world. The gist of the argument is as follows.

Refutable theories imply points that potentially clash with the real world. The more highly refutable a theory, the more points it implies that could clash with the real world or the more easily its points could clash with the real world. When a theory is corroborated—when it is tested at a refutable point and passes the test—it thus reveals something about the real world, at least at the point(s) where it was tested successfully. The more highly corroborated a theory, then, the more it reveals about the real world. On the other hand, when a theory is refuted—when it is tested at a refutable point and fails the test—it is shown incorrect about the real world at that point. Nevertheless, if a modified theory or new theory is corroborated at the same point, the modified or new theory reveals something about the real world that the initial theory did not. At least at such a point the modified or new theory has more to say about the real world; it is a "better" or "more progressive" theory. A number of comments are in order.

First, the key to the potential for theories to reveal something about reality is that theories be refutable. That seems obvious from the chain of reasoning just mentioned, but it cannot be emphasized enough. From a refutationist perspective, this means that theories in archaeology or any other field are potentially about the real world as long as they are testable. They reveal something about the real world when they pass tests or when they fail tests.

Second, corroborated theories reveal only something about the real world. Theories are composed of many statements, some implicit and some explicit. The combinations of statements that constitute a theory have many implications, and only *some* of those implications will be testable. Corroboration of a theory at test point(s) will reveal reality at those point(s), but one cannot be sure about the remainder of the theory. The latter will be consistent with reality revealed at the test point(s), so long as the theory itself is consistent, but so could other theories. In short, then, corroborated theories reveal parts of reality and a picture that is consistent with its corroborated points.

Third, the potential for theories to reveal reality certainly must have existed long before anyone knew anything about the refutationist view of science, or even scientific method for that matter. All that is required is that theories be testable, and pass at least some tests. Closer to home, testable theories in archaeology have almost certainly been revealing something about reality before, during, and after the positivist—anti-realist—fashion in methodological discussions.

In sum, as long as theories are refutable and are tested they can tell us something about the real world, or they can tell us where theories clash with the real world. In the latter case they can lead to modified or new theories that tell us more about the real world. That is why a realist interpretation of theories is always appropriate from a refutationist perspective. Furthermore, all the methodological challenges to realism did not and would not hinder the development of realist theories in practice *unless* such discussions had or would lead to compromising the development of refutable theories. Of course some archaeologists have compromised the development of refutable theories by taking methodological positions that challenge the importance of testability. That will be discussed in the next chapter. For the most part, fortunately, the compromise has not taken place. If the arguments in this book are correct, the New Archaeology has led in practice to increased development and testing of refutable theories, that is, to theories that reveal more about what really happened in the past.

Some Limitations of the Refutationist Approach

The refutationist view of science is focused on a worthwhile goal: Development of theory. Theory development, the generation of new understanding and insight, is enhanced when explanations serve as stepping-stones to other theories. In order to serve as stepping-stones, theories must be refutable. These broad features of the refutationist view are, I hope, very clear by now.

The refutationist approach also offers workable guidelines for searching out and exploiting error in received theories. Furthermore, the attitude toward error—that it is actually desirable and should be exploited—is a healthy relief from the inductive tendency to regard error as sin. These many advantages will become evident again in Chapter 8, where refutationist method is hammered into tools useful for developing at least some types of theories that incorporate human agency.

Despite the advantages of refutationist method, however, it does not provide methodological tools to meet all issues important for theory development in a field such as archaeology. Four limitations are discussed here: (1) Explanations testable in a particular context are not always testable in other contexts; (2) testability is not a criterion that can be used uncritically when selecting high-level theories; (3) refutationist method does not provide adequate criteria for deciding when refuted theories should be maintained and when they should be rejected; and (4) the refutationist view does not adequately encourage the generation of competing theories nor provide an account of how competing theories benefit theory development.

Testability and context

Explanations that can be tested, revised, and retested in a particular archaeological context cannot always be generalized for testing in other contexts. If such theories are generalized anyway, they may not lead to any new understanding and insight. Recall in Chapter 3 how the universalization of Wittfogel's theory enabled it to be tested in contexts far beyond the Asian one in which it was initially formulated and tested. As a matter-of-fact, the testability of Wittfogel's hydraulic theory in other contexts was a crucial reason why it contributed so much to theory development. Earle's explanation of the role of hydraulic activity in Hawaii, for example, grew from his refutation of Wittfogel's theory.

Earle's new and rather elaborate explanation of the role of hydraulic activities in social organization in one area of Hawaii was tested against the artifactual data from that context. His explanation passed the tests and was thus corroborated in that context. What I found bothersome, however, is that Earle's new theory does not seem generalizable so that it can be tested in other contexts. Earle did not even intend to make a claim such as "in all cases where there is significant large-scale hydraulic activity, the latter will reinforce social organization that is already in place prior to it." If Earle were to have made such a generalization it would have been quickly refuted; Wittfogel's own studies in Asia would have refuted it, as would other studies. In that case, however, nothing more would be known than prior to the generalization.

Incidentally, Earle's theory could certainly be suggestive for those developing explanations in other contexts. In that way Earle's theory could indirectly lead to new understanding and insight, but again in a localized context rather than a universalized one. It should be added that many other theories might be suggestive as well, including those that are inconsistent with Earle's. In any case, that theories successfully tested in some localized contexts can be suggestive for theorizing in other localized contexts is not the same as universalizing a theory for potential testing in all other relevant contexts. That is why such theories are unlikely to lead to as much new understanding and insight as universalized theories like Wittfogel's.

In brief, not all explanations of archaeological events can be successfully generalized for testing in other contexts. If they were so generalized, they might not contribute any more than what was known already. For a purist in the refutationist camp, that would be a severe handicap. Purists would likely even object to calling such localized and non-generalizable theorizing "Popperian" or "refutationist" even though the theorizing might be testable in a particular context. In my view, however, the difficulty is simply a limitation of the use of refutationist method in a field like archaeology. Perhaps the same limitation would apply for use of refutationist method in other social sciences, although that is a matter that lies beyond the scope of this book.

Testability and high-level theories

The high-level theories that inform development of explanations in the middle range can have a major influence on the testability of those middle-range explanations. Recall, for example, the two classic high-level theories that inform explanations of the formation of state structure: conflict theory and integration theory. It was argued in Chapter 3 that conflict theory can yield more highly testable explanations than can integration theory. The former identify one or a very few elements as causes, and imply that the existence of those causes will inevitably—universally—lead to state structure. That conflict theories normally entail only one or a few causes, and that they are so readily universalizable, enables them to be tested quite severely and in numerous contexts. On the other hand, the variety and multiplicity of causes in typical integration theories, along with the lack of inevitability about where those causes may lead, discourages or even forecloses on testability beyond the context in which an integration theory is generated.

If the selection of a high-level theory can have such a bearing on the testability of explanations informed by it, and if testability is so important for gaining understanding and insight into what happened in the past, the conclusion would seem obvious: Select only those high-level theories that will yield testable explanations at the middle range. Certainly there is much to be said for that conclusion; the importance of testability is underscored many times over in this book. I might add that the conclusion is a clear and inviolable mandate in the North American New Archaeology. Narrative histories and explanations that incorporate individualistic elements, for example, are informed by models that indeed do not readily yield testable explanations. That, in a nutshell, is why those in the North American camp exclude high-level models that would generate them.

But wait. Testability is very important, but it is not exclusively important. At least some events might have been unique, and narrative histories might at least explain them. Also, some events might have been influenced or even caused by the ideas and decisions of prehistoric peoples. To disallow high-level models that exclude such possibilities would be to shut the door on the study of possible realities in archaeological contexts. That consequence of the North American position might not be intentional, but it is not comforting either.

My suggestion is this. Attempt to select high-level models that yield testable explanations. All things being equal, select those models that yield the most testable explanations. On the other hand, if there are events that can be explained adequately only by using high-level models that yield less testable or nontestable theories, then use them with the following critical qualification: A high-level model should yield testable explanations at least in the context for which an explanation is generated. In other words, the models should yield testable explanations at the local level even if testing them beyond the local context is not feasible or is not productive.

If the qualification that theories be at least locally testable cannot be met, then there is one last viable option: An explanation should be very carefully induced from available artifactual data and should be very carefully stated so that it makes no claims beyond the range of its data and other statements strictly inferred from its data. This latter approach is inductive, and is not simply guesswork. This is the approach that will be taken in Chapter 9, which concerns theories about prehistoric cognition.

If the inductive option cannot be met, then I do recommend that speculation be curtailed, at least in a professional context. If not curtailed, I see no way to separate fantasizing from theorizing.

Rejection of theories

In his early work Popper devised conventions by which theories would be rejected if they were refuted (Popper 1959; Lakatos 1970). He later recognized that refuted theories should not necessarily be rejected. Two reasons emerge from the refutationist perspective. First, auxiliary hypotheses might be added to a refuted theory; retesting might then corroborate the reformulated theory. Second, even if a theory cannot be reformulated and tested with auxiliary hypotheses, it might still yield new understanding and insight despite being mistaken at some point(s). In short, it is important not to reject theories too easily. In refutationist jargon, it is important that at least some people maintain theories *tenaciously*.

The trouble is that refutationist method provides no clear criteria for deciding when refuted theories should be tenaciously maintained and when they should be rejected. Refutationist method does provide some abstract guidelines, to be sure: Be cautious about rejecting theories before adjustments and retesting lead to further refutation, and do abandon theories when they continue to fail tests after adjustment. Nevertheless, these abstract guidelines are difficult if not impossible to use as criteria in an applied context for deciding at what point a refuted theory should finally be rejected.

Incidentally, refutationist method is not alone in lacking applicable criteria for deciding when to reject theories. Neither the inductive nor the paradigmatic view provides such criteria, and neither does the anarchic view (discussed in the next chapter). The challenge is being put to the refutationist view, however, because it underlies the methodological approach endorsed in this book. The inductive, paradigmatic, and anarchic views are all heavily criticized in this book for other reasons anyway. Clearly they are not being endorsed as methodological frameworks for most work in archaeology.

There is a fallback position in the refutationist framework for dealing with the problem of deciding when to reject theories. It is this: In a community of investigators, it is desirable that some maintain refuted theories tenaciously and that others reject refuted theories. By pursuing both options, there is a much better chance that further benefits of a refuted theory will be realized, and that the benefits of exploring alternative theories will also be realized.

The modified position might be the best available even if it does not yield definite criteria for when theories ought be maintained and when they ought be rejected. The modified position does raise another difficulty in the refutationist framework, however; it presupposes the existence of multiple theories competing with each other, yet it does not directly encourage the generation of multiple and competing theories nor does it provide an adequate account of how competing theories benefit theory development.

Competing theories

Refutationist tools are designed to structure and assess an explanation in isolation from the surrounding theoretical landscape. That is a problem for a number of reasons. Testability is not entirely independent of other theories. Competing theories play a significant role in revealing possible error in other theories, and hence places where other theories should be tested. Competing theories are also necessary for rejection; theories are not rejected unless there are alternatives to replace them (Lakatos 1970). Finally, competing theories are necessary if a community of investigators is to reap the benefits of maintaining refuted theories as well as exploring alternative theories.

Weaknesses in a given theory are often only seen from the perspective of an alternative theory. The Michelson-Morley experiment in the nineteenth century suggested that light speed might not change. That is why the experiment is often interpreted as proof of the absolute speed of light and as a refutation of the theory (associated with Newtonianism) that light speed is additive. Historically, however, the Michelson-Morley experiment was designed to answer a millennia-old metaphysical question that also cropped up in Newtonianism: Is there an ether, or is there empty space? The experiment provided no clear answer to that question. The point is that interpretation of the Michelson-Morley experiment as a refutation of the additive theory of light speed only became acceptable when another theory about the speed of light (the absolute speed of the relativity theories) became available (Lakatos 1970).

Not only is empirical weakness difficult to recognize without the perspective of competing theories, but a theory will seldom if ever be abandoned unless there are alternatives to replace it. Newton's physics persisted despite many anomalies until the relativity theories were available. The evidence that mounted against the classical diffusionist theory because of radiocarbon dating in the 1950s was formidable, but it is difficult to imagine diffusionist theory being rejected without processual theories available as replacements.

Finally, as argued in the previous subsection, it is desirable that some investigators maintain refuted theories and that others reject them in favor of alternative theories. Such is not possible if there are no competing theories.

In brief, competing theories are crucial for recognizing anomalies in theories and for interpreting anomalies as refutations. Furthermore, anomalous data will seldom if ever lead to rejection of a theory unless there are plausible alternatives to take its place. Finally, competing theories are necessary if refuted theories are to be maintained by some but rejected in favor of alternative theories by others.

In conclusion, refutationist method does not encourage the generation of competing theories, nor does it account for the interplay between competing theories when they are generated. Other methodological tools are needed for these purposes. The anarchist view of knowledge provides them.

Suggested Readings

Testability is the most important concept in this book. The theory of testability used here emerges largely from the refutationist view of science. The reading selections for this chapter present and expound upon testability in the refutationist tradition.

1. Imre Lakatos, 1970, "Falsification and the Methodology of Scientific Research Programmes."
This essay recounts some misinterpretations as well as criticisms of the refutationist view. It also outlines a number of different interpretations and elaborations of the refutationist view.

2. Karl R. Popper, 1959, *The Logic of Scientific Discovery*.
Karl Popper's systematic formulation of the refutationist view of science is contained in this book, a translation of the German original of 1933. The arguments are sometimes quite complicated, but they are clear and so is the logical flow. Most issues are addressed in a manner more suited to professional philosophers than other scholars. Nevertheless, the implications of Popper's ideas for the practice of science are quite apparent and are frequently drawn out explicitly.

3. Karl R. Popper, 1962, *Conjectures and Refutations: The Growth of Scientific Knowledge*.
The essays in this collection highlight major themes in the refutationist view of science and explore its political and social implications. There are many arguments, but most are not overburdened with detail. These essays are preferable to *The Logic of Scientific Discovery* as an introduction to Popper's refutationist view, and to sample its intellectual ramifications for science and society.

Chapter 7   The Anarchic View of Science

The watchword of the anarchic vision is *anti-method*. Method constrains the development of theory: Methodological standards ossify the authority of received theories and inhibit consideration of novel ones. To advance knowledge, then, methodological considerations should be abandoned. Put positively, *anything goes* when formulating and supporting theory: fallacious reasoning, suppression of anomalous data, ad hoc adjustments, and deliberate propaganda.

The anarchic view of science is at odds with a book that advocates the use of method for making decisions about theories. Nevertheless, a brief discussion should be included. The anarchic view is the only one that rigorously exposes the limitations and abuses of method. Thus far in this book methodological views have served as positions from which to shed light on the limitations of alternative approaches. An example was seen in the last chapter, where the refutationist perspective was used to expose weaknesses in induction. The anarchic view, however, is the only one from which an assault has been launched on the use of *any* method whatsoever. A keen awareness of methodological misuse is particularly valuable for archaeologists. Without data that can be regenerated, and with the problematic status of much of the available artifactual data, archaeologists are forced to be especially cautious when generating and testing theories relevant to that data.

The anarchic view makes a number of other contributions. It reveals the complexity of theory formation—the "context of discovery"—that is largely ignored by the inductivist and refutationist approaches and is only partly addressed in the paradigmatic view.

Finally and most importantly, the anarchic view is the only one that emphasizes the importance of multiple and competing theories in the advance of knowledge.

To the contributions of the anarchic vision must be added a most disturbing drawback. It is assumed that no intellectual criteria are reliable for evaluating theories, or for judging among them. In other words, the anarchic vision implies relativism: the view that no theory can be "objectively" judged better than any other theory.

Although few if any archaeologists dare embrace relativism explicitly, anarchic themes—including relativism—are apparent in some of the postprocessual literature. The goals and approaches of postprocessual archaeologists vary, but they share skepticism or outright rejection of the scientific underpinnings of processual archaeology. Assaults on scientific standards usually foreshadow relativism. Testability is a casualty even if the attacks do not lead to full-blown relativism.

The initial task in this chapter is to trace the principal themes of the anarchic vision, and to explain why the anarchic view provides such an enticing rationale for relativism. I then highlight the benefits and drawbacks of the anarchic view. On the beneficial side, the anarchic view does expose abuses of method, and also encourages the generation of multiple and competing theories. These benefits can and should be exploited. The most disturbing drawback is the relativism that flows from the anarchic view. From the assumption that there are no objective standards by which to assess theories it is concluded that there are no rational criteria for preferring any particular theory. Contemporary relativists fill the rational void with a sociological interpretation of knowledge, that is, with the assumption that knowledge is the product of social forces rather than intellectual judgment. They typically claim that theories function as political and exploitative tools used by privileged groups, such as entrenched academic schools, to reinforce their dominance and to suppress opposition.

I then trace anarchic themes in the work of some well-known postprocessualists: Ian Hodder, Michael Shanks, and Christopher Tilley. Anarchic themes, or at least unmistakable shadows of anarchic themes, are found in the work of all three. Rather than use the benefits and discard the detriments, however, these postprocessualists embrace a sociological interpretation of knowledge. That is why they feel justified in ignoring rational standards, and why they can feel free to impose their own favored social and political views on their interpretations of the past. It is argued in the conclusion that theoreticians need not be stuck in the quagmire of relativism when exploiting the benefits of the anarchic view.

Incidentally, the anarchic themes in postprocessual archaeology dovetail with paradigmatic themes in postprocessual archaeology. The latter were discussed in chapter five, and included the following: Tenacious commitment to theories even in the face of anomaly, the assumption that competing theories are embedded in different "irreconcilable" outlooks (paradigms), and the tendency to view differences in competing theories as due to political and social influences rather than intellectual disagreement. That these paradigmatic themes tie in with anarchic themes is not surprising. Irrationalist assumptions underlie every theme in the anarchic view; they also inform numerous themes in the paradigmatic view.

An Outline of the Anarchic View

Paul K. Feyerabend has provided the most systematic formulation of the anarchic view of science, along with an extensive set of arguments in its support. His formulation is summarized in this section.

According to the anarchic view, the goal of science is to expand knowledge. Movement toward that goal is facilitated by generating theories of all types, and as rapidly as possible. Constraints that hinder or block the generation and consideration of theories must be confronted and removed. Methodological standards are a source of constraint. They function to legitimate the authority of received theories and to inhibit consideration of alternatives. Method thus hinders rather than helps the advance of knowledge.

Postulation of as many theories as possible, of any type whatsoever, encourages the advance of knowledge. There are numerous reasons. One cannot know which theory or theories will yield new understanding and insight, so the more theories available, the better the chances of gaining new knowledge. Also, the more quickly theories are propounded, the more rapidly their potential can be explored. Furthermore, weaknesses in theories are revealed by the light of competing explanations. The greater the variety of theories, then, the better the chance that anomalies will be recognized. Even explanations that yield little if any new knowledge can throw light on lacunae in other theories.

According to the anarchic vision, attention to method does not encourage the generation of theories. As a matter-of-fact, it curtails the number and variety of theories. There are a number of reasons. One is that method functions as a (mythical) standard by which select theories gain authority. Belief in method thus encourages false confidence in privileged theories. Another reason is that belief in method stultifies the generation and consideration of alternative theories. Because methodological standards are loaded in favor of established theories, it is difficult if not impossible for alternative explanations to meet those standards. That is also why method can be used to intimidate critics and dismiss their arguments.

Scientific institutions are also legitimated by commitment to method. The methodological rituals that supposedly deliver knowledge are considered the heart and core of scientific institutions, just as theologies are the heart and core of religious institutions. The methodological theology also provides the rationale for scientific institutions to impose authority. It is the stick with which those in scientific institutions beat down anyone who questions the truth or importance of science. Even worse, the authority of scientific institutions can and is used to promote the collective power and personal advantages of individual scientists.

Not only does belief in method inhibit the development of science, but it has never been important for science anyway. Nearly any methodological view can be used to reconstruct most every development in science. That is why inductivist histories, paradigmatic histories, and refutationist histories can and do explain the same historical developments. If any methodological view can explain the same developments, then none of them can be especially important. In short, method has been historically irrelevant except as a rhetorical and propagandistic tool.

In place of method, then, any means possible should be used to argue for preferred theories and against competing theories. Deliberate ad hoc adjustments, misleading interpretation of "supporting" data, suppression of anomalous data, invalid reasoning, and even propaganda are all acceptable means for gaining a hearing for favored theories and disparaging others. In short, *anything goes*.

A number of anarchic themes have been given attention in this book. One is that rigidly imposed method can function to stifle theoretical development. Another is that methodological guidelines are insufficient to explain the development of theory, historically or otherwise. Furthermore, the need for multiple and competing theories is a theme that constitutes one of the six critical issues in theory building and assessment. The anarchic conclusion—that method should be abandoned—does not validly follow, however. To explain why is to separate the benefits from the drawbacks of the anarchic view, the central task of this chapter. The next section lays the groundwork.

Roots

The anarchic view of science was systematically formulated by Paul K. Feyerabend in his 1978 book *Against Method*. He traced anarchic implications into social and public policy in his 1982 book *Science in a Free Society* (Feyerabend 1982). In his 1988 book *Farewell to Reason* he argues that reason is a startlingly inadequate tool for the personal and social development of the individual. Closeness to and empathy with family and friends are not rationally grounded, but they are the foundation of happiness and morality (Feyerabend 1988). Attention in this section is turned to arguments in *Against Method*.

From the anarchic perspective method cannot logically deliver science. Furthermore, method has not historically delivered science.

Following is a summary of the principal logical and historical roots from which Feyerabend's arguments grow.

Every methodological view is designed to deliver knowledge. For example, inductive method is designed to deliver theories that are true, or probably true, and refutationist method is designed to deliver theories that can lead to better theories.

Method purportedly delivers knowledge in two ways: by providing formulas for generating theories and standards by which to legitimate theories. Feyerabend argues that neither the methodological formulas nor the methodological standards assure that knowledge will be delivered.

Feyerabend's logical argumentation has two sides. The first is that generating new theories requires imagination, boldness, creativity, and even impudence. None of these can survive within the constraints of method. As a matter-of-fact, the generation of important new theories requires abandoning methodological constraints. The reason methodological constraints must be abandoned to generate new theories leads to the second side of Feyerabend's logical argumentation: that methodological standards are simply made up to justify accepted theories. In other words, method is the product of theory rather than theory being the product of method. It is hardly surprising, then, that method used to legitimate received theories must be disregarded when generating new theories.

The most absorbing arguments in Feyerabend's assault on method are historical. By far the dominant example is Feyerabend's reconstruction of Galileo's attack on the earth-centered view of the cosmos and support of the sun-centered view, highlights of which are presented here.

Feyerabend maintains that Galileo (1564–1642) did not and could not have adhered to accepted scientific standards when arguing for the heliocentric (sun-centered) theory. In a detailed presentation, Feyerabend argues that the Aristotelian or geocentric (earth-centered) view actually met the standards of science of the day better than the heliocentric view. Consider "simplicity," for example. The geocentric view requires complicated epicyclical orbits of the planets, the mathematics of which are considerably more complicated than the simpler mathematics of the heliocentric view. Other than that, however, the lengthy list of necessary assumptions required by the heliocentric view make it more complicated. For example, it is intuitively easier to accept that we are stationary, with other bodies moving around us, than to imagine that the earth is not only rotating on its axis but is also moving around the sun in a plane that is not perpendicular to its axis of rotation. Despite such complexities in the heliocentric view, Galileo tried to convince people that the heliocentric view was "simpler." Here is another example of Galileo's disregard for standards. The optical theory underlying telescopic observation was highly questionable at the time and was far from being established. Yet Galileo assumed optical theory in some of his crucial arguments for the heliocentric view. The multiple images created by the early lenses of the time were also visually confusing and even misleading. These are reasons why defenders of the geocentric view had good reason to question what they saw through the crude telescope that Galileo had constructed from information filtering down to him from Holland. With speculative optical theory and unclear visual images, it is no wonder Galileo's critics lacked confidence in the "factual" information about the four moons of Jupiter and two moons of Saturn, or in the observed structure of the terrain of our own moon.

Not only did Galileo's arguments for the heliocentric theory fail to meet standards of science in his day, but they also would not have met standards—refutationist or otherwise—deemed worthwhile today. As a matter-of-fact, Galileo's theories might never have been formulated had he tried to meet any methodological standards. He might have hesitated to put forth his views, or at least might not have had the confidence to argue for them so persistently. Instead of using scientific standards, Galileo employed blatantly fallacious techniques of argument. He even belittled those who maintained the geocentric view. In his book *Dialogue Concerning Two World Systems*, a character named "Simplicio" (Simpleton) mouths the geocentric ideas. In short, far from abiding by any conception of scientific standards in his argumentation for the heliocentric system, Galileo was a deliberate propagandist (Feyerabend 1978).

Feyerabend generalizes from the Galileo example (and others as well) that the "law and order" approach to science—the attempt to guarantee theories are scientific by insisting they meet a set of methodological guidelines—is fruitless and even harmful. Science cannot be captured by any preconceived view of its nature anyway, and the "law and order" approach would inhibit the vigorous generation of conflicting theories. Furthermore, Galileo exploited scientific "standards" as a rhetorical device himself. He claimed different standards—such as mathematical "simplicity"—to support his own theories. In other words, Galileo made up method to legitimate his own theories, rather than using method to guide the development of his theories. There was "law and order," all right; he made up his own law and ordered it to fit his theories.

Beneficial and Detrimental Themes

The anarchic view of science does yield a number of methodological benefits. The goal of the anarchic view is to advance theory development. It is the same goal that underlies the refutationist view.

The anarchic view also explains why multiple theories of different types are crucial in stimulating theory development. There are three reasons: the inability to predict which among competing theories will yield the most understanding and insight, the role of competing theories in revealing weaknesses in each other, and the need for alternative theories when established theories are ready to be replaced. It is more convenient to expound further on these three reasons later in the chapter than here.

The anarchic view also sheds light on the misuse and abuse of method. Using method to legitimate theory is fruitless. The time and energy wasted on trying to decide whether theories are "scientific" could be better used to explore the potential understanding and insight theories might provide. Remember that attempts to meet preconceived standards can serve to enshrine received theories while discouraging the generation and serious consideration of innovative ones. Method can and has been used in these ways to legitimate received theories and to discredit new theories within scientific communities. Method has been similarly used to buttress the authority of science against attacks from outside its walls.

Despite encouraging the generation of multiple and contrasting theories, and offering welcome medicine for misuses and abuses of method, there are a number of questionable assumptions and arguments within the anarchic view. The focus is on those that would hinder the development of theory, particularly in a field such as archaeology.

One mistaken assumption is that scientific standards are not important for the establishment of theory. In the longer run, for example, the discrepancy between the geocentric theory and the facts was crucial in the downfall of the geocentric theory. Also, the closer correspondence of the heliocentric view with the facts was of paramount importance for its establishment. Even granting that Galileo disregarded widely accepted scientific standards, his ad hoc arguments and propagandistic tricks would not have enabled the heliocentric theory to prevail if it had not eventually been corroborated by empirical evidence.

Furthermore, although Galileo did not share the Aristotelian standards of science of his opponents, he did embrace standards that seemed appropriate to himself. Optical theory may not have been developed sufficiently to allow his telescopic "evidence" to be accepted without question by the Aristotelians. Galileo apparently accepted optical theory to the point where *he* had confidence in the evidence revealed by the telescope. In short, Galileo may have embraced scientific standards even though those standards were different from the norm of the day.

In brief, then, Feyerabend does not acknowledge the importance of scientific standards in the eventual victory of the heliocentric view over the geocentric view, nor does he acknowledge the beneficial role that scientific standards may have played in Galileo's own thinking when arguing for the heliocentric theory. Why was Feyerabend able to avoid such points? One reason is that he focused on the context of discovery.

For Feyerabend to have concentrated his analysis on the context of discovery was not inappropriate. After all, the generation of theory is crucial in the development of science. He completely ignored the role of justification, however, and that is not warranted. Assessing theories by methodological standards is also crucial in the development of science, as I hope has been demonstrated by the comments on Galileo's own standards and the role of standards in the eventual acceptance of the heliocentric view.

It should be noted that Feyerabend's book was conceived as only one side of a debate about science, the irrational side of which was Feyerabend's and the rational side of which was to be argued by Imre Lakatos. Professor Lakatos' untimely death ended the joint project, the result of which was the publication of *Against Method* alone rather than in tandem with Lakatos' contrasting position. It may not be fair, then, to have expected Feyerabend to discuss the important roles played by scientific standards.

By far the most dangerous drawback to the anarchic view is relativism. The relativistic consequences of the anarchic view are explored next.

Anarchy and Relativism

There are different routes to relativism. The most common is to stumble upon it unwittingly and certainly unintentionally. How does such happen? Usually someone becomes disillusioned with standards of reason, that is, with methodological standards. Regardless of whether the standards are inappropriate, impossible, or just misunderstood, once faith in them is lost there is a rebound toward relativism. This may have happened to Ian Hodder. It seems that his disenchantment with positivistic science is a major reason for the relativistic tendencies in his contextual approach to archaeological explanation (Hodder 1991). The anarchic vision provides a more direct and audacious route to relativism. It contains not only an explicit rationale for relativism but also the immodest thesis that relativism is the best route to knowledge. These are also the reasons why anarchic themes can be used to justify relativistic approaches even if relativism is encountered via another route.

The reason the anarchic vision entails relativism is not difficult to find: If there are no reliable standards by which to assess theories, then there are no intellectual criteria by which to judge any theory preferable to others. The demise of rational standards inevitably leads to relativism.

It is clear that attacks on rational standards and support of relativism are two principal foci in Feyerabend's analysis of Galileo's heliocentric arguments in *Against Method*. Feyerabend was interested in more than just the intellectual consequences of relativism, however. In his book *Science in a Free Society*, published in 1982, Feyerabend draws out the political and social consequences of adopting relativism.

Feyerabend argues that the aura of respect for "science"—scientific theories and scientists as well—is unfounded. Science in the modern world takes the central place occupied by theology in the medieval world, complete with its aura of invincibility. In the popular eye science has become the only legitimate claimant to the truth. It is no wonder, then, that the methods of science—as mythical as they are—are considered crucial for legitimate inquiry. The label "social sciences" is a tribute to the prestige enjoyed by science.

The privileged position of scientific knowledge has also showered status onto scientists themselves. Scientists have become the new priests of knowledge, playing the role enjoyed by clerics during the Middle Ages. Scientists can and do abuse their position, wielding their status for personal gain and political power. For example, scientific consultants play an authoritative role in the adoption of many public policies, both as members of groups that draw up policy proposals and also as "expert" witnesses who testify in proceedings to consider policy proposals. Philosophers of science have added their voices to the chorus of those espousing the virtues of the scientific enterprise.

To counter the abuse of scientific theory and unwarranted influence of scientists, Feyerabend recommends countervailing political power. Citizens' groups should be formed to oppose the entrenched policies and privileges of scientific communities. For example, citizens' groups should form to oppose the building and use of nuclear-power generators. In brief, in a "free society" science would be recognized for what it is: just one among numerous claimants to influence and power. It should have to battle other viewpoints in the political arena, rather than holding an authoritative position because of its supposed objectivity.

It hardly needs to be said that Feyerabend's discussion of the social and political implications of his anarchic view of knowledge is heavily laden with relativistic overtones. In his view scientific theories and the scientists who espouse them have no claim on truth and do not warrant special status. Typical of those who downplay or argue against the intellectual foundations of science, Feyerabend assumes that scientific theories function principally as tools of power, illegitimately conferring authority on viewpoints that serve special interests. Also typical, he endorses the use of political and other sources of power to oppose scientific viewpoints and to strip influence from those with a vested interest in science. His call for "citizens groups" to control or even eliminate nuclear power, for example, is based on the assumption that the science underlying it is questionable, and that those who support it must only be acting in their own vested interest. Feyerabend does not mention that nuclear power also has some considerable benefits compared to the alternatives, such as being much less dependent upon nonrenewable resources and contributing very little hydrocarbon residue to the atmosphere.

Anarchic Themes in Postprocessual Archaeology

Both beneficial and detrimental themes of the anarchic vision are prominent in postprocessual archaeology. Three particularly striking themes are the following: (1) encouragement of a multiple and diverse set of theories, (2) attacks on rational methodological standards, and (3) flirtation or even endorsement of relativism.

The shear multiplicity of theoretical perspectives that populate the postprocessual movement are rather astounding. Among them are symbolic, structural, and Marxist approaches. As an observer of the postprocessual landscape quickly realizes, these and many other approaches have different meanings. That is a reason why, for example, some postprocessualists find Marxist approaches promising (Leone 1982a, 1982b), whereas others are not convinced that Marxist approaches are satisfactory (Hodder 1991). There are also subvarieties. Some postprocessualists, for example, call for a "structural Marxist" approach (Tilley 1981; Miller and Tilley 1984; Shanks and Tilley 1982). Furthermore, some approaches fall between the cracks of the major varieties. The contextual approach of Hodder (1991) is one.

A multiplicity of high-level theoretical perspectives certainly encourages the generation of diverse types of theories. In addition, however, postprocessual archaeologists typically endorse the value of generating a variety of theories. The rationale may not always be explicit, or thoroughly argued if it is. Nevertheless, there are good reasons for generating a multiplicity of diverse theories. The reasons are found in the anarchic view.

According to the anarchic view, a multiplicity of theories is crucial for the progress of theory. The reasons were mentioned earlier but are reviewed here again. First, because one cannot predict that theories will yield understanding and insight, pursuit of a variety of theories is likely to produce more rapid theoretical progress. Second, weaknesses in any given theory are normally only revealed from the perspective of competing theories. Because recognition of weaknesses in theories is crucial for theory development, a plethora of different and conflicting theories is important. And third, established theories seldom if ever disappear without alternative theories to replace them. It is thus necessary to have alternative theories available to "fill the void" when established theories approach the end of their fruitful use.

In short, the postprocessual insistence on a variety of diverse and contrasting theories can be beneficial. Furthermore, a diversity of theories does *not* in itself imply relativism. So long as theories are forced to meet scientific standards when being assessed, modified, or rejected it makes no difference how many or how different they may be.

In my view, processual archaeologists would also do well to encourage the generation of different and competing explanations of prehistoric phenomena. The benefits of multiple and divergent theories can be reaped in processual as well as postprocessual archaeology. The rationale is the same regardless of the camp in which one pitches his or her theoretical tent.

Incidentally, processual approaches continue to flourish despite the demise implicit in the prefix "post." Furthermore, important elements of the methodology associated with productive processual approaches can be used in the development of theories that incorporate individualistic elements. The next two chapters outline how that can be done. It will be all the more critical that processualists understand and exploit productive method as they enter a realm in which, according to their postprocessual critics, only radically different approaches can bear fruit.

As valuable as it is to have multiple and diverse theories, calls for diversity can easily become confused with two undesirable themes of the anarchic vision: a disregard for methodological standards and hence relativism. Both these themes have infiltrated the postprocessual movement. Infiltration usually takes place during attacks on methodological standards. Next is a reconstruction of how this occurs.

If there is one common element in the postprocessual movement, it is rejection of "positivism" as a methodology for the building and testing of theories. In Chapter 4 a number of different meanings of positivism were outlined. It was also pointed out that the meaning of positivism in archaeology is generally associated with at least the following three theses: (1) that there are universal "laws" in the structure and transformation of human institutions, (2) that explanations must be empirically verifiable, and (3) that individualistic elements, such as minds, might exist and might be influential in human events but theories that incorporate such elements are not verifiable.

Among some archaeologists, the expression "covering-law model" is an alternative label for positivism. Those two expressions would not be conflated in academic philosophy, but doing so is not entirely unjustified. Hempel's formulation of the covering-law model came during his early period, when his views had a positivistic slant (Hempel 1942). A more common practice in archaeology is to conflate positivism with the methods of science. This is a serious matter, because rejection of positivism is thought by some to be sufficient to reject scientific approaches (Bell 1987a).

For example, Ian Hodder states that "it will be necessary . . . in the quest for an adequate archaeology of mind, to ditch decisively the natural science, covering law approach" (Hodder 1991:32). He also conflates positivism with processual approaches, referring to "processual, positivist approaches" (Hodder 1991:ix). Processual archaeology is also identified with the New Archaeology, such as when he refers to "the whole of the New Archaeology or processual archaeology" (Hodder 1991:28). In sum, all five—natural science approaches, covering-law models, positivism, processual archaeology, and the New Archaeology are identified with each other. They should not be, and for many reasons (Bell 1987a), the most important being that some crucial elements of positivism compromise its productivity (Bell 1984, 1987a; Wylie 1982). According to Hodder's logic, however, the rejection of positivism (the covering-law model) entails the rejection of all natural science approaches, processual archaeology, and the New Archaeology (Bell 1987a).

Typical of the anarchic vision, the attack on rational standards (by Hodder in this case) leads to relativism. Like Feyerabend, Hodder replaces methodological standards with the belief that sociological factors, and especially "power," are the keys to understanding why theories are adopted (Hodder 1991). The Frankfurt school is one source of inspiration. The critical theory of Friedrich Adorno, Jurgen Habermas, and others in the Frankfurt school is highly sociological, to the point where ideas are interpreted to be the product of social and political forces rather than intellectual assessment (see Bronner and Kellner 1989). Another source of inspiration is Michel Foucault's view that power dominates human institutions, including intellectual institutions (see Foucault 1980; Rabinow 1984).

In other words, Hodder seems to be adopting the "strong program" in the sociology of knowledge. According to the strong program, sociological factors actually determine the very content of ideas that are supposedly the product of intellectual pursuit (see Barnes 1974; Bloor 1991). In the strong program, for example, an archaeologist's "theory" that women played a passive role in the development of agriculture would be no more than a projection of the Victorian view that women are by nature passive.

By the way, the strong program is much more sweeping than the "weak program" in the sociology of knowledge. According to the weak program sociological factors provide a directive context for the development of knowledge but intellectual factors still drive the generation and assessment of theories within that context. For example, access to funding to study AIDS might concentrate research on viruses, but the testing, modification, and rejection of theory about viruses would still be guided by scientific method.

Finally, like most relativists, Hodder can feel justified in playing the same intellectual power game that he thinks he has exposed. He feels free to impose his own pet political and social perspectives on the generation of theory—specifically, he endorses feminist approaches, indigenous approaches, and working-class approaches—but he seems quite undisturbed that the dogmatism in doing so could just as well be used to impose a plethora of political and social perspectives contrary to his own—such as that women are inherently inferior, that dominant civilizations are intrinsically superior, and that people flounder in the working class because they lack intelligence, imagination, or are lazy (Bell 1987a).

As Christopher Peebles so aptly points out, Michael Shanks and Christopher Tilley are also attracted to a sociological explanation of why some theories are adopted rather than others. Their view, which they call the "politics of truth," amounts to the assumption that truth is a product of politics. "We must be concerned to investigate what kinds of power and determinate social conditions make the truth of a text or a museum's representation of the past appear plausible" (Shanks and Tilley 1987b:198). That is why critical archaeologists must "take up an oppositional role to contemporary society" and embrace "a notion of archaeological discourse as being part of a war of position" (Shanks and Tilley 1987b:204). Like Hodder, Shanks and Tilley do not want to acknowledge any significant criteria for adopting theories other than political and power relations. That is why they, like Hodder, are not hesitant to impose their own political and social views onto archaeological theory (Peebles 1990).

The reconstructions of arguments in Hodder, Shanks, and Tilley all have a similar pattern: an attack on rational standards followed by a resort to social and political explanations of why people support certain theories as opposed to others. This underlying pattern can also be seen in a larger archaeological context. For more on the latter, I strongly recommend Bruce Trigger's article "Hyperrelativism, Responsibility, and the Social Sciences" (Trigger 1989c). Trigger places relativistic tendencies in archaeology within its anthropological framework, and even within the broader context of the social sciences.

In this chapter I have been quite critical of some methodological trends appearing in the postprocessual camp. Before concluding the chapter, however, it is important to add some qualifications.

First, the postprocessual approaches of people such as Hodder, Shanks, and Tilley include many ideas besides the methodological ones criticized here. Some of those ideas certainly merit serious consideration. For example, recognition that the thoughts, ideas, and decisions of prehistoric peoples may have influenced social structure and change is valuable. Indeed, that recognition has spurred some New Archaeologists—those in the British camp—to explore incorporating human agency into archaeological theory. Another example is the critique of positivism. As argued earlier, positivism is not used in productive processual archaeology. On the other hand, there has been much adulation of positivism in the methodological literature of the New Archaeology. Criticism is needed even if positivist method is not actually employed.

Second, the relativism that follows from attacks on rational standards has not been explicitly embraced. Indeed, there are attempts by Hodder, Shanks, and Tilley to discuss and assess theories in archaeology rather than simply proclaim any theory they wish. Hodder's contextual approach is an example (Hodder 1991). Shanks' and Tilley's *Re-Constructing Archaeology: Theory and Practice* (1987a) contains other examples, as does Michael Shanks recent book *Experiencing the Past: On the Character of Archaeology* (1992). Shanks' and Tilley's "Archaeology in the 1990s" (1989) has further examples.

When Hodder, Shanks, and Tilley move away from their attacks on positivism and flirtations with relativism, in other words, some of their actual methodological proposals seem to reflect the "weak program" in the sociology of knowledge. The weak program is quite sensible. Even if methodological standards are maintained within an intellectual community, it can hardly be denied that social, political, and other cultural factors can and do have some influence on the direction of knowledge. To acknowledge such is certainly not the same as embracing relativism and the strong program with which relativism is almost inevitably associated.

Third and finally, there are many varieties of approaches associated with postprocessual archaeology. Some were mentioned earlier in the chapter. To make a blanket claim that relativism permeates all of them would not be fair. For a thorough discussion see the *Norwegian Archaeological Review* with Shanks and Tilley's "Archaeology in the 1990s" followed by comments from Barbara Bender, Ian Hodder, Bjørnar Olsen, Frands Herschend, Jarl Nordbladh, Bruce Trigger, Robert Wenke, and Colin Renfrew, and a reply by Shanks and Tilley (Shanks and Tilley 1989).

The qualifications cited here do not lesson the dangers of attacks on rational standards. Testability is one of the casualties even if relativism is not embraced with open arms. Nevertheless, there are ideas in the postprocessual camp that should be taken seriously rather than dismissed categorically.

Conclusion

I conclude this chapter by discussing answers to a number of questions. First, is it surprising that some processualists fear a variety of approaches will be the downfall of methodological standards and leave archaeology open to relativism? As shown in the previous section, that fear is warranted. Some of the best known postprocessualists may not have been familiar with the anarchic view per se. Nevertheless, in widely discussed books they have adopted major anarchic themes, both beneficial and detrimental.

A second question is this: Must archaeologists of any theoretical leaning be condemned to accepting the disadvantages of the anarchic vision if the advantages are put into practice? The answer to that question is no, emphatically no. One can accept the beneficial themes, such as encouraging the generation of a variety of contrasting theories, but still insist on methodological standards when assessing, modifying, and even rejecting theories. Galileo's work and its fate provide a good example. It was argued that Galileo may have used his own standards even if they were at odds with those of the Aristotelians. Even more important, the geocentric theory was ultimately abandoned and the heliocentric theory accepted because of methodological standards: The former was empirically refuted and the latter empirically corroborated. Feyerabend does not tell his readers these important points about the role of method in Galileo's work and its acceptance. They are certainly a devastating blow to Feyerabend's arguments for relativism. They do not, however, weaken his arguments for the importance of multiple and competing theories.

From a slightly different angle the situation is as follows. Feyerabend associates the generation of a multiplicity of theories with relativism. What actually happened is that a multiplicity of theories sharpened the arguments, *including the empirical arguments,* for and against the competing geocentric and heliocentric theories. Eventually the empirical arguments prevailed in favor of the heliocentric view. In other words, a multiplicity of theories helped defeat relativism. That can be expected *so long as at least some of the theories are testable and are interpreted as testable.* What I fear is that the call of postprocessualists for a multiplicity of theories is associated with little or no insistence on the testability of theories.

The lesson is twofold. Archaeologists should encourage the generation of a multitude of competing theories. Nevertheless, archaeologists should also insist on methodological standards. Testability is essential when assessing, modifying, and rejecting theories. Theories that do not meet such rational standards might be interesting and they may even contain elements of truth. If there is no reliable way to discover in what ways they may be correct or mistaken, however, such theories are unlikely to serve as stepping stones to better theories. That is also why such theories are unlikely to play a significant role in the long-term improvement of archaeological knowledge.

Suggested Readings

Two books by Paul Feyerabend serve as a tandem for those wishing to explore the anarchic view and its social-political implications. Also annotated is a well-known book by Ian Hodder that incorporates numerous anarchic themes.

1. Paul K. Feyerabend, 1978, *Against Method*.
Against Method provides the best known criticism of the use of method and the possibility of the use of method. The book utilizes both logical argument and historical argument in its attack on method. The dominating historical example is Galileo's support of the sun-centered view of the cosmos and his attacks on the earth-centered view.

2. Paul K. Feyerabend, 1982, *Science in a Free Society*.
Having (supposedly) shown in *Against Method* that science is an irrational pursuit, Feyerabend traces the social and political ramifications in *Science in a Free Society*. He argues that science and especially science policy (like policy concerning nuclear power) should be held under close scrutiny by the public. Furthermore, scientists are to be regarded like any other self-interested group, and should be controlled through political opposition and power.

3. Ian Hodder, 1991, *Reading the Past: Current Approaches to Interpretation in Archaeology*, 2d edition.
The content of this book can be conveniently divided into three areas. In the early chapters Hodder criticizes positivistic approaches to archaeological

theory. He identifies processual archaeology with positivism. In the middle chapters he outlines his "contextual approach" for building theories about prehistoric experience. Emphasized is the uniqueness rather than universality of social context. In the later chapters he recommends contemporary political-social themes for interpreting prehistoric societies. In particular he supports the use of themes from the feminist movement, from working-class perspectives, and from indigenous archaeologies. The book may be the most influential in the postprocessual movement. It also incorporates nearly all beneficial and detrimental methodological ideas in that movement.

Part III   Individualism and Cognitive Archaeology

Chapter 8   Holism, Individualism, and Empathy

Incorporating human agency into theories about the unwritten past has moved high on the list of priorities among theoretical archaeologists, prompting reference to a "cognitive revolution." This chapter explores ways of incorporating the ideas, decisions, and actions of humans into archaeological theory. The methodological guidelines developed here will be applied to a detailed example in Chapter 9.

Different types of explanation either constrain or encourage inclusion of human agency, that is, inclusion of the ideas, decisions, and actions of humans. At one extreme are methodological approaches that exclude agency entirely, and at the other extreme are approaches that embrace agency uncritically. Although the extremes form the ends of an explanatory continuum, it is convenient to chop the continuum into three parts. Human agency plays a distinctly different role in each.

The first type of explanation, *holistic* explanation, invokes only forces transcendent to human agency. Holistic approaches assume that what humans think, wish, desire, believe, or will, is *not* a factor, or at least not a significant factor, in the development or structure of human organization. The second, *individualistic* explanation, incorporates human agency—the thoughts, decisions, and other willful elements of humans. Individualistic approaches assume that thoughts and decisions have had a significant impact on the structure and change of human organizations. The third, *empathetic* explanation, reconstructs not only thoughts and decisions, but also elements such as affective states, spiritual orientations, and experiential meanings. Empathetic approaches assume that the inner experience of humans is worthy of study for its own sake, and that study of the inner experience of humans provides a handle for interpreting human culture. The methodological assumptions underlying each of the three types of explanation are, in order, *holistic method*, *individualistic method*, and *empathetic method*.

Much can be gained by understanding the divergent rationales and contrasting guidelines of the three approaches. The strengths and limitations of each are clarified by thorough comprehension of the alternatives. Knowledge of each is also indispensable for shifting approaches, and for amalgamating elements from among them.

Methodological debate in archaeology has centered largely on the holistic and empathetic approaches, between which there is a vast gulf. Between those two is individualistic method. Use of individualistic method as an alternative for building archaeological theory is in its infancy, but it is being explored in this book not just because it is new. A much more important reason is that methodological individualism holds the greatest potential for developing theories that incorporate human agency and yet are still testable. Such theories are usually only weakly testable, to be sure. Nevertheless, they can provide at least some important understanding and insight. Even when such theories are nontestable, which some are, methodological individualism suggests an inductive approach for tying theory very closely and explicitly to the available data.

It has long been recognized that individualistic elements should not be ignored in archaeological theory (Collingwood 1946; Leone 1982b). The importance of individualistic elements has been recognized not just by those critical of holistic approaches (Deetz 1977; Hodder 1985, 1991), but even some closely identified with holistic approaches (Flannery 1968a, 1973; Sabloff et al. 1973; Renfrew 1982, 1987, personal communication 1987). There also have been probing discussions of ways to identify individuality, such as in prehistoric technology (Hill and Gunn 1977). Despite the recognition that humans are agents, and calls to incorporate individualistic elements into archaeological theory, more comprehensive discussions and examples are just now emerging (Gardin and Peebles 1992; Renfrew and Zubrow 1993). A more systematic account of the potential and limitations of individualistic method for archaeological theory is needed. Also needed are more specific guidelines on how to use methodological individualism when developing archaeological theory. This and the next chapter are attempts to fill those voids.

Incidentally, that archaeologists have just recently begun to incorporate individualistic elements into their theories does seem surprising. Methodological individualism has been in the air for much of this century and has been an active player on the philosophical stage for at least five decades. Furthermore, archaeologists have not been unaware of its presence (Sabloff et al. 1973), and individualistic method has an established tradition in anthropology, especially in economic anthropology (Halperin 1984, 1985).

A reason for the delay in the introduction of methodological individualism into theoretical archaeology may be the central role that has been played by holistic and other deterministic high-level models, such as biological and ecological models. Deterministic models have been used in processual archaeology over the past quarter century, but human agency clearly cannot be incorporated into theories that are exclusively informed by such models.

Holistic, Individualistic, and Empathetic Approaches

Prehistory commonly means history without the benefit of written records. That fact has encouraged students of prehistory—particularly archaeologists—to sidestep, or at least de-emphasize, speculation about the thoughts and decisions of prehistoric peoples. Avoiding such human elements in theories about the past has dovetailed with the *holistic* approaches to explanation that dominate the social sciences, that is, with the assumptions that super-human forces underlie social structure and that humans have no control over them. In short, to understand structure or change with holistic method is to search for forces transcending humans. Crude Marxist interpretations are holistic, as are explanations in the systemic phase of processual archaeology.

Incidentally, the meaning of holism here is different from that used in anthropology. The anthropological meaning of holism is that particular aspects of a culture, such as rituals or eating, can be understood only within the context of the culture as a whole (Honigmann 1977).

Because humans do think and sometimes act because of their thoughts, it also makes sense to try to incorporate elements like ideas and decisions into theories about prehistoric peoples. Incorporating such human elements rests on a number of assumptions. It assumes that thoughts and decisions do have agency—they are not just reflections of, or "superstructure" upon, underlying forces. It also assumes that collective actions and shared institutions can be interpreted as the products of the decisions and actions of individuals. These assumptions and related ideas constitute *individualistic method,* or *methodological individualism.* Cognitive archaeology, for example, the goal of which is to understand the thoughts, decisions, and similar ideational facets of prehistoric people, breaks sharply with holistic method by employing individualistic method. That schism is dramatic, and its ramifications are likely to shake the foundations of theory building in archaeology.

Attempts to reconstruct the feelings, hopes, experiential meanings, and other affective and spiritual elements of prehistoric peoples often utilize *empathetic method*: use of personal intuition to understand the inner lives of other people. Empathetic method assumes there is common structure to human experience. The common structure is the "bridge" that justifies an investigator's claims about the experiences of other people. Because there is a shared structure to experience, the feelings, hopes, and experiential meanings of an investigator are assumed to be similar to those of a target group. Emic approaches to theory building normally employ elements of empathetic method.

Philosophical Anthropology

The three approaches contain different methods for developing theory. Those methods are the focus in this chapter. Nevertheless, many other issues are implicit in the methodological views. What is the role of the biological side of man versus the cognitive or even spiritual side of man? At the social level, what roles do the cognitive and spiritual levels actually play, if any? Irrational elements may dominate both individuals and social organization, so is it plausible to assume that either can be effectively understood using rational procedures? If using rational procedures to understand man and society requires attention to universals, are there cultural universals and if so what are they and how can they be identified? These questions raise issues that come under the general topic of philosophical anthropology, or the philosophy of anthropology. Following are a number of comments on the philosophy of anthropology, especially as to how it is related to ideas in this chapter.

First, the issues in philosophical anthropology raised here are so closely associated with the methodological discussions in this chapter that the chapter itself might be viewed as the philosophy of anthropology, or at least as a chapter with implicit issues in philosophical anthropology. Labels, and even multiple labels are fine so long as they help one gain a perspective and are not misleading. There is no harm in viewing this chapter as philosophical anthropology, at least so long as one remembers that the discussion will be focused on methodological issues in theory building and that other issues will remain implicit to one degree or another.

Second, in the rather large store of literature on philosophical anthropology are five books that I find particularly relevant to the methodological issues addressed in this chapter.

The first is Joseph Agassi's *Towards a Rational Philosophical Anthropology* (1977). Agassi discusses five different perspectives on man. He traces the significant implications of each, including the implications on views of knowledge and method. The perspectives are man as machine, man as animal, man as rational, man as social, and man in the image of god.

The next two books are by Ian Jarvie. His 1984 *Rationality and Relativism: In Search of a Philosophy and History of Anthropology* is an exploration of the philosophy and history of anthropology. The particular focus is two-fold: on views of rationality and, as always is the case when rationality is assumed in a social context, on views of relativism. Jarvie's 1986 *Thinking about Society: Theory and Practice* is a collection of his papers on a wide-ranging series of issues in the social sciences in general and anthropology in particular. Included are papers on the differences between natural and social sciences, on realism in sociological theories, on the scientific character of social anthropology, and on ethnography.

The fourth book is Ernest Gellner's 1989 *Plough, Sword and Book*, which traces historical and thematic transformations in theories of rationality. Those changes are all placed within concrete social contexts, contexts that include economic institutions, religious institutions, and others as well.

The fifth book is Donald Brown's 1991 *Human Universals*. In it, Brown questions the wide-ranging skepticism about the possibility of human universals. Brown selects six specific types of human proclivity and investigates whether they are universal or not. His study ranges from how such universals can be conceptualized to how they can be explained.

Holistic Method versus Individualistic Method

Religious inclinations, or disinclinations, can be set aside when reading the following exchange between an atheist and a believer:

> *Atheist*: "Can you not see that the church is designed to control your life? Its theological doctrine mandates that you accept it as the broadcaster of wisdom, telling you what you can and cannot do. You also are expected to serve it, both in time and with money, in order to gain 'salvation,' whatever that is. You are expected to participate in its rituals, and submit to the proclamations of its prelate—that person who is supposedly in closer contact with its deity, if there is one. In other words, you are but a pawn of institutionalized religion and if you wish to understand it, you must see through your delusion of belief to realize how it represses and exploits you."

> *Believer*: "That's not at all how I conceive of my commitment. God has given me many blessings, and my church is an incarnate messenger of His word. I feel neither repressed nor exploited. As a matter of fact, I

have willingly given my life to God and his agent, the Church, and am thankful to have made the decision to do so."

Which of the above positions is correct? Overlooking one's own predispositions, the answer is rather trivial: They both are correct. Each offers understanding, although from quite disparate perspectives. What would clearly be a mistake, in my view, is uncritical adoption of one to the exclusion of the other.

The position of the atheist is purely holistic. It is also considered "scientific" by many. Its scientific status can seem especially assured to those strongly influenced by methodological visions that emphasize the function of institutions in repressing people. Marxist interpretations are an example.

To a holist, the expostulations of the believer are subjective, emotional, and impressionistic to the point of being irrational. Furthermore, they do not provide a basis for testable theories. Theories based on expostulations of this type could be used to explain anything, leaving nothing to refute them. The convictions of the believer, however, should not be simply dismissed because they do not fit a precast view of science. The thoughts and commitments of the believer can be interpreted as his or her choices, and those choices can be interpreted as a reason, even a necessary reason, for the existence of churches and other religious institutions.

To give serious attention to the believer's view, one must break from the holistic outlook, but the grip of holism is not easily severed. Its heritage is powerful in our intellectual tradition, especially because it is so often identified with the "scientific" study of mankind. The reasons will emerge in the upcoming section.

Holism

The principal tenets of holism can be summarized quite briefly. Holism is the belief that forces transcending humans explain social structure and change, and that even the thoughts, decisions, and actions of people are explained by those forces. Human agency has no significant influence on the holistic forces. Although this characterization of holism is extreme, holistic tendencies can dominate theory building to the point where individualistic and empathetic alternatives are excluded. The reasons are historical as well as intellectual.

Holistic roots in the Bronze Age

The view that man is not in control of his own destiny, either individually or collectively, extends far back into the religious and cultural heritage of civilization. It has been argued that such religious or quasi-religious beliefs were prominent in the Bronze Age, in Mycenaen Greece (1400–1100 B.C.). At that time there may have been no concept of a free will, much less a workable theory of rationality. Man's affairs were deemed to be in the hands of the Gods, and even the latter seemed to have little if any control over their own lives. In other words, fatalism prevailed, even before the notion itself was formulated (Snell 1982; also see Herzfeld 1982, for an ethnographic interpretation of fatalism in contemporary Greek culture).

Fatalistic views are by no means a figment of the past, as almost any observer of recent culture could attest. Apocalyptic religions assume the future is determined—usually featuring a cataclysmic event—and that we can only submit to that future. Another example is the crude Communist doctrine that inexorable economic "laws" dictate that collective socialism will replace capitalism. In short, the assumption that super-human forces underlie human affairs is as old as mankind and yet as contemporary as the present.

Hegel, Marx, and Comte

Although the roots of holism can be traced into the misty past of mankind, especially in religious and social outlooks, in the nineteenth century it came to be identified with attempts to uncover "scientific" explanations of human institutions (Hayek 1972). In technical idiom, this new version of holism assumes *sociological deter-*

minism: the view that humans are passive pawns shaped by social forces.

By the way, belief in physical determinism, such as in the physics of Isaac Newton, is surely one reason that sociological determinism can be attractive. Physical determinism and sociological determinism also work together in some cases, such as in the hydraulic theory of Wittfogel. The physical need for large-scale waterworks and the inexorable physical requirements of building and maintaining the waterworks makes inevitable—determines—the growth of state structure.

In any case, the view that sociological forces transcending humans are the "real" levers controlling our lives, dominating us whether we like it or not, can be traced to a number of thinkers of the last century. Hegel, Marx, and Comte figure prominently among them.

Georg Wilhelm Friedrich Hegel (1770–1831) maintained that the world is a product of what he called the *Weltgeist* (world spirit), or *Geist* for short. The manifestation of the *Geist* in space is "nature," to use Hegel's terminology, and its manifestation in time is "history." In short, all structure and change are the product of the *Geist*.

The *Geist* transcends human control. In Hegel's view, it controls us. We may deceive ourselves into thinking that we are agents of our own intentional action, and that those actions make a difference in the course of events. The *Geist* is the real causal agent, however. Humans are puppets whose strings are pulled by the *Geist* (Hegel 1977).

Karl Marx (1818–1883), who frequently acknowledged his intellectual debt to Hegel, adopted the latter's view that transcendent forces control both the structure and dynamics of society. In Marx's view the force is not an idea, like the *Geist* (Hegel was an *idealist*), but is matter, especially in economic structure (Marx was a *materialist*). From the Marxist perspective the economic structure of a society is the primary determinant of human phenomena—social, religious, cultural—and economic systems develop and disappear without regard to the plans, hopes, or control of humans. A "scientific" study of mankind, according to the Marxist view, must be focused upon the material forces (Marx and Engels 1961). The spread of holism in the contemporary world has perhaps been due more to Marx than anyone else. Along for the ride was, and still is, the belief that "scientific" explanations must be holistic.

Incidentally, the expressions *materialism, cultural materialism,* and *Marxist* have caused confusion in the archaeological literature. Similarities and differences are presented briefly here.

Materialism is simply the view that humans, prehistoric or otherwise, are predominantly occupied with activities that provide subsistence. In other words, human activity is mainly economic activity, a corollary of which is that the economic dimension of all institutions is crucially significant.

Another entirely different meaning of materialism is that archaeological theory should always be answerable to the material record. It is the view that theories in archaeology should have an empirical foundation. There certainly are substantial differences in views about the nature of the empirical side of archaeology and how it should be used. Those differences have gained considerable attention in this book. Nevertheless, all approaches to explanation in archaeology are materialist in this sense, with the exception of some recommendations coming from the postprocessual camp.

Cultural materialism is the view that all cultural phenomena are the epiphenomena of the economic orientation of man. It is normally associated with the ideas of Marvin Harris (1979). Cultural materialism is materialist in both senses: It assumes that humans are predominantly occupied with subsistence activities, and that theories in archaeology should have an empirical foundation. Cultural materialists insist that all cultural phenomena are the product of economic activity, however. Empirical materialists do not always assume that cultural phenomena are the product of economic activity.

Marxist approaches to explaining social organization and culture place ideational elements in dialectical relationship with economic factors. Some Marxist approaches incorporate cultural materialism because they give priority to the role of economic factors in the dialectic. Other Marxist approaches do not assume cultural materialism because they give priority to ideational elements in the dialectic (Trigger 1989b:341). Marxist theory in archaeology is also sometimes,

but not always, associated with Marxist historical and social doc-
trines, such as the belief that a class with advantages in a given
economic system will exploit classes less privileged in the system.
The Marxist heritage has left the impression that holistic forces are
always materialistic. It is important to realize, however, that holistic
forces can also be idealistic. Hegel's *Weltgeist* is an example already
cited. The "high structuralism" in contemporary anthropology also
gives holism an idealistic slant. High structuralism assumes that universal patterns in human mentality are the primary levers in the
formation of human social organization (Lévi-Strauss 1966). Humans
have no more control over those patterns than they do economic
forces, according to structuralist interpretations. Typical of holistic
approaches, uncovering universals—in this case, patterns of the
mind—is a primary goal. Another goal of high structuralism, however, is to uncover meaning in the lives of people. That is why structuralist approaches also have empathetic elements.

Auguste Comte (1798–1857) is another Continental thinker whose
intellectual influence on contemporary social science cannot be over-
estimated. He also left a heritage of holism, and identified science
with holism. A number of elements constitute Comte's holistic view.

Comte coined the expression "positivism" from the French verb
"positer"—to posit. This was pointed out in the discussion of positivism in Chapter 4. Specifically, Comte maintained that all scientific knowledge must be derivable strictly from what is posited to the
senses; speculation about causes or other metaphysical entities beyond what is posited to the senses should be excluded from science.
The anti-metaphysical face of Comte's positivism does contrast with
the economic metaphysics of Marx's materialism, but the similarities
in the two traditions are even more striking. Comte, like Marx, believed there were universal laws of social organization that transcend human agency and hence are not malleable. Just as for the
Marxists, a science of man requires uncovering those universal laws
(Comte 1968; Martineau 1855).

In short, the approaches of both Comte and Marx to the study of
man are holistic, and each identified science with his particular approach. Because the Marxist and Comtean traditions have been im-

mensely influential in the development of the social sciences, it is hardly surprising that holistic approaches tend to dominate, and that holistic approaches are commonly identified as "scientific."

Marxist theories, processual theories

Some meat can be added to the skeleton of holism with a few examples. These will also provide substance for a discussion of the advantages and disadvantages of holistic approaches.

Marxist theories place ideational elements—thoughts, ideas, religious belief, and other cognitive factors—in dialectical relation with material elements—economic structure and the roles into which it forces people. The underlying assumption is that the material elements dictate and constrain the formation and change of the ideational elements. At the extreme—in "vulgar" Marxism—the material elements determine the ideational elements, the latter being only a "superstructure" upon the former. In a modified form, the material and ideational components interact although material factors dominate.

Of particular importance to the present discussion is that Marxist theories de-emphasize the role of human agency, and discount it completely at the extreme. Explanations of social structure and change are not found in the agency of humans, but rather in economic institutions. Thoughts, decisions, and other ideational elements—"consciousness," to use Marxist terminology—are interpreted to be the product of a person's role in the economic structure of society rather than as pivotal in the formation of that structure. That is why Marxist explanations remain largely holistic despite the interest of some Marxists in the cognitive side of humans (Leone 1982a, 1982b; Tilley 1981; Tilley and Shanks 1987).

Processual theories of the systemic type are another well-known example of holistic explanation. Processual theories—theories that explain change from one state-of-affairs to another state-of-affairs—normally assume that the cause of change transcends human agency. Systemic approaches, which explain change in terms of endogenous dynamics (the "system") rather than exogenous factors, have been particularly favored by processual archaeologists.

In Marxist approaches social structure and change are attributed to the structure and change in economic institutions. In processual theories the role of individuals is removed even further because social institutions themselves, economic or otherwise, are interpreted to be products of entities like "systems" (Flannery 1968a). As a result systemic versions of processual approaches generally have provided even less room for the agency of humans than Marxist approaches (Hodder 1991).

Another reason for the exclusion of human agency is that processual explanations have been identified with positivistic method, the anti-metaphysical slant of which excludes speculative elements such as "minds" from scientific scrutiny. The belief that positivism underlies processual approaches, and the attempt to employ positivism rigorously by some (Binford 1972), have put a further methodological constraint on the inclusion of human agency in processual explanations.

Incidentally, processual archaeology should be identified with refutationist rather than positivistic method (Bell 1987a). Later it will also be seen that at least some processual problems—problems of explaining change—can be approached with individualistic method. That is why some processual archaeologists now talk of a new "cognitive phase" in processual archaeology (Renfrew and Zubrow 1993).

Benefits and Limits of Holistic Explanation

An advantage of holistic approaches is that the normal source of information on the thoughts, feelings, and decisions of humans— the written record—can be sidestepped. Because archaeological study focuses on the human past without written record, this advantage can hardly be overemphasized.

Another advantage is that a sizable portion of the artifactual record is appropriate for building and assessing holistic explanations.

Marxist approaches, for example, rely heavily upon utensils, tools, or anything else that might have been instrumental in the productive life of prehistoric peoples. Such remains can dominate the artifactual record. For the same reason, many processual theories address economic organization and change, or at least incorporate economic factors if the goal is to explain other types of social change.

The advantages cited here might tempt the conclusion that only holistic approaches should be used for theories that are assessed against the artifactual record. But there are two serious drawbacks to accepting that conclusion. Holistic approaches cannot account for the agency of humans, and cannot adequately explain social change unpredictable by holistic means. The example that follows brings out strengths of holistic approaches, and also reveals the two pitfalls.

The long-term cycles of economic expansion and contraction associated with Kondratieff—called Kondratieff cycles—are played out over fifty- to sixty-year periods regardless of catastrophic events or disruptive humans (Schumpeter 1964). Even the Second World War, one of the greatest man-made catastrophes in history, and Adolf Hitler, one of the most disruptive humans of all time, did not substantially alter the economic expansion predicted by Kondratieff theory. From the perspective of Kondratieff theory, World War II was emphatically *not* the cause of the expansion, as is popularly believed, because the upswing in capitalization and economic activity during and after the war was already in place before the war commenced. The drastic upheaval of the Second World War was only a ripple that might have accelerated the economic expansion in North America by a few years and delayed it in Europe by a few years. In short, the Second World War in general and Hitler in particular could just as well have been nonexistent, neither having more than a transitory effect on the Kondratieff wave of expansion.

If events such as the Second World War and someone such as Hitler have little to no effect on the march of economic expansion, then no unique events ever alter economic forces and no humans have agency. The conclusion is that only holistic approaches should be used when developing theories about human social organization and change.

But wait. Humans are agents, and not all events can be predicted. The first lacuna of holism—inability to account for human agency—would require ignoring the fact that Hitler's impact was startling, and the Second World War did have important consequences. There has been a near-universal disgust with fascism, at least in one of its more virulent forms. There has been a partial but significant unification of most of Western Europe. Unification of Europe was one of Hitler's dreams, although its present structure is not what he had envisioned. The point is that human thoughts, decisions, and actions—and events flowing from them—may indeed "make a difference."

It is reasonable to overlook weaknesses in holism when one's theoretical goals can be pursued in spite of them. Hitler's agency and World War II were insignificant for Kondratieff economic cycles. On the other hand, the Second World War drastically effected the lives of hundreds of millions of people and had a major impact on many political, social, and economic events. If one's theoretical goals require incorporating such effects, then holistic approaches may not be adequate. Unfortunately, those wed to holistic approaches can be blind to that fact. Instead of employing a non-holistic approach, the agency of humans and the unpredictability of certain events are likely to be considered unfit for "scientific" investigation and hence ignored. If they are not ignored, the possible agency of humans will be explained away in an ad hoc manner. Crude Marxists, for example, would insist that there is only one scientific route to explaining events like the Second World War: via economic structure and stresses within that structure. Interpretations incorporating human agency would be explained away as "mere ideational superstructure," or even "false consciousness:" ideas that do not accurately reflect the economic basis of human life.

The second lacuna—that holistic method cannot adequately account for unpredictable change—is related to the first. The reason is that ideas and decisions, and the actions following from them, can bring about change. But ideas are sometimes new, and new ideas are not always predictable. Neither are the changes resulting from new ideas always predictable. These points have been stressed by Karl Popper in *The Poverty of Historicism* (1957).

Popper argues that new scientific ideas grow from the weaknesses of received ones. Because it is not often possible to predict where crucial weaknesses will be found in received ideas, he reasons that the shape of new ideas is likewise unpredictable. Because ideas in science have a major impact on technology and technology has an enormous impact on events, future events are likewise unpredictable (Popper 1957). New ideas in science and the technology that flows from them can give a certain direction to change, but the changes themselves are not precisely predictable, especially over the long term. For example, the modern communications systems are a factor in directing the breakdown of totalitarian systems. Equipment such as fax machines and satellite phones cannot be so readily controlled by tyrants, and information about the outside world and their own government can give people the impetus to rebel against a repressive government. Where such rebellions might lead in the longer run is, of course, not always clear.

The unpredictability of change is magnified by the fact that actions have unintended consequences that sometimes prevail over the intended consequences. As a matter-of-fact, in human affairs events are usually the product of unintended consequences as well as intended ones. That many phenomena are unintended will be discussed further when reviewing methodological individualism.

There is yet another reason why the unpredictability of human events is overlooked. When restructuring the past, in which events have already transpired, it can seem as if there were no room for alternative occurrences. As a result, what has happened can appear as if it were "determined." That is why theories built upon historical investigation are prejudiced toward the predictability of events. Historical disciplines like archaeology can be slanted toward holistic approaches for this reason alone.

By the way, historians not shackled by a deterministic prejudice can produce interesting narrative accounts of events. The war histories of A.J.P. Taylor (1965, 1966) are an example. Taylor reconstructs wartime situations as perceived by the pivotal humans, tracing the rationale for their decisions and pointing out the consequences—often unintended—that followed. There is always the suggestion that alternative decisions might have yielded drastically different turns in the course of a war.

Incidentally, narrative histories are typically used to account for unique events in history, and hence are not designed to be testable. Those points were discussed in Chapter 3. But narrative histories do have the advantage of accounting for some (unique) events that are difficult if not impossible to account for otherwise, and they can suggest that decisions have a major impact on the course of history.

In sum, holistic approaches do not account for the potential role of human agency. Nor do holistic approaches allow for the possible unpredictability of at least some events in human history. The individualistic approach does overcome at least some of these lacunae. It is the subject of the next section.

Methodological Individualism

Individualistic method does provide room for human agency and a framework within which unpredictable change can be explored. The refutationist thrust of methodological individualism is another advantage. It encourages the formulation of testable theories, in this case testable theories about thoughts and decisions. The principal drawback is that individualistic method can be applied only to a rather confined—albeit important—range of archaeological theory.

Tenets of methodological individualism

Methodological individualism is a set of related ideas. It can be understood from a number of perspectives, depending upon which thesis or theses are chosen as a focus. For the purposes of this book two theses will be emphasized: (1) that thoughts do have *agency*, that is, that ideas and decisions, implicit and explicit, are crucial in the development of human societies, and (2) that collective institutions and dynamics, such as social structure and change, are the product of the decisions and actions of individuals. Many artifacts, by the way, can also be interpreted as the remnants of products made by the decisions and actions of individuals.

That ideas made a difference in early human affairs seems prima facie valid; it cannot be effectively denied. David Hume once argued that no testimony can establish the occurrence of miraculous events unless the contrary of the testimony is itself even more miraculous. In a similar vein it seems to me that denying the influence of ideas is more difficult to explain than assuming their influence. More significant than arguing for the agency of humans, then, is to ask what misconceptions lead to the conclusion it human agency is insignificant.

The first is the scientistic tendency to identify science exclusively with one type of method, in this case to identify science with holistic method. Even when human agency is acknowledged within a holistic perspective, it is not regarded as a legitimate component of scientific theories. As already pointed out, some explanations of social organization and change require no reference to human agency. It does not follow that no explanations require reference to human agency.

The second misconception is to interpret methodological assumptions as empirical statements rather than as heuristic tools. If method is interpreted empirically, attention turns to whether methodological components are "true" or "false," such as whether humans really do have minds (individualism) or not (holism). To be sure, arguing whether methodological assumptions are true or false can be valuable. For example, arguments for and against the existence of human universals can have a bearing on whether one has confidence to universalize theories in fields like anthropology and archaeology. Nevertheless, interpreting methodological assumptions only as empirical statements and then debating whether they are true or false is about as sensible as debating whether hammers and saws are true or false. Method is a tool, and attention should focus on delineating those situations in which a methodological approach can be productive or not so productive. For example, universalizing theories can increase testability and yield new understanding and insight even if there is no definitive answer as to whether human universals really exist.

Individualistic method can be fruitfully employed to build and assess theories when a theoretical problem-situation suggests that the thoughts and decisions of humans have been important. Holistic approaches can be productive when human agency need not be incorporated into theories.

The second thesis of individualistic method is that collective actions and entities are the product of the thoughts, decisions, and actions of individuals. For example, instead of citing a collective "spirit" as the cause of well-known events in late eighteenth-century France, individualistic method implies that the actions of many individuals, regardless of motives and ideas, dovetailed together into a partially collective movement referred to as the "French Revolution." Individualists avoid reifying collective notions such as the "spirit" of the revolution, or a "collective" movement, into causal entities. Instead, collectives are interpreted as derivative, the *result* of the decisions and actions of individual human beings. Even if some individuals do act because of dedication to a hypostatized entity, such as the "spirit" of a revolution, they do so out of their own choice.

A corollary is that the collective actions of individuals can be interpreted as the product of different and incompatible motives. More mileage can be squeezed from the example of the French Revolution. Some people may have joined the events because of commitment to revolutionary ideals, others because they feared the consequences of not doing so, yet others because they hoped for pecuniary gain, others because of the excitement, others because those close to them were involved, and others for a myriad of further reasons and motives, including spontaneous involvement with no motive whatsoever.

That a variety of motives underlie collective action provides a framework for explaining change, and particularly unpredictable change. Under given conditions collective actions can be dominated and directed by the ideas and motives of some individuals. As conditions change, however, others with alternative ideas and motives can rise to dominate. The result can be change, and even drastic change, in the collective actions of a group. That is why a revolution can turn into a monster quite discordant with the hopes that might initially have made it appealing.

It can now be seen that the two themes underlying individualistic method are closely related. The ideas, decisions, and actions of individuals explain change, but there are normally a wide variety of ideas and motives among individuals. Changing conditions encourage dominate motives and ideas to fade while facilitating others to emerge. The result, not surprisingly, is unpredictable change.

Unintended consequences

Unpredictable changes are also unintended. That is intuitively obvious, but individualistic method can be better understood by explicitly identifying three reasons why unintended consequences often arise in human affairs.

The first reason has already been discussed: Collective actions are the product of numerous and inconsistent motives and ideas. As conditions change, dominant ideas and motives tend to recede, while others ascend to the forefront.

The second reason was also outlined earlier: New ideas can and do arise. They can lead to decisions unforeseen prior to the advent of the new ideas. Consequences unintended from the perspective of prior conditions are the result.

The third reason for unintended consequences is that knowledge of motives and ideas of individuals is scanty. One must be particularly careful when analyzing collective action, the common behavioral features of which seldom if ever imply that the motives and goals of the participants are the same.

In brief, then, there are numerous reasons for the prevalence of unintended consequences, even in a world where individual humans believe they act intentionally. Of particular note is that unintended consequences are *not* explained by an appeal to forces transcending human agency. Individualists part company with holists at this point.

Even though holists and individualists both recognize that much of what occurs lies beyond the intentions of humans, the reasons are markedly different. Holists persist in believing that the consequences would be predictable if only the right universal "laws" were found. Individualists, on the other hand, contend that predicting consequences is tenuous at best and is intrinsically impossible in most cases. For individualists the future is *open*, to use philosophical terminology (Popper 1962). *Appeals to holistic forces will never enable all social structure and transformation to be predicted.*

Incidentally, that the future is open provides another criticism of the attempt to establish universals—"covering laws"—in historical fields such as archaeology. If the future is open, such "laws" are always suspect. Attempting to establish universals inductively is *not*, however, to be confused with universalizing theories. The former is not valuable or even possible, whereas the latter is very productive for theory development. These matters were discussed in Chapters 3 and 4.

Knowledge of individuals

Knowledge of the ideas and motives of particular individuals is scanty. This point is extremely important in the individualist framework: It implies that assumptions about people's goals and decisions should be made only with considerable caution, if at all. The corollary is that policies based upon such assumptions—collectivist policies, for example—should be avoided. The case against assuming knowledge of individuals, and the constraints it imposes on the use of individualistic method, will be discussed in more detail next. An explanation of how individualistic method can be and is effectively employed within those constraints follows.

It certainly is possible to catch glimpses of the ideas and motives of some people, especially of those with whom one is personally close. For a more distant set of people, however, and especially a large set—even when there is collective action—individualistic approaches cannot assume such knowledge. Furthermore, if one must be careful about presupposing knowledge of the ideas and motives of living people, one must be all the more so for those no longer on this earth and especially for those for whom there is little or no written record.

If the agency of humans is significant in the structure and transformations of human institutions, and yet knowledge of their ideas and motives can only be fragmentary, then individualistic tools for investigating human institutions would seem poor at best. In light of this argument, it would not be surprising if individualistic approaches were ignored or abandoned in favor of holistic ones.

Indeed, individualistic method is constrained by the variety, changeability, and opaqueness of individual ideas and motives. Where it can be effectively used are in those realms of human activity where the ideas or motives are shared. That is a reason why individualistic method can be employed to analyze the rudimentary economic behavior of individuals: All individuals need to make decisions about obtaining food and shelter and, in more developed economies, about other material goods and services such as medicine, transportation, and education. That individualistic method has an established tradition in economic anthropology is not surprising. Nor is it surprising in archaeology that individualistic method has been employed to analyze the decisions of individuals in the pursuit of game and other foodstuffs in hunter-gather societies (Mithen 1990), or in the making and management of tools for such pursuits (Perlès 1992). Individualistic method would be less useful for analyzing choices made by individuals for certain colors of clothing, however, or for their tastes in music. In such realms necessity does not constrain the variety of choice. Decision making can thus be more capricious, and, as a result, far more variegated. In addition to the economic realm, individualistic approaches can be employed to investigate other types of ideas shared by groups of people, such as ideas in mathematics and science. It comes as no surprise, then, that cognitive archaeology is focused on ideas shared by a group rather than on ideas that are less public and agreed upon (Renfrew 1987, personal communication 1987).

Ideas, decisions, and actions can and often do become constituents in the lives of people to the point where they seem to function like rocks, or weather. In philosophical terminology, that is a reason why cognitive elements are amenable to a *realist* interpretation: the view that ideas are attempts to describe the actual world. A corollary is that ideas become actual elements in the sphere of human decision and action, just like rocks, weather, and other natural entities (Popper 1972, 1983). "Traditions," for example, can and do become factors that both guide and constrain the lives of individuals. Traditions turn into "ideologies" when they are accepted and acted upon without critical reflection, even in the face of obvious counterevidence. As a matter-of-fact, the reality of cognitive elements is demonstrated by the prevalence of ideological thinking, in which ideas are taken to be more "real" than any evidence that can be marshalled against them.

Despite being real elements in our world, cognitive elements are amenable to change, even drastic change. Even ideologies come and go, sometimes with rather surprising alacrity. In other words, ideas shared by individuals, or decisions and actions common to different individuals, are not the same as holistic forces impounding upon individuals.

Holistic forces are always assumed to be beyond the control of humans and hence *in principle* do not change. That is why holistic approaches assume a future trajectory predictable from a model of an antecedent past, necessitating the belief that there *is* a model to make the predictions. Vulgar Marxist approaches assume that the future of human institutions is predictable from economic laws, for example. The ideas of humans cannot interfere because they are themselves a product of economic factors. Approaches that assume there are laws binding at all times for all societies ("covering laws") are another example.

The difference between the malleable status of shared ideas, decisions, and actions of individualistic approaches and the nonmalleable status of forces impounding on humans in holistic approaches cannot be overemphasized. Crumley and Marquardt (1987) use an individualistic approach in their study of the regional development of the Burgundy area of France. The interplay between ideational elements and material conditions is appropriately called a *dialectical* approach, rather than a Marxist approach, thus avoiding the political and holistic overtones of the latter. The methodological recommendations in the latest book by Shanks and Tilley on approaches to understanding the prehistoric past are more individualistic than holistic. For that reason labeling them "Marxist" might be misleading (Shanks and Tilley 1987a).

It should be clear by now that the "individual" in individualistic method is a *generic* individual: some individual or other rather than a particular individual. For example, it is assumed that a decision to hunt fauna rather than gather flora under specified conditions by the hunter-gatherers in the studies of Steven Mithen (1987, 1990) would be a decision made by most hunter-gathers of the Perigord rather than just the decision of some particular individual. In short, the ideas and decisions of the individual refer to the set of ideas and decisions that are common to (actual) individuals.

Applications of individualistic method in studies of the prehistoric past are limited to the generic individual. When a *particular* individual becomes a study of prehistorians, however, the goal is usually to identify particular humans with their products (Hill and Gunn 1977). The goal is similar to that of an art historian attempting to identify the painter of a landscape scene. This is different from the goal of using individualistic method, which is to explain social structure and change as the product of human agency. Both focus on individuals, but the particular individual should not be confused with the generic individual assumed in methodological individualism.

It is obvious by this point that the term "individualism" can be confusing. The choice of the word is plausible. The connotations of the word "individualism" imply that agency can and does play a crucial role in the structure and change of human institutions. Those connotations also contrast sharply with the pawn-like, robotic conception of humans in holistic views. Individualism has also become identified with the dignity of the individual and respect for individuality, and is associated with the social, economic, and political institutions that encourage those values. In the United States that meaning is conveyed by the expression "rugged individualism."

In addition to the plausible connotations outlined here, one must be careful not to read other connotations into the word "individualism." It does not connote that we know much about the great variety of ideas or motives of particular individuals. Quite the contrary, it cautions us against assuming such knowledge. It also does not connote that individuals must act on ideas and motives different from those of others; we can and do act on shared values. It does not even connote that people must act on ideas, or values, or any such things. They might simply react or act spontaneously in some other irrational way. The following historical comments shed more light on the numerous connotations of the word "individualism."

Historical Roots of
Methodological Individualism

Understanding the background to individualistic method will help unravel the confusions surrounding the meaning of "individualism." It will also shed light on why the individualistic outlook can arouse strong reactions, both positive and negative.

The roots of methodological individualism are frequently traced to the "Austrian" school of economics. The Austrian school was founded in the late nineteenth century by Carl Menger, who argued against the labor theory of value espoused by such diverse thinkers as Karl Marx and Adam Smith. The labor theory of value assumes that the value of a product is, or at least should be, equal to the human effort expended in its production. Menger contended that the value of a product is "subjective"; that is, the value of a product is due to demand for it. The labor invested in a product is only tangentially related to its value and sometimes is irrelevant.

After the First World War a number of members of the Austrian school dedicated themselves to exposing the faults of collectivist economic organization. Eugen von Boehm-Bawerk was one. Ludwig von Mises was another. Not surprisingly, von Mises argued for the advantages of free-market economic structure (von Mises 1949, 1962). Friedrich von Hayek, von Mises' protégé, has become the foremost spokesman of the Austrian school. Hayek clearly recognized the significance of the individualistic assumptions that underlie free-market theory. He has made those assumptions explicit, argued for them, and traced the ramifications into economic theory and social policy (Hayek 1944, 1948).

Methodological individualism is also associated with Karl Popper. Popper recognized the kinship of the individualistic outlook and his refutationist view of science. He used both in his criticisms of holistic interpretations of history, such as vulgar Marxism. Popper also employed methodological individualism in the development of his social philosophy.

The similarity between the individualistic views of Hayek and Popper is more than coincidental. They had known each other and had shared ideas for decades. Popper (1945) even dedicated his *The Open Society and Its Enemies* to Hayek.

In *The Road to Serfdom* (1944) and more explicitly in *The Counter-Revolution in Science: Studies on the Abuse of Reason* (1972), Hayek attacks holistic approaches in the social sciences. He also criticizes collectivist economic and social policies generated from holistic assumptions. In place of holistic approaches he advocates individualistic method. He offers a number of arguments for individualistic method. For example, he argues that the prerequisites for happiness vary greatly among individuals. One person may need wealth, whereas an ascetic life-style is crucial for another. Furthermore, humans have only limited knowledge of what is significant in the lives of different people, at least beyond the obvious need for food and a modicum of shelter. He concluded that humans should be constrained as little as possible in working out their own destinies.

Hayek also developed a set of arguments that are specifically economic. For example, the complexity and constant flux of an economy make it impossible to implement efficient and effective collective plans. Furthermore, as an economy becomes more complex planning becomes even less workable. Instead of collectivization, Hayek argues for a free-market, one that is determined by the ensemble of decisions of individuals and freely associating groups of individuals.

In short, Hayek's social and economic arguments for free-markets presuppose an individualistic outlook on people and institutions. He concluded that the best social structure is one within which individuals can maximize choices in pursuing their own goals. That is a liberal democratic society, the center of which is a free-market economy.

Popper's arguments for methodological individualism are also interwoven with his criticisms of holistic method. In *The Open Society and its Enemies* (1945) and *The Poverty of Historicism* (1957), Popper warns of the dangers of social and political theories based upon holistic assumptions. Such theories can become self-fulfilling prophecies, but only by intervention in the flow of human events, that is, by using dictatorial means. Popper argues for individualistic method in the social sciences, and the benefits of social and political policies framed within an individualistic outlook.

Individualistic method and refutationist method

Popper has been prominent in the development of methodological individualism for another reason: Individualistic method is closely associated with refutationist method. Similarities between individualistic method in the social sciences and refutationist method in the physical sciences are outlined next.

Implicit in the refutationist view is that parts of theories remain opaque to us. The parts of theories we know best are those components and implications that potentially clash with reality, that is, where theories are refutable and thus can be tested. Individualistic method provides the warning that our knowledge of the panorama of motives and ideas upon which individuals make their choices is quite limited. When an individual can learn, however, is when his or her ideas clash with reality. Scientific knowledge advances by developing theories which supersede errors in mistaken theories. Individuals learn by developing better ideas when others fail. The unpredictability of the future of knowledge from the refutationist perspective is similar to the unpredictability of the future of human events implied by individualistic method. The interpretation of scientific knowledge as a human creation and changeable by human agency is similar to the individualistic view of social institutions as human creations and as changeable by humans. Finally, the importance of a social framework in which ideas can be asserted boldly, but also criticized severely, is best guarded by attitudes implied by refutationist method, attitudes that encourage people to assert bold ideas and yet be open to criticism of those ideas. In short, individualistic method for the social sciences is the close relative of refutationist method in the physical sciences.

Individualistic method and social policy

As a formula for social policy, individualistic method can be summarized as follows: Leave individuals as free from constraint as possible in all realms of their lives. Individualistic method thus buttresses liberal democracy and free-market economic organization. Not surprisingly, then, individualistic method is also a formula with which to fight against collectivization, whether it be the collectivization of ideas or of production.

Holism, on the other hand, buttresses collectivization. The assumption that superhuman laws organize human events implies that all people are subject to those same laws. One corollary is that humans are largely the product of those laws. That leads to another corollary: The differences among individuals are minimal when compared to the similarities. Collectivist policies are supposedly sensible because they emphasize the similarities among humans. Collectivization is desirable because it (purportedly) provides an efficient and direct route to satisfying common needs.

In brief, then, individualistic assumptions legitimate free-market economies and holistic assumptions justify socialized economies. That is why commitment to individualism or holism can take on the drumbeat of conviction. The danger is all the greater, however, that conviction can also be drummed into ideology. Ideological attachment to either individualistic or holistic approaches can stifle the flexibility necessary for judicious use of either, in archaeology or any other realm. Fortunately there is a compromise.

Political and social commitment can provide the impetus to pursue certain types of theories. Someone particularly interested in the feminist movement, for example, might be motivated to study the role of women in prehistoric societies, or someone intrigued with socialist policies might attempt to understand welfare structure in prehistoric societies. If an archaeologist is uncomfortable with either holistic or individualistic method, and its disadvantages for his or her theoretical interests are not the reason, then an honest appraisal of one's own political-social orientation is in order. If political and social commitment exclude consideration of either individualistic or holistic approaches, theory development can clearly be constrained. Ideological commitment can blind one to the disadvantages of the approach wed to one's own political and social convictions, as well as masking the advantages of an alternative approach. It is important to be aware of these potential dangers and to have the courage to counter them.

Before concluding the historical commentary, two alternative reconstructions of the historical background of individualistic method should be mentioned. The first focuses on unintended consequences, the second on the individuality and agency of humans.

That human institutions and events are a mixed product of purposeful human actions with unintended consequences is attributable to Max Weber (1864–1920). Methodological individualism can thus be interpreted as an outgrowth of the Weberian tradition (Weber 1962). Karl Marx (1818–1883) preceded Weber and can also be given a historical note because of his emphasis on the unintended consequences of economic activity. As pointed out earlier, Marx's philosophy is largely holistic: The unintended consequences of economic activity were explained by economic laws not controlled by individuals. Furthermore, regimes that have identified with Marxism are not noted for embracing the dignity of the individual or other values and institutions normally associated with an individualistic outlook. Despite the irony, it is no historical mirage to trace one root of methodological individualism to Karl Marx's recognition of the unintended consequences of human actions.

A focus on the individuality of humans and on individual responsibility is a hallmark of existentialism, especially that of Jean-Paul
Sartre (1956, 1957). It is also illuminating, then, to link the emergence of individualistic method with the existentialist movement
that grew before and during World War II, and that exploded onto
the scene after the war. That interpretation of the historical roots of
individualism has been offered by Mark Patton (1986).

Holistic Method and Individualistic Method

Tools are designed to help with particular problems. In theoretical
pursuits, a *problem-situation* is the context that makes an explanation
interesting. Normally an explanation arouses interest when it illuminates or is in conflict with the empirical record, when it ramifies or
conflicts with another explanation, or when it supports or calls into
question a broad metaphysical outlook (Popper 1983). It is not un-
common for an explanation to be interesting for two or more of the
reasons just mentioned. For example, the evolutionary theories of
Darwin provided a shock for all three reasons. It conflicted with accepted dating chronology for the human past, it was inconsistent
with the accepted theory of Archbishop Ussher (1581–1656) that the
origin of man dated from 4004 B.C., and it challenged the standard
Biblical account of the origins of life and mankind.

The decision to employ either holistic or individualistic method
should depend upon its promise for generating and improving explanations in a given problem-situation. In some problem-situations
in archaeology, institutions, social structure, and social dynamics are
best interpreted as transcendent to human agency. In those contexts
there is little if any need to invoke the thoughts, will, or acts of
individuals. For investigation in those realms holistic methods are
appropriate. In other problem-situations those institutions, structure, and dynamics can better be interpreted as the intended and
unintended products of human agency. In those realms individualistic method would be appropriate. There are more specific criteria

that can help archaeologists who would like to decide which approach to utilize.

It is clear there is no algorithm or effective procedure that will guarantee the most fruitful decision. One can clarify theoretical goals, however, and then make a decision on method relative to the goals. For example, if there is to be an interpretation of the longer-range trading patterns within a region of prehistoric settlements, relationships among populations, tools, agricultural productivity, and other such parameters without concern for other particularities would suggest holistic approaches. In such cases holistic assumptions might deliver comprehensive and testable explanations. It must be remembered that theoretical goals can change, however, and often in unforeseen ways. Suppose that in the course of investigating field data to test a holistic explanation for the problem-situation mentioned, one discovers a rather startling rise in the trade of a certain type of figurine. The figurine seems to function as an icon, and may thus indicate a significant alteration in thought patterns. The discovery could provide the impetus to use individualistic method. One might consider the possibility of a cognitive change, and search for evidence that could bear upon such a change.

In short, there are investigative situations in which holistic approaches are promising and others in which individualistic method are promising. It cannot be decided a priori which is preferable, but a particular context can indicate which might be best pursued, at least initially. Furthermore, approaches can be switched when necessary. Although holistic and individualistic method are inconsistent, they can be used as complements, as in the example above. Switching methods is no more surprising than using a saw for cutting wood, and then resorting to a hammer to nail it to a sideboard. Uncritical attachment to one approach or the other can prevent a switch to a more productive alternative.

It was pointed out earlier that strongly held social and political viewpoints can result in uncritical attachment to either holistic or individualistic approaches. There is also an intellectual reason for uncritical attachment: Method productive in one area is assumed— sometimes mistakenly—to be productive in all areas. Another reason for uncritical attachment is professional: Adherence to a particular method can identify a subspecialty. Although there is need for professional niches, defining them by method carries the danger of excluding consideration of alternative methods that might prove useful. Yet another reason for uncritical attachment is that methodological commitment can help a grant application, the funding of which is sometimes more dependent upon proposed method than research goals.

Despite the multiple pressures, there is no need to be caught in an ideological trap over method. Simply remember that method is a tool, chosen in light of one's research goals, and that method can and should change when an alternative shows more promise or when one changes goals. That, along with keeping one's professional, political, and social proclivities in abeyance, should help one pick an appropriate approach in a given problem-situation. Nimble use of multiple approaches is more difficult to practice than to preach, of course, but it certainly is possible.

Methodological Individualism and Theoretical Archaeology

Some implications of individualistic assumptions for theoretical archaeology are explored in this and the following sections. First is a review of ways that understanding the individualistic outlook can be helpful for those using holistic approaches. Second is an outline of the potential for applying individualistic method to build testable theories about prehistoric social organization and change. Explaining social structure via individual decision making is one area of use. Another is employing individualistic method to an inductive reconstruction of prehistoric ideas. This last use will be discussed with the help of a detailed example in the next chapter.

Understanding individualistic method

It is unlikely that holistic approaches have borne their last fruit. Despite the obituary notice implied by the expression "postprocessual" archaeology, processual approaches and materialism as well may only be yielding initial harvests. The factors that help facilitate holistic studies of prehistoric peoples, such as requiring no written records and the availability of a potentially abundant material record for theory assessment, are not entirely helpful for individualistic approaches. In fact, the material remains that bear witness to the ideas and decisions of prehistoric peoples are not generally obvious or even accessible. For those who wish for these or other reasons to continue pursuing holistic approaches, however, much can still be gained by understanding individualistic method. There are a number of reasons.

First, familiarity with individualistic approaches can serve as a reminder that holistic approaches miss aspects of human culture when they push human agency off the theoretical playing field. Realizing that alone should help prevent ideological attachment to holism.

Second, holistic approaches do not always yield adequate explanations of some phenomena, such as some types of societal collapse. These can become anomalies in holistic explanations. Awareness of the potential for individualistic approaches make it less tempting to treat such anomalies in an ad hoc fashion, such as blindly assuming that more holistic research will inevitably account for the anomaly, downplaying the significance of the anomaly, or ignoring it all together. One might not personally choose to resolve an anomaly with individualistic tools, but one might at least be open to an individualistic alternative pursued by someone else.

Incidentally, there is no reason not to attempt to resolve an anomaly in a holistic explanation by adding auxiliary hypotheses that are also holistic. A resolution might be found, after all. That would be far better than explaining an anomaly away by ad hoc stratagems.

Decisions at the level of the individual

Individualistic method can be useful for developing explanations that incorporate decisions of individuals. The studies of Steven Mithen on the decision making of hunter-gathers in pursuit of food is an example already mentioned. Instead of building theories on a data base referring only to cumulative group behavior, Mithen uses theories about the choices of individuals to explain the cumulative behavior (Mithen 1987, 1990). It is analogous to explaining gas pressure and volume at the macro-level by the action of molecules at the micro-level.

Mithen has also used the artifactual record to test his theories. Individualistic theories, like holistic theories, must be assessed against the material record. Because the material remains of economic activity in prehistory can be more abundant than material remains from other types of activity, the focus will often be on individual choices made in the economic sphere.

In earlier discussions of testability it was noted that some theories are highly testable because they can be universalized and hence assessed in many different contexts. Wittfogel's hydraulic theory was the primary example used in this book. Other theories are testable and can be improved in a particular context, but generalizing them for testing beyond the context is of questionable value even though they can be suggestive for theory development in other contexts. Earle's modified hydraulic theory for the Halelea District of Kauai was an example. The testability of Steve Mithen's theory about individual choice seems more like the latter. Even when generalized just to other hunter-gatherer groups, the variations in available flora and fauna would almost certainly dictate different choice preferences. If Mithen's theory were generalized, then, it would almost surely be quickly refuted. The suggestive value of his approach is certainly worth noting, however: Hunter-gatherers will have choice preferences. The mathematical formulations used by Mithen to predict those choices might also be adapted for use in other contexts.

It is also worth stating again that individualistic theories generally must focus upon a prehistoric activity that is largely the same for most individuals under given conditions. A particular hunter-gatherer in the Perigord region of Southwest France in Mithen's studies, for example, is likely to have similar nutritional needs as other hunter-gathers and to be familiar with the same traditional hunting techniques as other hunter-gatherers. Personal peculiarities and preferences would be much more difficult if not impossible to identify in the material record. Fortunately, such preferences are unlikely to have much if any influence on shared activities. Whether one male hunter-gatherer had brown hair and liked shorter women, for example, whereas another had blond hair and preferred taller women, would not likely have any direct bearing on the hunting activities of either one.

In sum, exploring individual decisions among prehistoric peoples requires a focus on activities that leave a material record and which are common to people rather than particularities that differentiate people from each other. For both reasons economic activity is often the focus of study, and the individual decisions to be investigated will be those of the generic individual rather than those of particular individuals.

Using individualistic method to explore decisions does require that the choices of individuals be stipulated, but it does not require speculation about the ideas behind those choices. A hunter-gatherer, for example, may choose to pursue game instead of gather root plants, but one need not know whether that person "thought" abstractly about the consequences of his or her choices, made the choices spontaneously without thought, or did something in between.

Analyzing decisions at the level of the individual is one way to use individualistic method. Individualistic method can also be used to speculate about the thoughts of prehistoric peoples. That is one aim of cognitive archaeology.

Methodological Individualism in Cognitive Archaeology

The broad goal of cognitive archaeology is to incorporate mental, ideational, symbolic, and other such elements into theories about prehistoric peoples. Within that broad framework are a panorama of specific goals. At one extreme are attempts to capture such abstruse elements as the feelings of prehistoric peoples, their experiences, and the variety of meanings that engulfed their existence (Hodder 1991). At the other extreme are guarded attempts to gain partial insight into some of the ideas held by prehistoric peoples (Renfrew 1982). The latter approach is endorsed here. Individualistic method provides the guidelines, the reasons for which are explained below.

The individualistic view not only implies that ideas are important in the development of human institutions, but also that ideas can and are sometimes willfully used to change those institutions. That is why theories about prehistoric cognition cannot be generated by holistic method, which by definition excludes human agency as significant in the structure and transformation of human institutions. Theories about prehistoric cognition could be generated with empathetic method. The trouble is that they are unlikely to be testable at all. Like empathetic attempts to capturing feelings and experiential meanings, empathetic attempts to understand prehistoric cognition run the risk of being mere speculation rather than speculation subject to testing. The refutationist orientation of methodological individualism, on the other hand, puts an empirical constraint on theories about prehistoric cognition: Such theories should be testable. If such theories are not testable, then the spirit of requiring testability can at least be applied. More specifically, if theories about prehistoric cognition are not testable, theories about prehistoric cognition must be very carefully induced from the available data and limited to statements strictly inferred from that data.

The next chapter is devoted to explaining the mechanics of using individualistic method to develop theories about prehistoric cognition. Rather than say more about the mechanics here, then, the remainder of this section is devoted to presenting more background to the use of individualistic method in cognitive archaeology and explaining the reasons for turning to methodological individualism for that purpose.

Incidentally, a surprise is in store. A few comments here might cushion the shock. New Archaeologists in the American camp are quite skeptical of any attempts to use nondeterministic high-level models. Because methodological individualism does not imply a deterministic view of either humans or social development, those New Archaeologists will be very skeptical. Strange as it may seem to them, however, one of the primary reasons for turning to methodological individualism is that it provides a framework for advancing the processual goal of explaining change. More specifically, individualistic method provides an opportunity to explain changes due to ideas.

Calls to understand the ideas of people and how they influence historical development have a long tradition, including calls from some who have had considerable influence on the thinking of archaeologists (Collingwood 1946). Archaeologists have also made such calls (for example Leone 1982b and Hodder 1991). Exploring the ideas of people in prehistory with individualistic method, however, is quite recent. The most explicit example are the methodological proposals for cognitive archaeology offered by Colin Renfrew. Renfrew's attention to methodological constraints, and his careful use of individualistic theses—although he has no particular label for them—make his work particularly exemplary.

Immediately following are comments on reasons for exploring prehistoric ideas. It is crucial to be familiar with those reasons to understand why Renfrew, a devoted processual archaeologist, would consider much less use an individualistic approach. The discussion then turns to the individualistic method utilized in Renfrew's approach to cognitive archaeology.

Goals of cognitive archaeology

A primary reason for cognitive archaeology is interest in how people may have thought. That in itself would justify pursuing theories about the cognition of prehistoric peoples. There are other reasons, however. One is that ideas may have been crucial in human affairs in the past, even in prehistory. In order to gain a more complete picture of prehistoric peoples, then, attempts to understand the ideas woven into their lives are warranted. A further reason for exploring the cognition of prehistoric peoples is the need to find adequate explanations of change in prehistoric societies. This reason is not as obvious as the others.

Explaining change in human societies has been a dominant goal of theoretical archaeologists during the past few decades. The goal of *process*-ual archaeology *is* to explain change, after all, and it is a goal of Marxist approaches as well. As has been seen, however, both processual and Marxist explanations have been largely holistic: They assume that the dynamics of change transcend human thought and decision. That is a strength of holism, but its Achilles heel as well. Holistic approaches assume that future trajectories can always be plotted from the present and past, and that human agency will have no significant influence on those trajectories. Holists also assume that there must be holistic resolutions to any anomalous predictions.

As already argued, the future is not always predictable and some features may not be predictable at all. The refutationist view that the future is "open" has already been presented. There is additional evidence, however, from sources as diverse as new ideas in systems theory and mathematics, and as old as the intuitive notion that the ideas and decisions of humans do play a role in creating change.

Some systems are *complex systems*, those that change in ways not explicable from past structure or dynamics. Parameters of the past and present in these systems are not adequate to explain how they change, which is why they tend toward "chaos." Interestingly enough, many complex systems do reorder themselves, but in unpredictable forms.

A primary source of insights and ideas on complex systems has been the work of Ilya Prigogine. Following his work in thermodynamics, Prigogine and his proteges have been employing complex systems to understand organization and change in physical as well as social systems (Prigogine 1980; Prigogine and Stengers 1984). Some have already been exploring the potential for interpreting prehistoric social organization and change as complex (van der Leeuwe 1981). Another conceptual and practical tool for understanding complex systems is the mathematical fractal theory of Benoit Mandelbrot (1982) and others (Peitgen and Richter 1986). With fractal geometry it has been possible to delineate form in the path of a lightning bolt, for example, the path of which had previously been thought to be totally chaotic.

Yet another way to explain unpredictable change in prehistoric societies is to interpret change as the product of human agency. The focus on prehistoric cognition, then, can serve processual goals. *It is another way of searching for new explanations of change in prehistoric societies.* This reason for interest in cognitive archaeology will, I predict, lead more and more processual archaeologists to individualistic method.

Employing refutationist method

Another reason that processual archaeologists can find individualistic approaches attractive is that the latter share the refutationist method employed in effective processual archaeology. Three related themes in the refutationist view should be given attention when using individualistic method: recognition that one can only capture some aspects of the ideas of other people, that theories about ideas should be testable, and that theories should not be merely empathetic projections. Each theme is discussed in turn.

It has been pointed out that formulating and assessing theories about the ideas of prehistoric peoples is frustrated by the lack of a written record. Quite surprisingly, the sparse material record does hide an advantage. When using the individualistic framework one assumes that only some aspects of peoples' thoughts are accessible. The upshot of having only a sprinkling of material remains for theory building and testing, and a methodological prescription that warns against presumptuous claims about people's ideas and motives, is that attempts to "restructure" anything approaching a "world view " or "totality of thought" would be highly suspect. Not surprisingly, then, Renfrew (1982, 1987, personal communication 1987) insists that statements about the ideas of prehistoric people can give only partial insights.

Building theories about the thoughts of prehistoric peoples should be done in such a way that they can be tested against the material record. If they are not testable, then they must be induced carefully from the data and must be limited to statements that can be inferred directly from the data. In either case, it is important to separate more speculative elements of theories about ideas from those that are more testable or at least can be inferred directly from the data.

The way to separate the former from the latter is to make a *logicist* analysis of the ideas, to use the terminology of Jean-Claude Gardin (1992; see also Gardin 1980). A logistic analysis separates the components of the ideas and the inferential steps connecting them. Renfrew does such an analysis in his theorizing about cognition, thus enabling distinctions to be made between what can be known with reasonable confidence and what is more speculative. The logistic analysis leaves a "cognitive map" or *mappa* (Renfrew's terminology). The components of a *mappa* are either induced directly from the material record or are inferred carefully from the components induced directly from the material record. The latter components are thus also inferred from the data. The mechanics of building a *mappa* occupies a substantial part of the next chapter.

In sum, theories about prehistoric ideas should be confined to limited aspects of prehistoric thinking, and those aspects should be testable against the material record or at least induced carefully from the material record. These two requirements lead to the third: The theories about ideas should not merely be empathetic projections. Theories confined to statements about ideas contrasts sharply with theories that emerge from empathetic approaches. In the latter, one projects his or her own experience into those of others.

Statements open to empirical assessment can be *distanced* from the investigator; that is, they can become objects for theoretical exploration regardless of the cultural and other presuppositions of the investigator. When the presuppositions of the investigator do become parts of a cognitive map, they can at least be made explicit and opened to assessment by logicist analysis. This is markedly different from projecting one's own ideas into the minds of others. Projected ideas become *self-referential*; that is, the "truth" of the idea is largely the product of the person making the claim. The danger is amplified in archaeological contexts precisely because there are no written records against which to check a self-referential claim.

In practice, distinguishing between testable statements about ideas and nontestable, self-referential claims is not always easy. When using individualistic method one should *try* to form statements that can be tested against the material remains or induced carefully from it. Do recognize, however, that there will normally—

perhaps always—be a "subjective" side to theories about prehistoric ideas: the impetus provided by an investigator's own interests. More specifically, archaeologists like others would be inclined to explore ideas that are related to areas of particular interest.

Despite the research direction given by a person's particular interests, there is no reason why the testability of theories need be compromised. Such "subjective" direction can be eliminated if one distances ones own proclivities through logistic analysis, and limits oneself to theories that are testable against the material record or that are induced carefully from the material record.

Careful methodological use of individualism is also exemplified in the work of Henri-Paul Francfort. He and his group at the Centre Nationale de la Recherche Scientifique in Paris and others are exploring, at the level of the generic individual, the manufacture, maintenance, and management of tools in prehistory (Francfort 1992; Perlès 1992; Roux 1992). Their models even enable one to recognize symbolic use of tools: Disruption of the normal parameters for choice of materials and style can indicate a symbolic role that overrides the usual utilitarian function of tools (Perlès 1992). The work of these people exemplifies the refutationist hallmarks of methodological individualism: the recognition that only partial insights into the ideas of the generic individual are possible, the use of logistic analysis to separate those components that are testable or induced and those components that are not, and care in avoiding self-referential components that come from empathetic projections.

Empathetic Method and Individualistic Method

The goal of reconstructing the feelings, hopes, and other affective and spiritual elements in the experiential lives of prehistoric peoples is much broader than that of gaining insight into some of their ideas. For such an all-inclusive goal one typically turns to *empathetic method*: the use of personal intuition to understand the inner lives of other people. Empathetic method assumes there is a common structure to human experience. The assumed common structure is used to justify claims about the experiences of other people. More specifically, the investigator's experience is assumed to be similar to that of others, including those who left no written record.

One obvious difficulty is that the experience of people may not be similar, and can be utterly different. Furthermore, empathetic constructions tend to be far too speculative to meet the refutationist constraints of individualistic method. The upshot is that empathetic theories cannot be assessed against the artifactual record with any confidence. In fact, empathetic method can be viewed as individualistic method that has lost its refutationist rudder, that is, individualistic method that has transcended the bounds within which statements can be effectively tested against the material record or at least inferred carefully from the material record.

It is important to bear in mind that "empathetic method" is a generic expression used to cover quite a range of approaches. At one extreme it merges with individualistic method, adopting the goals and constraints of the latter. At the other extreme empathetic method incorporates the broad goals and intuitive approach that characterize pure empathy. At this extreme it is assumed one can "know" how others think and feel via (self-referential) intuitions. The structuralism of Lévi-Strauss (1966) lies in this direction. More often than not there will be an amalgamation of individualistic and empathetic elements. An example is Hodder's "contextual structuralism" for uncovering the experience of prehistoric peoples (Hodder 1991; Bell 1987a).

In this section the pure form of empathetic method is discussed briefly. The reason is not because it is commonly employed, but because understanding it can help one recognize and avoid empathetic tendencies when using individualistic method.

To begin, empathetic method does have a number of similarities with individualistic method. Both are contraries to the holistic focus on trans-human forces and dynamics. Advocates of empathetic and individualistic method both recognize that holistic approaches cannot possibly capture the full richness of human life and activity. They would likely find, for example, more telling insight in the testimony of the believer than that of the atheist previously discussed. Furthermore, human agency is important in the eyes of both individualists and those wedded to empathetic approaches. The ideas, decisions, and other human elements are not considered insignificant in the organization of human institutions.

Despite the similarities between individualistic and empathetic method, there are major differences in goals, and approaches to the goals. First, empathetic method is aimed at painting a comprehensive portrait of the affective, spiritual, and cognitive elements in human experience. Individualistic method restricts theories to those elements for which the material record can provide some evidence. Second, empathetic approaches are not used for the processual goal of explaining change. The empathetic assumption that there are unchanging universal structures of the human mind draws out elements that are static rather than dynamic. Methodological individualism, on the other hand, implies that the thoughts, decisions, and actions of people are in flux, and can be used to explain change. Third and finally, empathetic method does not provide feasible ways of testing theories, whereas individualistic method does. That is why empathetic approaches do not easily yield conjectures that can be empirically assessed and then improved. Empathetic portraits are more like a final product rather than a sketch that can be tested, altered, and hence used to gain further understanding.

Incidentally, pure empathetic approaches are sometimes called *high structuralism.* Underlying universals in human experience are not only assumed, but are also stipulated explicitly and are claimed to dominate the generation of cultural forms and human institutions. Lévi-Strauss's high structuralism is the best-known example. High structuralist approaches are like holistic approaches: Humans are viewed as pawns of structures that transcend their control. The difference is that principal causes of social structure are internal in high structuralism whereas they are external in holistic approaches.

Conclusion

Methodological individualism has been the focus of this chapter. Understanding its potential and limitations required discussion of holistic and empathetic approaches as well. As usual when studying

a methodological approach, comparison with the alternatives increases knowledge of its benefits and weaknesses. That knowledge
helps one make more judicious methodological choices.

Empathetic approaches have commonly been assumed to be the
only alternative to holistic approaches. Individualistic method as an
alternative is, however, entering the theoretical scene in archaeology. It sometimes shares common ground with holism, such as the
goal of explaining social structure and change. It shares with empathetic method the focus on human agency as a crucial component in
explaining human life and institutions. Individualistic method has
refutationist roots. For that reason it is designed to produce explanations that are testable against the data, and hence revisable in light
of the data. It shares these qualities with processual approaches but
not with empathetic approaches.

In the eyes of many, only holistic approaches merit the label "scientific." That view is not implausible: Holistic theories are often ones in
which error can be found and exploited to gain further understanding
and new insight. The training that numerous archaeologists receive
within the context of the social sciences can reinforce the belief that
holistic assumptions are the only route to a "scientific" study of man.
Individualistic method is also rooted in the refutationist view of science. That is why it can be used to formulate, test, and improve at
least some theories that incorporate decision making in prehistory.
That is also why it can be used to formulate testable theories about
prehistoric thinking, or at least theories that are tied closely to the material record. The individualistic framework can also be used to explain
some major transformations in human societies not explicable by holistic means. For these reasons methodological individualism should take
its place among the theory-building tools of archaeologists.

Suggested Readings

There are numerous philosophical and economic works that lay out the
foundations of methodological individualism. The books by Popper and
Hayek discussed here are among the most useful for understanding applied

methodological individualism. By way of contrast, the book by Harris is a manifesto for cultural materialism, one of the most holistic of approaches. Cultural materialism and the systemic types of processual approaches have been the pillars of the holistic movement in archaeological theory.

1. Marvin Harris, 1979, *Cultural Materialism: The Struggle for a Science of Culture*.

Pertinent to discussions on holism, individualism, and theoretical archaeology.

This widely known book presents the materialist approach toward understanding social structure and culture. Cultural materialism is a traditional holistic approach to theory development in anthropology and archaeology.

2. Friedrich A. von Hayek, 1944, *The Road to Serfdom*.

Pertinent to discussions of individualism versus holism

The Road to Serfdom is a criticism of collectivist economic organization and the holistic assumptions that buttress it. Hayek's individualistic outlook on society and man underlies his criticism. The association of holism with collectivist views and individualism with free-market views is emphatically clear throughout the book.

3. Karl R. Popper, 1945, *The Open Society and its Enemies*, and 1957 *The Poverty of Historicism*.

Pertinent to discussions of holism versus individualism.

These two works contain Popper's many arguments against holistic social organization and for institutions based upon individualistic assumptions. The (misdirected) association of holism and science are given particularly detailed criticism by Popper. His recommendation of individualism is informed by its relationship with the refutationist view of science. Some of the most important historical roots of holism are uncovered in *The Open Society and its Enemies*.

Literature devoted to the systematic use of methodological individualism in archaeology is rare at this point. There have, however, been archaeological studies informed by individualistic themes. *Towards an Archaeology of the Mind* by Colin Renfrew (1982) is annotated in Chapter 9. Annotations here also include a number of other works that have spurred archaeologists to consider individualistic themes.

4. James Deetz, 1977, *In Small Things Forgotten*.

Pertinent to discussions of methodological individualism and archaeology.

This book reminds us to avoid romanticized reconstructions of the past, especially of the historical past. Archaeological evidence is used to help dispel the glossed-over portraits that have been based upon historical sources. A more accurate picture of the past is also facilitated by exploring the individual and his or her life rather than the large-scale generalities that buttress romanticized reconstructions. This short, readable book leaves one with an acute awareness of how incomplete are the pictures of life painted only with large-scale brushes.

5. Jean-Claude Gardin and Christopher S. Peebles, Christopher, eds., 1992, *Representations in Archaeology*.

Pertinent to discussions on methodological individualism, and holistic method.

Representations in Archaeology is a collection of essays from a 1987 conference on symbolic, structural, and semiotic approaches in archaeology. Included in the volume are papers on philosophical and methodological aspects as well as papers on more specific and more concrete archaeological studies, including those that originate in particular archaeological or anthropological research projects. The papers in this volume provide a wealth of material upon which one can reflect using the methodological ideas in this chapter.

6. James N. Hill, and Joel Gunn, eds., 1977, *The Individual in Prehistory: Studies of Variability in Style in Prehistoric Technologies*.

Pertinent to discussion of holistic and individualistic method.

The essays in this well-known book focus on techniques of recognizing individuality in prehistoric artifacts. The "particular individual" in these studies is not the "generic individual" of methodological individualism. Nevertheless, the break from holistic assumptions is a precondition for such investigations.

7. Ian Hodder, 1985, "Postprocessual Archaeology."

Pertinent to discussions of holistic, individualistic, and empathetic method.

In this article Ian Hodder presents his reasons for focusing on human agency when theorizing about prehistoric peoples. As the title implies, the themes in Hodder's recommendations do contrast sharply with those in his characterization of processual archaeology. Most troubling is that Hodder's methodological theses do not render theories testable. Hodder's proposals for method in archaeology are traced into greater detail in his 1987 book *Reading the Past*, a new edition of which was published in 1991. The latter is annotated in the suggested readings for Chapter 7.

8. Mark P. Leone, 1982b, "Some Opinions about Recovering Mind."
Pertinent to discussions of holistic and individualistic method and archaeology.

This review article by Mark Leone reflects his interest in exploring the experience of prehistoric peoples. Leone's knowledge of the literature and critical reflections upon it make this article particularly valuable reading for those who wish to explore nonholistic approaches to prehistory.

9. Claude Lévi-Strauss, 1966, *The Savage Mind.*
Pertinent to discussions of empathetic and individualistic method.

The Savage Mind presents a classic example of "high structuralism" in the formulation of theories about prehistoric thinking. Although the focus is on thought patterns, the patterns ("structures") are like holistic forces in that they transcend human control and not malleable. That crucial patterns of thought are common to all is an assumption underlying many empathetic approaches.

Chapter 9   Cognitive Archaeology

Exploration of the prehistoric mind has become part of the cognitive revolution in archaeology. The methodological issues raised by the revolution are not revolutionary, however. They concern how empirical studies of prehistoric thinking should be used and what method(s), if any, should guide theory structure. Those familiar issues are addressed in this chapter by the development of specific guidelines for generating and assessing theories about prehistoric thinking.

Methodological guidelines need to be particularly explicit and carefully applied in cognitive archaeology. Theories about prehistoric thinking can only be weakly testable at best. Explicit and careful use of method is required to help prevent theorizing about cognition from turning into fantasizing about cognition.

Methodological individualism provides the broad framework within which the guidelines are developed in this chapter. That point was made in the last chapter, but it is repeated here as a reminder. Although the specific guidelines are informed by methodological individualism, the explication and application of those guidelines will be so preoccupying in this chapter that there will be no room for further reference to that broad framework.

Before beginning in earnest, one final matter needs to be addressed. In this book the word "theory" and its various locutions have been used interchangeably with "explanation" and its locutions. In this chapter another word and its locutions will also be used: "interpretation." It may seem trivial to point out that interpretations can range along a methodological continuum from testable to nontestable and that the factors that enhance or decrease the testability of interpretations are no different than those discussed throughout the book. The reason I introduce "interpretation" here, however, is that it has a connotation that is particularly appropriate for discussing prehistoric cognition. Unlike "theory" and "explanation," "interpretation" often connotes an understanding that is confined to a limited set of data emerging from a specific context, and competing "interpretations" normally share data from the same context. Because studies of prehistoric thinking are usually focused on a specific (and often rather small) set of data in a specific context, "interpretation" fits the situation better than "theory" or "explanation."

Incidentally, because interpretations of prehistoric thinking are often confined to a small data base in a particular context, they normally will not be generalizable for testing in other contexts. In effect this means that the interpretations are induced from the data base and limited to that data base.

Interpretations: Testable and Nontestable

Formal presentations can be a curse in academic writing, at least in the eyes of some. Although I usually try to avoid formality, a rather abstract exposition does provide a convenient way to pinpoint the similarities and differences between testable interpretations and nontestable interpretations. As boring as it may be, I plead with the reader to spend a few extra moments to digest the material in this short section.

Any interpretation, testable or nontestable, requires (1) data to be explained. The interpretation itself consists of (2) other assumptions or entailments that enable the data in (1) to be explained. Furthermore, an interpretation should be (3) internally consistent: The contents of (1) and (2) should not contain contradictory elements.

When making nontestable interpretations, (4) the assumptions or entailments of (2) can be altered, deleted, replaced, or ramified in almost any way to explain (or ignore) the data, even anomalous data, in (1). Action (4) is not allowed when making testable interpretations, however. The statements in testable interpretations cannot be loosely altered, deleted, replaced, or ramified to account for data, especially anomalous data. By now one hardly needs reminding that testable interpretations cannot undergo ad hoc changes to explain away refuting data. Statements in testable interpretations can be changed, to be sure, but they can only be changed in ways that allow them to remain testable.

A "careful" induction to an interpretation from a data base can now be understood more clearly. A carefully induced interpretation will not only be tied closely to the data—a matter to be explained in the next section—but will also not ignore potential refuting data. In other words, a careful induction will lead to a testable interpretation.

It is now time to make sense of these abstractions. The upcoming section provides a detailed analysis of one example of the development of a testable interpretation of prehistoric cognition. Quite specific methodological guidelines will be extrapolated from the analysis. Those guidelines are also presented systematically in the conclusion so that readers will have a methodological "checklist" for use in their own theorizing. Even if one is not actively working in cognitive archaeology, it might be instructive to use the checklist to analyze the specific studies in *The Ancient Mind* (Renfrew and Zubrow 1993) and *Representations in Archaeology* (Gardin and Peebles 1992). Some of those studies meet the guidelines better than others.

Testability in Interpretations of Prehistoric Cognition

The methodological discussion will be built around the reconstruction of cognitive elements found in the analysis of the Indus Valley stones. This example is well known, especially because Colin Renfrew employed it in his inaugural lecture as Disney Professor of Archaeology at Cambridge University (Renfrew 1982:16–19). A brief synopsis of the artifactual data will set the stage for further discussion.

The stones come from the 4,000-year-old civilization of the Indus Valley, from the site of Mohenjodaro. They are cubical, and colored, and apparently had to be imported from a considerable distance. Of most interest, the stones are multiples of a constant unit of weight, the weight equivalent to 0.836 grams of mass. The weights are multiples of integers such as 1, 4, 8, continuing to 64, and then 320 and 1,600. Scale pans were also found at the site.

From the archaeological data Renfrew formulated a number of statements. The relationship of these statements (the "theory") to artifactual data is of paramount importance in testable approaches to prehistoric cognition. For that reason these statements formulated by Renfrew are reproduced verbatim:

1. That the society in question had developed a concept equivalent to our own notion of weight or mass.
2. That the use of this concept involved the operation of units, and hence the concept of modular measure.
3. That there was a system of numeration, involving hierarchical numerical categories (like tens and units), in this case apparently based on the fixed ratio of 16.
4. That this weight system was used for practical purposes (as the finding of scale pans corroborates), constituting a measuring device for mapping the world quantitatively as well as qualitatively.
5. That there existed a notion of equivalence, on the basis of weight among different materials (unless we postulate the weighing of objects of one material against others of the same material), and hence, it may follow, a ratio of value between them.
6. That this inferred concept of value entailed some constant rate of exchange between commodities (Renfrew 1982:17).

The set of statements is sizable. Despite that, additional statements were asserted in a later paper (Renfrew 1987), and in an unpublished lecture even more were added (Renfrew, personal communication 1987). In any case, is there justification for associating the six statements above with the artifactual data? Or are these statements so loosely connected that they are merely speculative? In other words, is Renfrew generating a testable set of interpretative statements or is he just weaving a nontestable interpretation?

First, the statements are *about* the thinking of prehistoric people;

they are emphatically *not* attempts to restructure their exact thoughts. For example, Renfrew does not claim that those ancient inhabitants of the Indus Valley had an idea of weight or mass that was precisely the same as it is for us today. In other words, Renfrew's broad goal is to unveil some elements of the thinking of prehistoric people. In his own terminology, he aims to create a "cognitive map," or *mappa*. A map is not to be confused with that which is mapped, but a map can indicate some features of that which is mapped.

Incidentally, Renfrew's wording in statement (1) is not entirely clear. He states that the inhabitants of the Indus Valley "had developed a concept equivalent to our notion of weight or mass" (Renfrew 1982:17). Particularly bothersome is the word "equivalent." What does it mean in this context? Renfrew's claim has been clarified in other papers and lectures, as well as in personal communications: that one feature of cognition in the Indus Valley was a notion of comparative weight (Renfrew 1987).

Second, it should be noted that some of the statements arise directly from the artifactual data, and that other statements are connected to those by logical relationship. The notion of weight (statement 1) stems from the fact that the stones are calibrated against each other, and that calibration in units leads to (statement 2). That the units are themselves arranged in a hierarchy suggests a system of numeration (statement 3). The fact that scale pans were found indicates that there was a quantitative weighing purpose for the stones (statement 4), and that there was a notion of (weight) equivalence (statement 5). The use of the scale for weighing implies that there was value associated with weight, and that weight may then have been used as a measure to determine exchange value (statement 6).

Third, the logical connections between statements are not just "logical" from the perspective of a particular archaeologist. Similar if not precisely the same statements would likely be made by archaeologists whether British, French, Greek, or Chinese; female or male; young or old; liberal or conservative; or characterized in any other way. In other words, the logical connections are more like those in mathematics, which hold regardless of the background, inclinations, or prejudices of the person using the mathematics.

The three features identified here above—restricting statements to claims about cognition, linking statements closely to artifactual data or with each other by logic, and taking care that the logical connections are not subjective projections of a theoretician—all dovetail to render the set of statements testable.

The first feature is that statements are restricted to assertions about thinking; they are not attempts to restructure exact thoughts. One can understand this point by tracing the consequences of attempting to restructure exact thoughts. Claims about what prehistoric peoples were "actually thinking" cannot be tested, because a potential refutation of such a claim would be another contrary claim about what prehistoric people were actually thinking. No test would be possible because the latter could not be found in prehistoric artifacts any more than the former. The precise thoughts of prehistoric peoples could only be found in written documentation.

Although claims about exact thoughts are not testable, statements about some features of the thinking of prehistoric peoples are considerably more amenable to testing. For example, if similar stones had been found that did not demonstrate weight ratios, then Renfrew's theory (his statements) would be refuted. Or, if there were evidence of trade in weighable items of reasonable value, then one would anticipate discovering similar weighing systems in the trade area of the Indus Valley civilization. Admittedly, failure to discover such would not refute Renfrew's claim; weighing might have been controlled centrally, and hence might have only been done when objects were brought to Mohenjodaro. Nevertheless, the discovery of similar weighing systems in the Indus Valley trade area would provide further support for the assertion that the weighing system had a practical function in exchange. Indeed, there is evidence of such in Bahrain, and the stones are the weights typical of the cities in the Indus civilization (Bibby 1969:354–355, 358–359).

The second feature is that some statements are linked closely to the artifactual data, and other statements are tied to the former by appropriate logic. The importance of linking at least some assertions in a cognitive map very closely to the artifactual data seems so obvious it hardly need be discussed. Nevertheless, the methodological reason cannot be overemphasized: to maintain testability. If Renfrew had leaped from the existence of the proportional stones to the inference that weights were central to the religious outlook of the Indus Valley civilization, his assertion would have been virtually nontestable. It is crucial to avoid such nontestable speculation if one hopes to distinguish what is empirically plausible from what might be a phantom of the imagination.

Statements not directly linked to artifactual data must be tied to others that are directly testable by artifactual data. The reason is that assertions not arising directly from data can only be vulnerable to empirical refutation if they are associated in a tight logical relationship with assertions that can be put to a direct test. For example, Renfrew's statement (3) that there was a system of numeration, involving hierarchical numerical categories, is tied logically to his statements (2) and (1). Statement (3) could not be directly tested by artifactual data; direct evidence of numeration would have to be written. Discovery of similar stones but without weight relations would not only refute (1) directly, but would also refute (2) and (3) as well because of the logical connection of (2) and (3) to (1).

The third feature is that the logical connections that bind statements together must not be just subjective projections of a theoretician. The way to assure they are not is captured in the preceding paragraph: The logical relationships between statements in a cognitive map must be close enough so that all statements are at least indirectly subject to testing. What makes such logical relationships adequate? Two properties stand out: entailment and consistency.

Entailment

Entailment, or implication, is one of the most controversial concepts in logical theory. The literature in mathematical logic devoted to explicating and interpreting entailment is vast, not to mention the literature devoted to entailment in the sciences. Fortunately, for methodological purposes an adequate understanding can be grasped quite readily: if X entails Y then a mistake in Y indicates that there is a mistake in X. This is simply a version of the *modus tollens* principle discussed in Chapter 6. *Modus tollens* is the logical heart of the refutationist view.

Suppose that a system of numeration entails a concept of units. It would follow that if there were no units, then there would be no system of numeration. This example might seem rather simple, but the methodological point is indeed quite simple. If a set of statements (a theory) is to be testable, then statements not directly testable themselves must entail statements that are directly testable.

It was noted in the previous section that both testable and nontestable interpretations can be modified to account for anomalous data, but that if a testable interpretation is to remain testable, it cannot be modified to explain away anomalous data. From a logical perspective the difference can now be understood as follows. When a nontestable interpretation is altered to account for anomalous data, additional assumption(s) are introduced that do *not* entail statements that are potentially refutable. In methodological terminology by now very familiar, ad hoc hypotheses are added. In everyday terminology, an interpretation is modified to "explain away" anomalous data. When a testable interpretation is modified to account for anomalous data, on the other hand, the additional assumption(s) must still enable the interpretation to entail statements that are testable. In methodological idiom, auxiliary hypotheses are added to the interpretation. Remember that hypotheses auxiliary to an interpretation maintain or even increase its testability.

Incidentally, there is little if any harm in using less arcane terminology to characterize the relationship between statements in a testable interpretation. For example, suppose an archaeologist formulates statements about prehistoric cognition and asserts that the statements "must be close to the data," or that "the statements cannot speculate far from the data." Such terminology seems quite appropriate so long as the meaning is understood; that is, that statements that are not directly testable must entail statements that are.

Universal statements

A few comments on universal statements are in order. Remember that generalized statements, often called "universal statements," are perfectly appropriate and even desirable *so long as they entail testable implications*. As a matter-of-fact, generalization can *increase* testability because a more sweeping claim can entail a greater number of testable implications. As counterintuitive as it may seem, that is why universalization can actually bring theoretical statements "closer" to the data. Bringing a theory closer to the data means bringing it closer to the data that can be used to test it. As argued earlier in the book, Wittfogel's universalization of his hydraulic theory brought it closer to the data that was used to test it.

On the other hand, the less data available for testing the more care should be taken when universalizing. The reason is that the less the available data, the less likely that generalizing will increase the number of implications that can be directly tested. To illustrate, consider the difference between theories that entail a relative cornucopia of artifactual data and theories that do not. Many theories about prehistoric economic and social organization can and have been beneficially universalized because of the abundance of artifactual data against which they can be tested. Even though the artifactual data appropriate for testing interpretations of prehistoric cognition may be more than is now realized, and even though further research will almost certainly increase the amount, there may never be an abundance of data appropriate for testing interpretations of prehistoric thinking. If so, cognitive archaeologists should be all the more careful about generalizing their interpretations.

I do hope the preceding cautionary note will not be used to discourage generalization of cognitive interpretations when there is enough potential data for testing. I hope it will discourage generalization when there is little or no potential data for testing.

To summarize, interpretations should be "close" to the data: They should be directly testable themselves or they should entail other statement(s) that are directly testable. Interpretations can be generalized, and indeed should be generalized, if it would increase the number of testable implications. On the other hand, interpretations should not be generalized if it would not increase the number of testable implications.

Consistency

Entailment is a critical property of the logical relationship between statements in a testable interpretation. It is not a difficult concept to understand. Applying it can be quite exacting and subtle, however, as was evident in Renfrew's generation of statements about the Indus Valley stones.

Consistency is the other important property of the logical relationship between statements in a testable interpretation. It is not so subtle; indeed, to most it is self-evident that the statements constituting an interpretation should be consistent. The use of consistency for methodological purposes is also quite easy to understand: Try to find inconsistencies, and if they are found use them as a springboard to search for error. The logical reason for consistency is not so obvious, however. A brief discussion is in order.

Consistent statements are statements that can all be true in at least one interpretation. The reason consistency is important is as follows: If statements are inconsistent, that is, if they cannot all be true in any interpretation, they validly imply any statement whatsoever. This has been an accepted principle of logic ever since it was established by Aristotle in the fourth century B.C. If there is inconsistency within the statements of an interpretation, then, the interpretation will entail any statement including any potential refuting statements. The upshot is that *no empirical information can possibly refute inconsistent statements.* In other words, *an inconsistent interpretation cannot be testable.*

Few thinkers have endorsed inconsistency. One who did, however, has had a enormous influence on Western intellectual currents since the middle of the nineteenth century. Hegel (1977) reasoned that contradiction was more likely than consistency in the cosmos, and hence that theories can reflect those contradictions. Perhaps that is why the Hegelian intellectual tradition is so replete with vagueness, ambiguity, and outright contradiction, all dressed out in a writing style that is as confusing as its ideas. The most recent outbreak of the Hegelian tradition is the postmodernist movement, the irrational flavor of which has infected some well-known postprocessual archaeologists. Along with the reasons identified in Chapter 7, the irrational tradition stemming from Hegel also helps explains why some postprocessual interpretations of the experience of prehistoric peoples are so nontestable.

Fortunately, aside from Hegel and his followers few would argue that contradictions should be tolerated. One would certainly hope that archaeologists would take care to avoid inconsistencies in their interpretations of prehistoric thinking.

Conclusion

In this chapter I focused on how cognitive archaeology ought be done rather than on criticism of alternative approaches. That is why only passing comment was made on the consequences of ignoring the guidelines that make testability possible.

The principal methodological points in this chapter are summarized next. They are intended as a checklist for those working in archaeology of the mind. The checklist is not likely to be useful unless one is familiar with the underlying concepts, but it should help one recall the methodological guidelines without having to reread the entire chapter.

1. Testable interpretations are vulnerable to empirical error; that is, they can potentially be shown to be mistaken by at least some data. If they are not testable, they can at least be induced very carefully from the available data.
2. Statements in testable interpretations cannot be arbitrarily altered, deleted, replaced, or ramified to account for anomalous data. If the statements in a testable interpretation are altered, the change must be done in such a way that anomalous data are not simply explained away.

3. Testable interpretations in cognitive archaeology consist of statements *about* prehistoric thinking; that is, the statements can highlight some features of prehistoric thinking. They cannot capture the precise thoughts of prehistoric or nonliterate people.

4. As with any testable theory, interpretations about prehistoric cognition must be structured so that they are close to the data. That means that the statements must be either directly testable or must entail other statements that are directly testable.

5. The relationship between statements not directly testable to those that are directly testable is characterized by the logical property of entailment. Also, the statements must be consistent.

6. A statement entails another statement if an error in the latter indicates an error in the former. Consistent statements are statements that contain no contradictions; in other words, they are statements that can all be true under some interpretation.

7. Generalized statements, or universal statements, can increase testability if they entail more testable implications. Interpretations should be generalized if they can become more testable.

8. Generalization should be avoided if there would be no increase in testability. In cognitive archaeology there may not always be artifactual data available or discoverable that is appropriate for testing generalized statements. In that case an interpretation can be induced from the available data. Be sure that the induction is done carefully: Statements must be either directly linked to the artifactual data or must entail statements directly linked to the artifactual data.

Suggested Readings

1. Jean-Claude Gardin and Christopher S. Peebles, eds., 1992, *Representations in Archaeology*.

Representations in Archaeology was included in the annotated bibliography for the last chapter. It is recommended for this chapter as a source of specific studies on prehistoric thinking, each of which can be assessed against the methodological guidelines developed in this chapter. Some of the studies adhere closely to the guidelines whereas others do not.

2. A. Colin Renfrew, 1982, *Towards an Archaeology of Mind*.

Colin Renfrew's inaugural lecture as Disney Professor of Archaeology at Cambridge University was published as this short volume. The importance of exploring human agency in prehistory is recognized by Renfrew, as is the importance of employing careful method in formulating theories about the thinking of prehistoric peoples. The expression "methodological individualism" does not appear, but the methodological recommendations discussed and used by Renfrew clearly reflect individualistic method. The brevity and clarity of this manuscript make it accessible and useful.

3. A. Colin Renfrew and Ezra Zubrow, 1993, *The Ancient Mind: Elements of Cognitive Archaeology* (tentative title), to be published by Cambridge University Press.

This volume has many case studies on prehistoric thinking, most of which closely follow the methodological guidelines developed in this chapter. As with the preceding bibliographical reference, it will provide archaeologists with specific studies that can be assessed against the methodological guidelines.

Conclusion

Philosophers of science often argue about and discuss method. After all, method is a cornerstone of our professional field. In this book I wanted much more, however. I wanted to create a manual for use by practitioners, in this case archaeologists. My most cherished hope is that archaeologists would apply the ideas to their own work. For some archaeologists this might entail a change in the way they approach theory generation and assessment. It will not change the approach of others, but it might offer a clearer understanding of why they approach theory the way they do. For all archaeologists it should clarify the rationale behind the myriad of methodological positions that have bombarded their field. That should help them sort out and apply what is more productive from what is less so, a task that is not as easy as I believe it should be, unfortunately. There are a number of reasons for this.

Many misuses of method in archaeological theory are an outgrowth of misconceptions about scientific method. The beliefs that there is *a* method of science, that method should function to legitimate theory, and that legitimate ("scientific") theories will guarantee progress are deeply rooted in our intellectual and cultural tradition. These beliefs have understandably evoked criticism, but the reaction has also led to additional misconceptions: That theories cannot be empirically tested, that methods of science are fruitless or even harmful for theory development, that there are no rational guidelines for building or assessing theory anyway, and that method really functions to establish authority and intimidate critics in intellectual power games. These themes form the core of relativism, shades of which have infiltrated postprocessual archaeology. One of these themes—nontestability—is also shared by what has been called the "radical critique" (Earle and Preucel 1987), "pseudo-archaeology" (Sabloff 1982), and "cult archaeology" (Cole 1980).

Creating further confusion for those applying method is that intellectual communities, including scientific communities, are not always paragons of rationality. They are subject to historical influences, political pressures, and other sociological constraints. Studies in the ethnology of science have provided some of the more interesting insights into the irrationalities and thoughtless habits that are part of scientific life. Bruno Latour compares the confusion in scientific practice to the incredible disorientation on a battlefield, where one's best laid plans are constantly interrupted, altered, or destroyed by developments beyond anyone's effective control (Latour 1988). A classic in the field at this point, Latour and Steve Woolgar's ethnological study *Laboratory Life: The Social Construction of Scientific Facts* paints a picture that is implied by its title: Scientific facts are social constructions (Latour and Woolgar 1979). A critic of science, Joseph Schwartz (1992), does a masterful job in pointing out the warts and bruises of irrationality on scientists as well as science itself.

If rational procedures are so difficult to apply in real intellectual work, one can understand why some archaeologists would exhort colleagues to avoid the most mercurial of all tasks: theory development. Indeed, from time-to-time archaeologists are warned about the dangers of indulging in theory building. M. A. Smith's 1955 article "The Limits of Inference in Archaeology" is an early example of the reaction against theorizing. Given the misconceptions about method that have emerged during the past few decades, it is not surprising that archaeologists are again being exhorted to avoid theory (Courbin 1988). By focusing strictly on fieldwork and artifact description one can sidestep the host of methodological confusions surrounding archaeological theory.

Despite the potential pitfalls, interest in theory is what attracts many to fields like archaeology and anthropology (Jarvie 1964). Perhaps that is why theoretical archaeology is here to stay. Given that it is, attention must turn to method. Despite all the pushes and pulls within intellectual communities, I at least am convinced that careful attention to method can enhance theory development in any field, including archaeology. Just as police, attorneys, judges, and juries are subject to all sorts of pressures in their work, keeping their eye on principles of justice makes all the difference in whether a legal system functions reasonably well or not. The same can be said about keeping ones eye on methodological principles when doing intellectual work.

In the course of generating and assessing explanations, some methodological decisions are rather simple whereas others can be quite complicated. Even when complicated, however, the reasons for making a decision should always be clear and comprehensible. Used well, even in difficult situations, methodological guidelines should seem like truisms: almost "obvious," or "self-evident." Confusion, on the other hand, provides the impetus to rethink a theoretical problem-situation. In that case methodological tools should help one analyze problem-situations more effectively and solve or resolve problems more productively.

Applied philosophy is an exciting alternative for one often skeptical of the assumptions that sometimes inform his own profession, not to speak of the fashions that can drive work in his field. But why apply philosophy to archaeology? Understanding the unwritten past is interesting in itself, and can provide a valuable perspective on the present. Another reason is more personal. As recounted in the Preface, I fell in love with archaeology over fifteen years ago. The romance is still flourishing and I suspect it will never end.

Bibliography

Adams, Robert McC. 1966. *The Evolution of Urban Society*. Chicago: Aldine Press.

———. 1974. "Historic Patterns of Mesopotamian Irrigation Agriculture." In Theodore E. Downing and McGuire Gibson, eds., *Irrigation's Impact on Society*, pp. 1–5. Tucson: University of Arizona Press.

Agassi, Joseph. 1963. *Towards an Historiography of Science*. The Hague: Mouton.

———. 1964. "The Nature of Scientific Problems and Their Roots in Metaphysics." In Mario Bunge, ed., *The Critical Approach to Science and Philosophy*, pp. 189–211. New York: Glencoe.

———. 1975. *Science in Flux*. Boston: D. Reidel.

———. 1977. *Towards a Rational Philosophical Anthropology*. The Hague: Martinus Nijhoff.

Aldenderfer, Mark S. 1981. "Creating Assemblages by Computer Simulation: The Development and Uses of SBSIM." In Jeremy A. Sabloff, ed., *Simulations in Archaeology*, pp. 67–117. Albuquerque: University of New Mexico Press.

Arnauld, Antoine, and Pierre Nicole. 1964. *The Art of Thinking: Port-Royal Logic*. Indianapolis: Bobbs-Merrill.

Barnes, Barry. 1974. *Scientific Knowledge and Sociological Theory*. London: Routledge and Kegan Paul.

———. 1982. *T. S. Kuhn and Social Science*. New York: Columbia University.

Barrett, John. 1989. Abstract of "Archaeology in the Age of Uncertainty." Paper presented at the Theoretical Archaeology Group Conference, Newcastle-upon-Tyne, England.

Bayes, Thomas. 1963. "Essay Towards Solving A Problem in the Doctrine of Chances." In *Facsimiles of Two Papers by Bayes*, pp. 370–418. New York: Hafner. Originally published 1763, in *Philosophical Transactions of the Royal Society, London*, vol. 53, pp. 370–418.

Becker, Marshall J. 1979. "Priests, Peasants, and Ceremonial Centers: The Intellectual History of a Model." In Norman Hammond and Gordon R. Willey, eds., *Maya Archaeology and Ethnohistory*, pp. 3–20. Austin: University of Texas Press.

Bell, James A. 1981. "Scientific Method and the Formulation of Testable Computer Simulation Models." In Jeremy A. Sabloff, ed., *Simulations in Archaeology*, pp. 51–64. Albuquerque: University of New Mexico Press.

———. 1984, Review of *Philosophy and Archaeology* by Merrilee H. Salmon. *North American Archaeologist* 5(4):337–43.

———. 1986. "On Applying Quantitative and Formal Methods in Theoretical Archaeology." *Science and Archaeology* (28):3–8.

———. 1987a. "Reason vs. Relativism: Review of Ian Hodder's *Reading the Past*." *Archaeological Review from Cambridge* 6(1):75–86.

———. 1987b. "Simulation Modelling in Archaeology: Reflections and Trends." *European Journal of Operational Research* 30:243–45.

———. 1991. "Anarchy and Archaeology." In Robert W. Preucel, ed., *Processual and Postprocessual Archaeologies*, pp. 71–80. Carbondale: Southern Illinois University Press.

———. 1992a. "On Capturing Agency in Theories about Prehistory." In Jean-Claude Gardin and Christopher Peebles, eds., *Representations in Archaeology*, pp. 30–55. Bloomington: University of Indiana Press, Bloomington.

———. 1992b. "Universalization in Archaeological Theory." In Lester Embree, ed., *Metaarchaeology*, pp. 143–63. Boston Studies in the Philosophy of Science Vol. 147. Dordrecht, Netherlands: Kluwer Academic Publishers.

———. 1993. "Interpretation and Testability in Theories about Prehistoric Thinking." In Colin A. Renfrew and Ezra Zubrow, eds., *The Ancient Mind: Elements of Cognitive Archaeology* (tentative title) Cambridge, England: Cambridge University Press. Manuscript in preparation.

Bell, James A., and James F. Bell. 1980. "System Dynamics and Scientific Method." In Jorgen Randers, ed., *Elements of the System Dynamics Method*, pp. 3–22. Cambridge, Mass.: MIT Press.

Bernoulli, Jacques. 1969. *Ars Conjectandi*. In *Die Werke von Jakob Bernoulli*, Vol. 3. Original published in 1713. Basel, Switzerland: Birkhaeuser Verlag.

Bibby, G. 1969. *Looking for Dilmun*. New York: Alfred A. Knopf.

Binford, Lewis R. 1962. "A New Method of Calculating Dates from Kaolin Pipe Stem Samples." *Southeastern Archaeological Conference, Newsletter* 9(1):19–21.

————. 1972. *An Archaeological Perspective*. New York: Academic Press.

————. 1983a. *In Pursuit of the Past: Decoding the Archaeological Record*. New York: Thames and Hudson.

————. 1983b. *Working at Archaeology*. New York: Academic Press.

Binford, Lewis R., and Sally R. Binford, eds. 1968. *New Perspectives in Archaeology*. Chicago: Aldine.

Binford, Lewis R., and Jeremy A. Sabloff. 1982. "Paradigms, Systematics, and Archaeology." *Journal of Anthropological Research* 38(2):137–53.

Bloor, David. 1991. *Knowledge and Social Imagery*, 2d edition. Chicago: University of Chicago Press.

Broad, William, and Nicholas Wade. 1983. *Betrayers of the Truth*. New York: Simon & Schuster.

Brodbeck, May. 1962. "Explanation, Prediction, and "Imperfect" Knowledge." In Herbert Feigl and Grover Maxwell, eds., *Scientific Explanation, Space and Time*. Minneapolis: University of Minnesota Press.

Bronner, Stephen E., and Douglas M. Kellner, eds. 1989. *Critical Theory and Society: A Reader*. New York: Routledge.

Brown, Donald E. 1991. *Human Universals*. Philadelphia: Temple University Press.

Bucha, V. 1970. "Evidence for Changes in the Earth's Magnetic Field Intensity." *Philosophical Transactions of the Royal Society*, Series A, 269, pp. 47–55.

Carneiro, Robert L. 1970. "A Theory of the Origin of the State." *Science* 169:733–38.

Cazeau, Charles J., and Stuart D. Scott, Jr. 1979. *Exploring the Unknown: Great Mysteries Reexamined*. New York: Plenum Press.

Childe, V. Gordon. 1958. "Retrospect." *Antiquity* 32:69–74.

————. 1962. *The Prehistory of European Society*. London: Cassell.

Clarke, David L. 1968. *Analytical Archaeology*. London: Methuen.

————. 1972a. "Models and Paradigms in Contemporary Archaeology." In David L. Clarke, ed., *Models in Archaeology*, pp. 1–60. London: Methuen.

————. 1972b. Review of *Explanation in Archaeology: An Explicitly Scientific Approach* by Patty Jo Watson, Steven A. LeBlanc, and Charles Redman. *Antiquity* 46(183):237–39.

————. 1973. "Archaeology: The Loss of Innocence." *Antiquity* 47: 6–18.

Cohen, Ronald, 1978. "Introduction." In Ronald Cohen and Elman R. Service, eds., *Origins of the State: The Anthropology of Political Evolution*, pp. 1–20. Philadelphia: Institute for the Study of Human Issues.

Cohen, Ronald, and Elman R. Service, eds. 1978. *Origins of the State: The*

Anthropology of Political Evolution. Philadelphia: Institute for the Study of Human Issues.

Cole, John R. 1980. "Cult Archaeology and Unscientific Method and Theory." In Michael B. Schiffer, ed., *Advances in Archaeological Method and Theory*, vol. 3, pp. 1–33. New York: Academic Press.

Collingwood, Robin G. 1936. *Human Nature and Human History*. London: H. Milford.

———. 1946. *The Idea of History*. Oxford: Clarendon Press.

———. 1960. *The Idea of Nature*. New York: Oxford University Press.

Comte, Auguste. 1957. *A General View of Positivism*, John H. Bridges, trans. New York: R. Speller.

———. 1968. *System of Positive Polity*, John H. Bridges, trans. New York: B. Franklin.

Courbin, Paul. 1988. *What is Archaeology: An Essay on the Nature of Archaeological Research*, Paul Bahn, trans. Chicago: University of Chicago Press.

Crumley, Carole L., and William H. Marquardt. 1987. "Regional Dynamics in Burgundy." In Carole L. Crumley and William H. Marquardt, eds., *Regional Dynamics: Burgundian Landscapes in Historical Perspective*, pp. 609–23. Orlando: Academic Press.

Dahrendorf, Ralf. 1959. *Class and Class Conflict in Industrial Society*. Stanford: Stanford University Press.

Deetz, James. 1977. *In Small Things Forgotten*. New York: Anchor Books.

Doran, James E. 1986. "Formal Methods and Archaeological Theory: A Perspective." *World Archaeology* 18(1):21–37.

Doran, James E., and F. R. Hodson. 1975. *Mathematics and Computers in Archaeology*. Edinburgh, Scotland: Edinburgh University Press.

Dray, William H. 1980. *Perspectives on History*. London: Routledge and Kegan Paul.

Dray, William H., ed. 1966. *Philosophical Analysis and History*. New York: Harper and Row.

Dunnell, Robert. 1986. "Five Decades of American Archaeology." In David J. Meltzer, Don D. Fowler, and Jeremy A. Sabloff, eds., *American Archaeology, Past and Future*, pp. 23–49. Washington, D. C.: Smithsonian Institution Press.

Earle, Timothy K. 1973. *Control Hierarchies in the Traditional Irrigation Economy of Halelea District, Kauai, Hawaii*. Ph.D. dissertation, University of Michigan, Ann Arbor.

———. 1977. "A Reappraisal of Redistribution: Complex Hawaiian Chiefdoms." In Timothy K. Earle and Jonathon Ericson, eds., *Exchange Systems In Prehistory*, pp. 213–29. New York: Academic Press.

———. 1978. *Economic and Social Organization of a Complex Chiefdom: The Halelea District, Kaua'i, Hawaii.* Anthropological Papers, No. 63. Ann Arbor: Museum of Anthropology, University of Michigan.

Earle, Timothy K., and Allen W. Johnson. 1987. *The Evolution of Human Societies: From Foraging Group to Agrarian State.* Stanford: Stanford University Press.

Earle, Timothy K., and Robert W. Preucel. 1987. "Processual Archaeology and the Radical Critique." *Current Anthropology* 28(4):501–13.

Ellul, Jacques. 1964. *The Technological Society.* New York: Knopf.

Embree, Lester, ed. 1992. *Metaarchaeology: Reflections by Archaeologists and Philosophers.* Boston Studies in the Philosophy of Science, vol. 147. Dordrecht, Netherlands: Kluwer Academic Publishers.

Feyerabend, Paul K. 1978. *Against Method.* Thetford, England: Verso Press. First edition published in 1975 by New Left Books.

———. 1982. *Science in a Free Society.* Thetford, England: Verso Press.

———. 1988. *Farewell to Reason.* New York: Verso Press.

Flannery, Kent V. 1968a. "Culture History vs. Cultural Process: A Debate in American Archaeology." *Scientific American* 217:119–22.

———. 1968b. "The Olmec and the Valley of Oaxaca: A Model for Interregional Interaction in Formative Times." In Elizabeth P. Benson, ed., *Dunbarton Oaks Conference on the Olmec*, pp. 79–110. Washington, D.C.: Dunbarton Oaks Research Library and Collection.

———. 1973. "Archaeology With A Capital 'S'." In Charles L. Redman, ed., *Research and Theory In Current Archaeology*, pp. 47–53. New York: Wiley Intersciences.

———. 1982. "The Golden Marshalltown: A Parable for the Archaeology of the 1980s." *American Anthropologist* 84:265–78.

Foucault, Michel. 1980. *Power-Knowledge: Selected Interviews and Other Writings, 1972–1977.* New York: Pantheon.

Fowler, Don D., David J. Meltzer, and Jeremy A. Sabloff, eds. 1986. *American Archaeology, Past and Future.* Washington, D.C.: Smithsonian Institution Press.

Francfort, Henri-Paul. 1992. "The Sense of Measure in Archaeology: An Approach to the Analysis of Proto-Urban Societies with the Aid of an Expert System." In Jean-Claude Gardin and Christopher S. Peebles, eds., *Representations in Archaeology*, pp. 291–314. Bloomington: University of Indiana Press.

Frank, Philipp. 1947. *Einstein: His Life and Times*, trans. by George Rosen, edited and revised by Shuichi Kusaka. New York: Alfred A. Knopf.

Fritz, John M., and Fred T. Plog. 1970. "The Nature of Archaeological Explanation." *American Antiquity* 35:405–412.

Galilei, Galileo, 1953. *Dialogue Concerning the Two Chief World Systems*, Stillman Drake, trans. Berkeley: University of California Press.

Gallay, Alain. 1986. *L' Archeologie Demain*. Paris: Belfond.

Gandara, Manuel. 1981. "Archaeology and Dogmatic Falsificationism: The Hawaiian Refutations." Manuscript produced for Anthropology 658, Winter 1981, University of Michigan, Ann Arbor.

Gardin, Jean-Claude. 1979. *Une Archeologie Theorique*. Paris: Hachette.

———. 1980. *Archaeological Constructs: An Aspect of Theoretical Archaeology*. Cambridge, England: Cambridge University Press.

———. 1992. "Semiotic Trends in Archaeology." In Jean-Claude Gardin and Christopher S. Peebles, eds., *Representations in Archaeology*, pp. 87–104. Bloomington: University of Indiana Press.

Gardin, Jean-Claude, and Christopher S. Peebles, eds. 1992. *Representations in Archaeology*. Bloomington: University of Indiana Press.

Gellner, Ernest. 1974. *The Legitimation of Belief*. Cambridge, England: Cambridge University Press.

———. 1989. *Plough, Sword and Book*. Chicago: University of Chicago Press. Reprint of original 1988 edition, published in London by Collins Harvel.

Gero, Joan M., and Margaret W. Conkey, eds. 1991. *Engendering Archaeology: Women and Prehistory*. Oxford: Basil Blackwell.

Gibbon, Guy. 1989. *Explanation in Archaeology*. Oxford: Basil Blackwell.

Giere, Ronald. 1988. *Explaining Science: A Cognitive Approach*. Chicago: University of Chicago Press.

Goldfrank, Esther S. 1978. *Notes on an Undirected Life*. Flushing, N.Y.: Queens College Press.

Goode, Terry M. 1977. "Explanation, Expansion, and the Aims of Historians: Toward an Alternative Account of Historical Explanation." *Philosophy of the Social Sciences* (7):367–84.

Goodyear, Albert ,C., L. Mark Raab, and Timothy C. Klinger. 1978. "The Status of Archaeological Research Design in Cultural Resource Management." *American Antiquity* 43(2):159–71.

Gray, Robert F. 1963. *Sonjo of Tanganyika*. Oxford: Oxford University Press.

Hacking, Ian. 1975. *The Emergence of Probability*. Cambridge, England: Cambridge University Press.

Halperin, Rhoda H. 1984. "Polanyi, Marx, and the Institutional Paradigm in Economic Anthropology." *Research in Economic Anthropology* 6:245–72.

———. 1985. "The Concept of the Formal in Economic Anthropology." *Research in Economic Anthropology* 7:339–68.

Harding, Sandra. 1986. *The Science Question in Feminism.* Ithaca, N.Y.: Cornell University Press.

Harrington, Jean C. 1954. "Dating Stem Fragments of Seventeenth and Eighteenth Century Clay Tobacco Pipes." *Quarterly Bulletin of the Archaeological Society of Virginia* 9:6–8.

Harris, Marvin. 1979. *Cultural Materialism: The Struggle for a Science of Culture.* New York: Random House.

Hayek, Friedrich A. von. 1944. *The Road to Serfdom.* Chicago: University of Chicago Press.

———. 1948. *Individualism and Economic Order.* Chicago: University of Chicago Press.

———. 1972. *The Counter-Revolution of Science: Studies on the Abuse of Reason.* Indianapolis: Liberty Press.

Hegel, Georg Wilhelm Friedrich. 1977. *Phenomenology of Spirit,* A. V. Miller, trans. New York: Clarendon Press.

Held, D. 1980. *Introduction to Critical Theory.* London: Hutchinson.

Hempel, Carl G. 1942. "The Function of General Laws in History." *The Journal of Philosophy* 39:35–48.

———. 1952. *Fundamentals of Concept Formation in Empirical Science.* Chicago: University of Chicago Press.

———. 1962. "Deductive-Nomological vs. Statistical Explanation." In Herbert Feigl and Grover Maxwell, eds., *Scientific Explanation, Space and Time,* pp. 98–169. Minneapolis: University of Minnesota Press.

———. 1965. *Aspects of Scientific Explanation and Other Essays in the Philosophy of Science.* New York: Free Press.

———. 1966. *Philosophy of Natural Science.* Englewood Cliffs, N.J.: Prentice Hall.

———. 1988. "Provisoes: A Problem Concerning the Inferential Function of Scientific Theories." *Erkenntnis* 28:147–64.

Hempel, Carl G., and Paul Oppenheim. 1948. "Studies in the Logic of Explanation." *Philosophy of Science* 15:135–75. Reprinted in Carl G. Hempel, 1965, *Aspects of Scientific Explanation and Other Essays in the Philosophy of Science,* pp. 245–90. New York: Free Press.

Herzfeld, Michael. 1982. "The Etymology of Excuses: Aspects of Rhetorical Performance in Greece." *American Ethnologist* 9:644–63.

―――. 1987. *Anthropology Through the Looking Glass: Critical Ethnography in the Margins of Europe*. Cambridge, England: Cambridge University Press.

Hill, James N., and Joel Gunn, eds. 1977. *The Individual in Prehistory: Studies of Variability in Style in Prehistoric Technologies*. New York: Academic Press.

Hodder, Ian. 1985. "Postprocessual Archaeology." In Michael B. Schiffer, ed., *Advances in Archaeological Method and Theory*, Vol. 8, pp. 1–26. New York: Academic Press.

―――. 1991. *Reading the Past: Current Approaches to Interpretation in Archaeology*, 2d edition. Cambridge, England: Cambridge University Press.

Honigmann, John Joseph. 1977. *Understanding Culture*. Westport, Conn.: Greenwood Press.

Hosler, Dorothy H., Jeremy A. Sabloff, and Dale Runge. 1977. "Simulation Model Development: A Case Study of the Classic Maya Collapse." In Norman Hammond, ed., *Social Process in Maya Prehistory: Studies in Honour of Sir Eric Thompson*, pp. 553–590. London: Academic Press.

Hull, David L. 1988. *Science as Process*. Chicago: University of Chicago Press.

Hume, David 1907. *An Enquiry Concerning Human Understanding*. Chicago: Open Court.

―――. 1958. *A Treatise of Human Nature*. Oxford: Clarendon Press.

Hunt, Eva, and Robert C. Hunt. 1974. "Irrigation, Conflict, and Politics: A Mexican Case." In Theodore E. Downing and McGuire Gibson, eds., *Irrigation's Impact on Society*, pp. 129–57. Tucson: University of Arizona Press.

Jarvie, Ian C. 1964. *The Revolution in Anthropology*. New York: Humanities Press.

―――. 1972. *Concepts and Society*. London: Routledge & Kegan Paul.

―――. 1984. *Rationality and Relativism: In Search of a Philosophy and History of Anthropology*. London: Routledge & Kegan Paul.

―――. 1986. *Thinking About Society: Theory and Practice*. Boston Studies in the Philosophy of Science, Vol. 93. Dordrecht: D. Reidel.

Johnson, Allen W., and Timothy K. Earle. 1987. *The Evolution of Human Societies*. Stanford: Stanford University Press.

Johnson, Matthew. 1989. "The Englishman's Home and its Study." Paper presented at the Theoretical Archaeology Group Conference, Newcastle-upon-Tyne, England.

Kant, Immanuel. 1934. *Critique of Pure Reason*, J.M.D. Meikljohn, trans. New York: E. P. Dutton and Company.

Kaplan, Abraham. 1964. *The Conduct of Inquiry.* San Francisco: Chandler.

Keegan, William F. 1991. "Culture Process and Culture Realities." In Robert Preucel, ed., *Processual and Postprocessual Archaeologies: Multiple Ways of Knowing the Past,* pp. 183–96. Carbondale: Southern Illinois University Press.

Keegan, William F. 1992. *The People Who Discovered Columbus: The Prehistory of the Bahamas.* Gainesville: University Press of Florida.

Keegan, William F., and Michael J. DeNiro. 1988. "Stable Carbon-and-Nitrogen-Isotope Ratios of Bone Collagen Used to Study Coral-Reef and Terrestrial Components of Prehistoric Bahamian Diet." *American Antiquity* 53:320–36.

Kelley, Jane H., and Marsha P. Hanen. 1988. *Archaeology and the Methodology of Science.* Albuquerque: University of New Mexico Press.

Kroeber, Alfred L. 1940. "Stimulus Diffusion." *American Anthropologist* 42(1):1–20.

Kuhn, Thomas S. 1962. *The Structure of Scientific Revolutions.* Chicago: University of Chicago Press.

———. 1970a. "Logic of Discovery or Psychology of Research?" In Imre Lakatos and Alan Musgrave, eds., *Criticism and the Growth of Knowledge,* pp. 1–23. Cambridge, England: Cambridge University Press.

———. 1970b, "Reflections on My Critics." In Imre Lakatos and Alan Musgrave, eds., *Criticism and the Growth of Knowledge,* pp. 231–78. Cambridge, England: Cambridge University Press.

———. 1977. *The Essential Tension: Selected Studies in Scientific Tradition and Change.* Chicago: University of Chicago Press.

Lakatos, Imre. 1970. "Falsification and the Methodology of Scientific Research Programmes." In Imre Lakatos and Alan Musgrave, eds., *Criticism and the Growth of Knowledge,* pp. 91–196. Cambridge, England: Cambridge University Press.

Lakatos, Imre, and Alan Musgrave, Alan, eds. 1970. *Criticism and the Growth of Knowledge.* Cambridge, England: Cambridge University Press.

Lanning, Edward P. 1967. *Peru before the Incas.* Englewood Cliffs, N.J.: Prentice-Hall.

Latour, Bruno. 1988. *The Pasteurization of France.* Cambridge, Mass.: Harvard University Press.

Latour, Bruno, and Steve Woolgar. 1979. *Laboratory Life: The Social Construction of Scientific Facts.* Beverly Hills, Calif.: Sage Publications.

Leach, Edmund R. 1961. *Pul Eliya: A Village in Ceylon.* Cambridge, England: Cambridge University Press.

Lees, Susan H., 1973. *Sociopolitical Aspects of Canal Irrigation in the Valley of Oaxaca*. Prehistory and Human Ecology of the Valley of the Oaxaca, vol. 1. Anthropology Memoir No. 6. Ann Arbor: Museum of Anthropology, University of Michigan.

Leeuwe, Sander van der, ed. 1981. *Archaeological Approaches to the Study of Complexity*. Amsterdam: University of Amsterdam Press.

Leone, Mark P. 1982a. "Childe's Offspring." In Ian Hodder, ed., *Symbolic and Structural Archaeology*, pp. 179–84. Cambridge, England: Cambridge University Press.

———. 1982b. "Some Opinions about Recovering Mind." *American Antiquity* 47(4):742–60.

Lévi-Strauss, Claude. 1966. *The Savage Mind*. Chicago: University of Chicago Press.

Libby, Willard F. 1963. "The Accuracy of Radiocarbon Dates." *Science* 140:278–80.

Lowe, John W. G. 1985. *The Dynamics of Apocalypse: A Systems Simulation of the Classic Maya Collapse*. Albuquerque: University of New Mexico Press.

Mandelbrot, Benoit B. 1982. *The Fractal Geometry of Nature*. San Francisco: Freeman.

Martineau, Harriett. 1855. *The Positive Philosophy of Auguste Comte*. New York: Blanchard.

Marx, Karl, and Friedrich Engels. 1961. *The Communist Manifesto*. New York: New York Labor News.

Masterman, Margaret. 1970. "The Nature of Paradigm." In Imre Lakatos and Alan Musgrave, eds., *Criticism and the Growth of Knowledge*, pp. 59–89. Cambridge, England: Cambridge University Press.

Meltzer, David J. 1979. "Paradigms and the Nature of Change in American Archaeology." *American Antiquity* 44(4):644–57.

Meltzer, David J., Don D. Fowler, and Jeremy A. Sabloff, eds. 1986. *American Archaeology, Past and Future*. Washington, D.C.: Smithsonian Institution Press.

Merton, Robert K. 1968. *Social Theory and Social Structure*. New York: Free Press.

Michels, Joseph W. 1973. *Dating Methods in Archaeology*. New York: Seminar Press.

Miller, Daniel, and Christopher Tilley. 1984. "Ideology, Power, and Prehistory: An Introduction." In Daniel Miller and Christopher Tilley, eds., *Ide-*

ology, Power, and Prehistory, pp. 1–15. Cambridge, England: Cambridge University Press.

Millon, René, Clara Hall, and May Diaz. 1961. "Conflict in the Modern Teotihuacan Irrigation System." *Comparative Studies in Society and History*, Vol. 4, pp. 494–521. The Hague: Mouton.

Mises, Ludwig von. 1949. *Human Actions: A Treatise on Economics*. New Haven: Yale University Press.

———. 1962, *The Free and Prosperous Commonwealth: An Exposition of the Ideas of Classical Liberalism*. Princeton, N.J.: Van Norstrand.

Mithen, Steven J. 1987. "Modelling Decision Making and Learning by Low Latitude Hunter Gatherers." *European Journal of Operational Research* 30: 240–42.

———. 1990. *Thoughtful Foragers: A Study of Prehistoric Decision Making*. Cambridge, England: Cambridge University Press.

Moivre, Abraham de. 1967. *The Doctrine of Chances: Or, A Method of Calculating the Probabilities of Events in Play*. New York: Chelsea Publishing.

Moore, James A., and Arthur S. Keene, eds. 1983. *Archaeological Hammers and Theories*. New York: Academic Press.

Newman, Robert P. 1992. *Owen Lattimore and the "Loss" of China*. Berkeley: University of California Press.

Nicole, Pierre, and Antoine Arnauld. 1964. *The Art of Thinking; Port Royal Logic*. Indianapolis: Bobbs-Merrill.

Parsons, Talcott. 1967. *Sociological Theory and Modern Society*. New York: Free Press.

Patton, Mark. 1986. "Questioning the Fundamentals: The Epistemological Basis of a Social Archaeology." Paper delivered at the World Archaeological Congress, Southampton, England.

Peebles, Christopher S. 1990. "From History to Hermeneutics: The Place of Theory in the Later Prehistory of the Southeast." *Southeastern Archaeology* 9(1): 23–34.

———. 1991. "Annalistes, Hermeneutics, and Positivists: Squaring Circles or Dissolving Problems?" In John Bintliff, ed., *The Annales School and Archaeology*, pp. 108–24. Leicester, England: Leicester University Press.

———. 1992. "Rooting Out Latent Behaviorism in Archaeology." In Jean-Claude Gardin and Christopher S. Peebles, eds., *Representations in Archaeology*, pp. 357–84. Bloomington: University of Indiana Press.

Peitgen, Heinz-Otto, and Peter H. Richter. 1986. *The Beauty of Fractals: Images of Complex Dynamical Systems*. Berlin: Springer-Verlag.

Perlès, Catherine. 1992. "In Search of Lithic Strategies: A Cognitive Approach to Prehistoric Chipped Stone Assemblages." In Jean-Claude Gardin and Christopher S. Peebles, eds. *Representations in Archaeology*, pp. 223–47. Bloomington: University of Indiana Press.

Popper, Karl R. 1945. *The Open Society and Its Enemies*. London: G. Routledge.

———. 1957. *The Poverty of Historicism*. London: Routledge and Kegan Paul.

———. 1959. *The Logic of Scientific Discovery*. New York: Basic Books.

———. 1962. *Conjectures and Refutations: The Growth of Scientific Knowledge*. New York: Basic Books.

———. 1970. "Normal Science and Its Dangers." In Imre Lakatos and Alan Musgrave, eds., *Criticism and the Growth of Knowledge*, pp. 51–58. Cambridge, England: Cambridge University Press.

———. 1972. *Objective Knowledge: An Evolutionary Approach*. Oxford: Clarendon Press.

———. 1983. *Realism and the Aim of Science*. London: Hutchinson.

Prentice, Guy. 1986. "Origins of Plant Domestication in the Eastern United States: Promoting the Individual in Archaeological Theory." *Southeastern Archaeology* 5:103–19.

Preucel, Robert W., ed. 1991. *Processual and Postprocessual Archaeologies*. Carbondale: Southern Illinois University Press.

Preucel, Robert W., and Timothy K. Earle. 1987. "Processual Archaeology and the Radical Critique." *Current Anthropology* 28(4):501–13.

Price, Barbara J. 1971. "Prehistoric Irrigation Agriculture in Nuclear America." *Latin American Research Review* 6:3–30.

Prigogine, Ilya. 1980. *From Being to Becoming: Time and Complexity in the Physical Sciences*. San Francisco: W. H. Freeman.

Prigogine, Ilya, and Isabelle Stengers. 1984. *Order Out of Chaos: Man's New Dialogue With Nature*. New York: Bantam Books.

Putnam, Hilary. 1974. "The 'Corroboration' of Theories." In Paul A. Schilpp, ed., *The Philosophy of Karl Popper*, Vol. 1, pp. 221–40. LaSalle, Ill.: Open Court.

Rabinow, Paul, ed. 1984. *The Foucault Reader*. New York: Pantheon.

Randers, Jørgen. 1980. *Elements of the System Dynamics Method*. Cambridge, Mass.: MIT Press.

Reichenbach, Hans. 1938. *Experience and Predictions: An Analysis of the Foundations and Structure of Knowledge*. Chicago: University of Chicago Press.

———. 1951. *The Rise of Scientific Philosophy*. Berkeley: University of California Press.

Renfrew, A. Colin. 1973a. *Before Civilization: The Radiocarbon Revolution and Prehistoric Europe.* London: Jonathan Cape.

———. 1973b. *The Explanation of Culture Change: Models in Prehistory.* Pittsburgh: University of Pittsburgh Press.

———. 1982. *Towards an Archaeology of Mind.* Cambridge, England: Cambridge University Press.

———. 1987. "Problems in the Modelling of Socio-cultural Systems." *European Journal of Operational Research* 30:179–92.

———. 1989a. *Archaeology and Language: The Puzzle of Indo-European Origins.* London: Penguin Books.

———. 1989b. "Archaeology: Humanity or Science?" Paper presented at the Theoretical Archaeology Group Conference, Newcastle-upon-Tyne, England.

Renfrew, A. Colin, and Paul Bahn. 1991. *Archaeology: Theories, Methods, and Practice.* New York: Thames and Hudson.

Renfrew, A. Colin, and Ezra Zubrow, eds. 1993. *The Ancient Mind: Elements of Cognitive Archaeology* (tentative title). Cambridge, England: Cambridge University Press. Manuscript in preparation.

Rouse, Irving. 1973. "Analytic, Synthetic and Comparative Archaeology." In Charles L. Redman, ed., *Research and Theory in Current Archaeology,* pp. 21–31. New York: John Wiley.

———. 1986. *Migrations in Prehistory Inferring Population Movement from Cultural Remains.* New Haven: Yale University Press.

———. 1992. *The Tainos: Rise and Decline of the People Who Greeted Columbus.* New Haven: Yale University Press.

Roux, Valentine. 1992. "Logicist Analysis, Exterior Knowledge, and Ethnoarchaeological Research." In Jean-Claude Gardin and Christopher S. Peebles, eds., *Representations in Archaeology,* pp. 277–90. Bloomington: University of Indiana Press.

Ruggles, Clive N.L. 1986. "You Can't Have One Without The Other?: I.T. and Bayesian Statistics and Their Possible Impact Within Archaeology." *Science and Archaeology* 28:8–15.

Sabloff, Jeremy A. 1982, "Introduction." In Jeremy A. Sabloff, ed., *Archaeology: Myth and Reality,* pp. 1–26. San Francisco: W. H. Freeman.

Sabloff, Jeremy A., ed. 1981. *Simulations in Archaeology.* Albuquerque: University of New Mexico Press.

———, ed. 1982. *Archaeology: Myth and Reality.* San Francisco: W. H. Freeman.

Sabloff, Jeremy A., Thomas W. Beale, and Anthony J. Kurland, Jr. 1973. "Recent Developments in Archaeology." *The Annals of the American Academy of Political and Social Science* 408:103–18.

Sabloff, Jeremy A., and Lewis R. Binford 1982. "Paradigms, Systematics, and Archaeology." *Journal of Anthropological Research* 38(2):137–53.

Sabloff, Jeremy A., Don D. Fowler, and David J. Meltzer, eds. 1986. *American Archaeology, Past and Future*. Washington, D.C.: Smithsonian Institution Press.

Sabloff, Jeremy A., and Gordon R. Willey. 1980. *A History of American Archaeology*, 2d edition. San Francisco: W. H. Freeman.

Sahlins, Marshall D. 1962. *Moala*. Ann Arbor: University of Michigan Press.

Salmon, Merrilee H. 1982. *Philosophy and Archaeology*. New York: Academic Press.

Salmon, Wesley C., Richard C. Jeffrey, and James G. Greeno. 1971. *Statistical Explanation and Statistical Relevance*. Pittsburgh: University of Pittsburgh Press.

Sanders, William T., and Barbara J. Price. 1967. *Mesoamerica: The Evolution of a Civilization*. New York: Random House.

Sartre, Jean Paul. 1956. *Being and Nothingness*, Bernard Frechtman and Hazel Barnes, trans. New York: Citadel Press.

———. 1957. *Existentialism and Human Emotions*, Hazel Barnes, trans. New York: Philosophical Library.

Schilpp, Paul. 1951. *Albert Einstein: Philosopher-Scientist*. New York: Tudor Publishing.

———. 1974. *The Philosophy of Karl Popper*. La Salle, Ill.: Open Court.

Schumpeter, Joseph A. 1964. *Business Cycles: A Theoretical, Historical, and Statistical Analysis of the Capitalist Process*. New York: McGraw-Hill.

Schwartz, Joseph. 1992. *The Creative Moment: How Science Made Itself Alien to Modern Culture*. New York: HarperCollins.

Service, Elman. 1962. *Primitive Social Organization*. New York: Random House.

———. 1975. *Origins of the State and Civilization: The Process of Cultural Evolution*. New York: Norton.

Shand, Alexander H. 1984. *The Capitalist Alternative: An Introduction to Neo-Austrian Economics*. New York: New York University Press.

Shanks, Michael. 1992. *Experiencing the Past: On the Character of Archaeology*. London: Routledge.

Shanks, Michael, and Christopher Tilley. 1982. "Ideology, Symbolic Power, and Ritual Communication: A Reinterpretation of Neolithic Mortuary Practices." In Ian Hodder, ed., *Symbolic and Structural Archaeology*, pp. 129–54. Cambridge, England: Cambridge University Press.

———. 1987a. *Re-Constructing Archaeology: Theory and Practice*. Cambridge, England: Cambridge University Press.

———. 1987b. *Social Theory and Archaeology*. Cambridge, England: Polity Press.

———. 1989. "Archaeology in the 1990s." *Norwegian Archaeology Review* 22(1):1–54.

Shennan, Stephen. 1988. *Quantifying Archaeology*. Edinburgh: Edinburgh University Press.

Shrader-Frechette, Kristin. 1988. Review of *The Science Question in Feminism* by Sandra Harding. *Synthese* 76:441–46.

Silverberg, Robert. 1968. *Mound Builders of Ancient America: The Archaeology of a Myth*. Greenwich, Conn.: New York Graphic Society.

Smith, Bruce D. 1987. "The Independent Domestication of the Indigenous Seed-Bearing Plants in Eastern North America." In William Keegan, ed., *Emergent Horticultural Economies of the Eastern Woodlands*, pp. 3–47. Carbondale: Southern Illinois University Press.

Smith, Laurence D., 1986. *Behaviorism and Logical Positivism: A Reassessment of the Alliance*. Stanford: Stanford University Press.

Smith, M. A. 1955. "The Limitations of Inference in Archaeology." *Archaeological Newsletter* 6:3–7.

Snell, Bruno. 1982. *The Discovery of the Mind in Greek Philosophy and Literature*. New York: Dover Publications.

Snow, Charles Percy. 1959. *The Two Cultures and the Scientific Revolution*. Cambridge, England: Cambridge University Press.

Spaulding, Albert C. 1968. "Explanation in Archaeology." In Sally R. Binford and Lewis R. Binford, eds., *New Perspectives in Archaeology*, pp. 33–39. Chicago: Aldine.

Sprat, Thomas. 1966. *History of the Royal Society*. St. Louis: Washington University Press.

Sterud, Gene. 1973. "A Paradigmatic View of Prehistory." In A. Colin Renfrew, ed., *The Explanation of Cultural Change: Models in Prehistory*, pp. 3–17. Pittsburgh: University of Pittsburgh Press.

Steward, Julian. 1955. *Irrigation Civilizations: A Comparative Study*. Pan American Union Social Science Monograph 1. Washington, D.C.: Department of Cultural Affairs.

Taylor, Alan J. P. 1965. *English History, 1914–1945*. Oxford: Oxford University Press.

———. 1966. *From Sarajevo to Potsdam*. London: Thames and Hudson.

Taylor, Royal E. 1987. *Radiocarbon Dating: An Archaeological Perspective*. Orlando: Academic Press.

Thomas, David Hurst. 1978. "The Awful Truth about Statistics in Archaeology." *American Antiquity* 43(2):231–44.

Tilley, Christopher. 1981. "Conceptual Frameworks for the Explanation of Sociocultural Change." In Ian Hodder, Glynn Isaac, and Norman Hammond, eds., *Pattern of the Past: Studies in Honor of David Clarke*, pp. 363–68. Cambridge, England: Cambridge University Press.

Toulmin, Stephen E. 1970. "Does the Distinction Between Normal and Revolutionary Science Hold Water?' In Imre Lakatos and Alan Musgrave, eds., *Criticism and the Growth of Knowledge*, pp. 39–47. Cambridge, England: Cambridge University Press.

Trigger, Bruce. 1978. *Time and Traditions: Essays in Archaeological Interpretation*. Edinburgh: Edinburgh University Press.

———. 1989a. "Comments on Archaeology into the 1990s." *Norwegian Archaeological Review* 22(1):28–31.

———. 1989b. *A History of Archaeological Thought*. Cambridge, England: Cambridge University Press.

———. 1989c. "Hyperrelativism, Responsibility, and the Social Sciences." *Canadian Review of Sociology and Anthropology* 26(5):776–91.

Turner, Stephen P. 1982. "On the Relevance of Statistical Relevance Theory." *Theory and Decisions* 14:195–205.

Ulmen, Gary L. 1978. *The Science of Society: Toward an Understanding of the Life and Work of Karl August Wittfogel*. The Hague: Mouton.

Wade, Nicholas, and William Broad. 1983. *Betrayers of the Truth*. New York: Simon & Schuster.

Watkins, John W. N. 1952. "Ideal Types and Historical Explanation." *British Journal for the Philosophy of Science* 3:22–43.

———. 1970. "Against 'Normal Science'." In Imre Lakatos and Alan Musgrave, eds., *Criticism and the Growth of Knowledge*, pp. 25–37. Cambridge, England: Cambridge University Press, Cambridge.

Watson, Patty Jo, and Mary C. Kennedy. 1991. "The Development of Horticulture in the Eastern Woodlands of North America: Women's Role." In Joan M. Gero and Margaret W. Conkey, eds., *Engendering Archaeology: Women and Prehistory*, pp. 255–75. Oxford: Basil Blackwell.

Watson, Patty Jo, Steven A. LeBlanc, and Charles L. Redman. 1971. *Explanation in Archaeology: An Explicitly Scientific Approach*. New York: Columbia University Press.

―――. 1984. *Archaeological Explanation: The Scientific Method in Archaeology*. New York: Columbia University Press.

Watson, Richard A. 1991. "What the New Archaeology Has Accomplished." *Current Anthropology* 32(3):275–91.

Weber, Max. 1962. *Basic Concepts in Sociology*. New York: Citadel Press.

Whewell, William. 1858. *History of the Inductive Sciences, from the Earliest to the Present Times*, 3d edition. New York: D. Appleton. Originally published 1837.

―――. 1967. *The Philosophy of the Inductive Sciences, Founded Upon Their History*. London: Johnson Reprint. Originally published in 1840.

Willey, Gordon R., and Jeremy A. Sabloff. 1980. *A History of American Archaeology*, 2d edition. San Francisco: W. H. Freeman.

Wilson, David. 1975a. *Atoms of Time Past*. London: Allen Lane.

―――. 1975b. *The New Archaeology*. New York: Alfred A. Knopf.

Wittfogel, Karl A. 1931. *Wirtschaft und Gesellschaft Chinas, Versuch der wissenschaftlichen Analyse einer grossen asiatischen Agrargesellschaft*. Leipzig: C. L. Hirschfeld Verlag.

―――. 1935. "The Foundations and Stages of Chinese Economic History." *Zeitschrift für Sozialforschung* 4(1):26–60.

―――. 1938. "Die Theorie der orientalischen Gesellschaft." *Zeitschrift für Sozialforschung* 7(½).

―――. 1957. *Oriental Despotism*. New Haven: Yale University Press.

Wittgenstein, Ludwig. 1953. *Philosophical Investigations*. New York: Macmillan.

―――. 1961. *Tractatus Logico-Philosophicus*. New York: Humanities Press.

Wobst, Martin. 1983. "We Can't See the Forest for the Trees: Sampling and the Shapes of Archaeological Distributions." In James A. Moore and Arthur S. Keene, eds., *Archaeological Hammers and Theories*, pp. 37–85. New York: Academic Press.

Wolf, Eric, and Angel Palerm. 1955. "Irrigation in the Old Acolhua Domain, Mexico." *Southwestern Journal of Anthropology* 11:265–81.

Wylie, M. Alison. 1982. *Positivism and the New Archaeology*. Ph.D. dissertation, Department of Anthropology, State University of New York, Binghamton. University Microfilms, Ann Arbor, Michigan.

―――. 1985a. "Between Philosophy and Archaeology." *American Antiquity* 50(2):478–90.

———. 1985b. "The Reaction against Analogy." In Michael B. Schiffer, ed., *Advances in Archaeological Method and Theory*, vol. 8, pp. 63–111. Orlando: Academic Press.

———. 1991. "Gender Theory and the Archaeological Record." In Margaret Conkey and Joan Gero, eds., *Engendering Archaeology: Women and Prehistory*, pp. 31–54. Oxford: Basil Blackwell.

Zubrow, Ezra. 1981. "Simulation as a Heuristic Device in Archaeology." In Jeremy A. Sabloff, ed., *Simulations in Archaeology*, pp. 143–88. Albuquerque: University of New Mexico Press.

Index